94

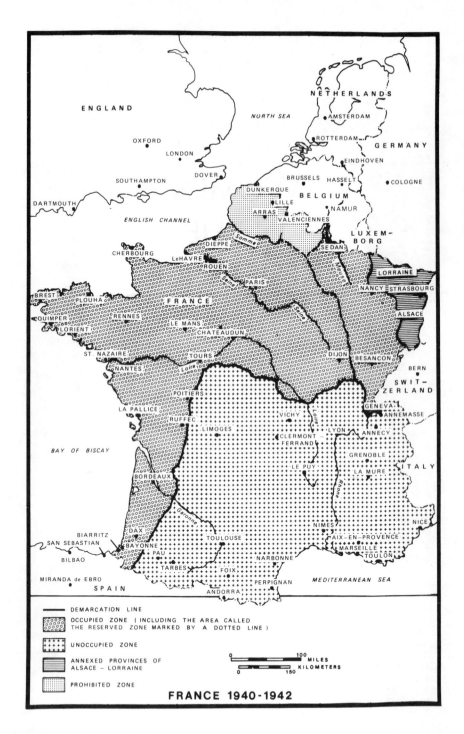

FRANCE 1940-1942

DEMARCATION LINE

OCCUPIED ZONE (INCLUDING THE AREA CALLED THE RESERVED ZONE MARKED BY A DOTTED LINE)

UNOCCUPIED ZONE

ANNEXED PROVINCES OF ALSACE – LORRAINE

PROHIBITED ZONE

Map by David W. Nelson

WOMEN
IN THE
RESISTANCE

Margaret L. Rossiter

14 6402

PRAEGER

PRAEGER SPECIAL STUDIES • PRAEGER SCIENTIFIC

New York • Philadelphia • Eastbourne, UK
Toronto • Hong Kong • Tokyo • Sydney

Library of Congress Cataloging-in-Publication Data

Rossiter, Margaret L.
  Women in the resistance.

  Bibliography: p.
  Includes index.
    1. World War, 1939–1945 – Underground movements –
France. 2. World War, 1939–1945 – Women – France.
3. France – History – German occupation, 1940–1945.
I. Title.
D802. F8R595   1985   940.53′44   85-16746
ISBN   0-03-005338-2   (alk. paper)
ISBN   0-03-005339-0   (pbk. : alk paper)

Published in 1986 by Praeger Publishers
CBS Educational and Professional Publishing, a Division of CBS Inc.
521 Fifth Avenue, New York, NY 10175 USA

© 1986 by Praeger Publishers

6789   052   987654321

Printed in the United States of America on acid-free paper

INTERNATIONAL OFFICES

Orders from outside the United States should be sent to the appropriate address listed below. Orders from areas not
listed below should be placed through CBS International Publishing. 383 Madison Ave., New York, NY 10175 USA

Australia, New Zealand
Holt Saunders. Pty. Ltd., 9 Waltham St., Artarmon. N.S.W. 2064, Sydney, Australia

Canada
Holt, Rinehart & Winston of Canada, 55 Horner Ave., Toronto, Ontario, Canada M8Z 4X6

Europe, the Middle East, & Africa
Holt Saunders. Ltd., 1 St. Anne's Road, Eastbourne. East Sussex, England BN21 3UN

Japan
Holt Saunders. Ltd., Ichibancho Central Building. 22-1 Ichibancho, 3rd Floor, Chiyodaku, Tokyo, Japan

Hong Kong, Southeast Asia
Holt Saunders Asia. Ltd., 10 Fl, Intercontinental Plaza, 94 Granville Road, Tsim Sha Tsui East, Kowloon,
Hong Kong

**Manuscript submissions should be sent to the Editorial Director, Praeger Publishers, 521 Fifth Avenue,
New York, NY 10175 USA**

TO MY HUSBAND, TED

CONTENTS

PREFACE

Although many women were engaged in the underground struggle to liberate France from the German occupation, the names of relatively few have figured in accounts of the French resistance. My purpose in writing this book has been to find out more about the part women played in the various resistance groups and to evaluate not only their contribution to the Nazi defeat but also its possible effect on the political status of French women. Did it, for example, have any bearing on their being enfranchised in 1944?

Information about women participants in the clandestine operations described here was difficult to obtain, and bits and pieces of their stories had to be gleaned from many sources. Books and articles by or about some individual heroines in the resistance have appeared, and I have drawn on those published sources to some extent. But a great deal of the material here comes directly from my interviews and correspondence with individuals who took part in the resistance or can speak authoritatively about it. I also include hitherto unpublished information uncovered in my searches through military and other government records, and the reports of private organizations in the United States and abroad.

Beginning in 1974, I interviewed 64 women and 36 men in France, England, Belgium, and the United States, almost all of whom permitted me to tape-record their recollections of events.[1] Some of those interviewed volunteered to lend me unpublished memoirs and other documents from their personal archives. In the course of this study I also corresponded with more than 100 former members of resistance groups and with other well-informed people. They answered countless questions, and 23 sent me extensive information.[2]

In addition, I read the *témoignages* (statements) that many resisters made in interviews conducted soon after the war under the auspices of the Comité d'Histoire de la Deuxième Guerre Mondiale in Paris.[3]

Information also turned up in the collection of clandestine newspapers at the Bibliothèque Nationale, and in a few documents at the Bibliothèque Marguerite Durand in Paris and at the Bibliothèque de la Documentation Internationale Contemporaine at Nanterre. Documents about some OSS women, missions, and intelligence chains in France were acquired from the Central

Intelligence Agency under the Freedom of Information Act, but only after a delay of four years.

As my research advanced, I discovered that the best available documents about women in the resistance were those describing their work in escape lines. Reports from U.S. servicemen who received help from escape lines are in the National Archives, Washington National Records Center, in Suitland, Maryland.[4] Chapters 2, 3, and 4 of this book contain much detail drawn from the 3,000 firsthand accounts of downed American airmen who evaded capture or escaped from German hands and managed to return to England thanks to the help of resistance networks. The stories the soldiers told in their interrogations by army intelligence officers contain a wealth of information about women who fed and sheltered them, and often guided them on their way to the next safehouse.

For security reasons, evaders usually knew their benefactors only by their pseudonyms or first names, but I was able to trace many individuals through materials compiled by the tripartite Awards Bureau, set up in Paris while the war was still in progress in an effort to identify the civilian patriots who had risked their lives to help Allied aviators.[5] The American section began functioning in October 1944 with a card file of about 3,000 names picked up from the escape and evasion reports.

Identifying the people who dared not give their real names to the men they were helping was a major problem for the Awards Bureau, but when one person was traced, the trail might lead to three or four others. The French press cooperated by urging anyone with information about escape lines to report the facts to the Awards Bureau. Once helpers were located, they were asked to fill out questionnaires describing their work, identifying the airmen they helped, and naming others in the group. Official recognition of resisters had to begin at the local level, with a declaration by the individual, which was then sent to the organization's headquarters.[6] American awards in the form of the newly established Medal of Freedom, letters of appreciation, or financial reimbursement were based on some 5,000 dossiers, many of which are now in the Washington National Records Center, along with detailed histories by American intelligence officers about some of the largest escape lines.

The intelligence records in the Washington National Records Center were made available to me under Executive Order 11652 of 1972, which provided that security classified information would be declassified after 30 years under certain conditions. The documents were subject to review for security and for information that might constitute an invasion of privacy; they were declassified as I requested them.

Information about women engaged in other kinds of work for the resistance is harder to find, and the same difficulties arise concerning their identity. During the many months spent sifting through records, I was constantly aware that all the networks included valiant women who received no official recognition, particularly those in the lower echelons who could devote only part of their time to the cause.

More people and organizations have helped with this book than I can acknowledge here. My greatest thanks go to the diminishing band of men and women who served the resistance and generously gave me information that I could get nowhere else. Many received me in their homes. Others wrote and talked to me by telephone. In particular instances their information helped me to clear up misconceptions created in earlier accounts.

Research in France and the United States was made possible in part by grants from the American Philosophical Society and the Josephine Keal Fund. The staffs of several institutions greatly aided my research. At the Comité d'Histoire de la Deuxième Guerre Mondiale, Henri Michel, the secretary-general, made suggestions about sources and gave me access to the archives; Françoise Mercier, archivist, and Michel Rauzier, librarian, provided me with documents and books. In the United States at the National Archives, John Taylor of the Modern Military Branch not only provided me with many military and OSS documents, but also put me in touch with people associated with the OSS. At the Washington National Records Center, archivists George Chalou and Frederick Pernell were most cooperative in providing me with essential documents. My cousin Virginia Giltner performed valuable services by searching through countless boxes of evasion records at the WNRC.

At Eastern Michigan University the library staff obtained many books through interlibrary loan. My colleague Prof. Daryl Hafter made helpful suggestions about the organization and content of the book, and Prof. Brigitte Robert Muller assisted me with the translation of some French paragraphs into English; unattributed translations are my own. One of my former students, Carole Edgerton, translated many letters into French and typed them as well. Constance Greenbaum, who is now working on a thesis at the University of Paris, served as my research assistant. In addition to checking documents, she helped to locate resisters for whom I was searching and interviewed five people in my stead.

Ralph Patton, president of the Air Forces Escape and Evasion Society, provided me with a great deal of material. In addition, 132 members of the society (60 percent) responded to my questionnaire asking for details about important assistance given to them by women. Pierre Bauset, president of the Royal Air Forces Escaping Society, Canadian Branch, also contributed information.

Special thanks are due Rosannah Steinhoff of Ann Arbor, who read the entire manuscript and made valuable suggestions about its organization and style. Arlene Phillips of Eastern Michigan University was most cooperative in typing the manuscript. Finally, I want to thank my editors at Praeger, Dotty Breitbart and Susan Alkana, who shepherded my manuscript through the various stages with enthusiasm and skill.

Notes

1. Their names are listed in the bibliography.
2. Their names are listed in the bibliography.
3. After the Comité went out of existence at the end of 1980, the *témoignages* and other documents, such as agents' reports, letters, and personal records, were transferred to the Archives Nationales. Staff members were transferred to the Institut d'Histoire du Temps Présent.
4. See Guide to Frequently Cited Sources.
5. The Awards Bureau represented the joint efforts of the U.S. Awards Section, P/W and X Detachment, G-2; the British MI 9; and the French Direction Générale d'Etudes et Recherches (DGER). In September 1944 the 6801 MIS-X Detachment was organized (but not activated until May 1945) to carry on the work of the U.S. Awards Section.
6. The DGER was interested in all types of resistance; the British and the Americans, only in escapes and evasions.

1 PRELUDE TO ACTION

1 FRANCE ON BERLIN TIME

Much is known about the resistance to the Nazi conqueror that developed throughout the country after France's defeat by Germany in 1940, but the part played by women has not been adequately recorded. This book will tell the story of what women did in the resistance: how they rescued Allied airmen shot down by the Germans by serving as leaders, hostesses, and guides of escape lines, thus making it possible for airmen to return to their bases in England, and how they gathered military intelligence, managed clandestine newspapers, and carried out sabotage and guerrilla operations. Women served in all capacities from typists to organizers and chiefs of resistance networks. As "combattantes sans uniforme" they helped immeasurably to undermine the foundations of the German occupation and hasten the defeat of the enemy.

The part women played in the resistance will be best understood against the background of events that began with the German invasion of the Netherlands and Belgium on May 10, 1940. The blitzkrieg of the German Panzer divisions abruptly ended the "phony war" that had existed on the Western Front since the Nazi conquest of Poland in September 1939. French armies and the British Expeditionary Force (BEF) rushed to support the Belgians in accordance with the French War Plan and in response to a last-minute appeal from King Leopold, whose country had put its faith in neutrality.

The Allied defense plan was derailed when General von Kleist's Panzer group smashed through the supposedly impassable Belgian Ardennes and hurled two armored corps across the Meuse River in eastern France. General Guderian then raced with his armored divisions to the Channel coast. By this daring maneuver the Germans cut the Allied forces in two. The Belgian army and the supporting British and French troops were caught in a net. Efforts to break out failed, and the weary Belgians surrendered on May 27,

1940.[1] The BEF and remnants of three French armies were forced back to Dunkerque.

During 9 frantic days, from May 26 to June 4, rescuers plucked 338,226 soldiers from the beaches in what was called the "miracle of Dunkerque." Almost 200,000 of these were British; the rest, French and Belgian. This gallant action had its repercussions, however. Although 130,000 trapped French soldiers had been saved at Dunkerque by an impromptu fleet of British and French ships, the French were bitterly aware that 40,000 others were left to be taken prisoner by the Germans. They firmly believed that the British had withdrawn prematurely from the Continent, leaving them to face the enemy alone.[2]

There was no respite after Dunkerque. On June 5 Hitler opened the Battle of France by unleashing 100 divisions in a mighty 4-pronged attack. The Germans advanced so rapidly, supported by the Luftwaffe, that the French had little time for effective counterattack. On June 10, sensing that France was about to fall and hoping to gain credit with his Axis partner, the fascist dictator Mussolini declared war on France.

Shaken by these events, the French cabinet, led by Premier Paul Reynaud, abruptly left Paris and moved to Tours. On June 14 the Germans triumphantly entered an almost deserted capital, which had been declared an open city, and raced toward the Loire River. The French government withdrew to Bordeaux in southwestern France.

Meanwhile, Premier Reynaud and British Prime Minister Winston Churchill made desperate efforts to keep France in the war. Churchill supported the usually energetic French premier. Reynaud, at first backed by a majority of his cabinet, believed that if the German offensive could not be halted, the French government should go to North Africa to continue the war. He was opposed by his new supreme commander, Gen. Maxime Weygand, and by his vice-premier, the 84-year-old Marshal Henri Philippe Pétain, the World War I hero of Verdun. They insisted that the government remain in France and seek an armistice.[3]

By June 16 the French armies were collapsing. On the same day Churchill, in a last-ditch effort to head off a capitulation by the French, supported a dramatic plan of Franco-British union. The terms of the plan were telephoned to Reynaud by Brig. Gen. Charles de Gaulle, his undersecretary for national defense, who was in London conferring with Churchill. Reynaud immediately took the proposal to his cabinet, but without success. His colleagues were suspicious of the British motives; and in any case they believed the situation was hopeless. Reynaud resigned in despair.[4]

He was promptly replaced by Marshal Pétain, who was appointed premier by Albert Lebrun, president of the Third Republic. In his radio address to the people, Pétain praised the army for fighting with a heroism worthy of its traditions against an enemy superior in number and arms. Then he said:

"I give to France the gift of my person to attenuate her misfortune. . . . It is with a heavy heart that I say to you today that the fighting must cease." He then added that he had asked the Germans for an armistice.[5]

Many French troops, hearing reports about the marshal's speech, believed that the war was over. They threw down their weapons and joined the exodus of several million people choking the roads as they fled before the Germans. Most French civilians were relieved that the fighting was over. Marie Madeleine Fourcade, who became a prominent resistance leader, reported: "Women smiled, people kissed one another. In the cafes the crowds drank to the health of the old marshal."[6] Young Brigitte Robert, a secretary in the Commerce Department in Paris, who moved with the government to Vichy, remarked that "our army had been defeated and the fighting had to stop. There was an instinctive feeling of relief."[7]

At the same time the French were stunned by the humiliating debacle after only six weeks of fighting. They had believed in their army, supposedly the best in Europe, and the security of the Maginot Line. Military collapse was a new and traumatic experience. Like many others, Marie Madeleine Fourcade felt an immense wave of anguish engulf her.

The armistice terms imposed by a jubilant Hitler on June 22 were severe. France would be divided into occupied and unoccupied zones, with a rigid demarcation line between the two. The Germans would directly control three-fifths of the country, an area that included northern and western France and the entire Atlantic coast. The remaining section of the country would be administered by the French government under Marshal Pétain.[8]

According to other provisions of the armistice, the French army would be disbanded except for a force of 100,000 men to maintain domestic order; France would pay the occupation costs of German troops;[9] the French government would prevent members of its armed forces from leaving the country and forbid its citizens to fight against the Germans. The government was also required to surrender upon demand any Germans living in France, most of whom were Jews. Pending the conclusion of a peace treaty, French prisoners of war, numbering approximately 1.5 million, would remain in captivity. By this decree thousands of women were left without husbands, brothers, or sons and had strong reason to join the later resistance.

One of the armistice terms posed a special threat to Great Britain. The Germans demanded that the French navy, the second most powerful in Europe, be interned in ports under Axis control. Although Hitler pledged not to use the fleet, the British questioned the value of such an assurance. If the Germans seized the French navy, it could mean the defeat of the English in the approaching Battle of Britain. Churchill, deciding that the risk was too great, ordered a naval force to Mers-el-Kebir, Algeria, where the French Atlantic squadron was berthed. The British sealed off the harbor with mines and then delivered an ultimatum giving the French commander three choices:

to fight with the British, to sail to British ports to be interned, or to sail to French Caribbean bases. When the ultimatum was rejected on July 3, the British opened fire on the French squadron, killing 1,267 sailors and sinking all but one cruiser and three destroyers. A wave of anti-British indignation swept across France, and the Pétain government broke diplomatic relations with its recent ally.[10]

By this time the French government had transferred to Vichy, a small resort city in unoccupied France noted for its mineral springs. There the Chamber of Deputies and the Senate of the Third Republic, in joint session as the National Assembly, gave Pétain full powers to draft a new constitution. The vote, a lopsided 569 to 80, indicated the revulsion that the members of Parliament, numbed with shock, felt against the republic that had brought them to defeat. Conversely, it showed their hope for strong leadership from Pétain, who became head of the French state.[11]

The old marshal was a father figure. He reminded the people that he had been with them in the glorious days of the past and that he would remain with them in the somber days of the present. He urged them to stay at his side and he would atone for the country's misfortune.[12] Like many other conservatives, Pétain believed that France had been defeated because of its lack of discipline and zeal. France was guilty of laxness, and the defeat was therefore merited. Suzanne Borel, who was attached to the Office of Information in Vichy, ironically summed up the government's attitude: "We were defeated, but with honor. It wasn't our fault; it was the fault of the English, the Jews, the unpatriotic schoolteachers. Of course it was not the fault of the generals. It was a kind of morphine."[13]

For two years the Vichy regime acted as a partial screen between the French in the unoccupied zone and the Germans. Here the conqueror was not visible, as he was in the north and west, and many believed that Pétain would save France from the terrible fate of Poland. Others were convinced that the marshal was playing a double game by only pretending to collaborate with the Germans. Was it not realistic to adopt a policy of *attentisme* – to wait and see what developed?

Meanwhile, however, another army officer, Charles de Gaulle, was following a dramatically different path. An exponent of mechanized warfare, he had been promoted to brigadier general in May 1940 because of his aggressive use of tanks against the Germans. At age 49 he was the youngest general in the French army when his old friend Premier Reynaud appointed him undersecretary for national defense. De Gaulle feared that it might be too late to win the Battle of France, but he forcefully advocated a fighting retreat to Brittany and the later transfer of the government and armed forces to French North Africa.[14]

Because of de Gaulle's determination to continue the fight, Reynaud sent him to London on June 16 to ask Churchill for help in transporting

French troops to North Africa. He was also to urge Churchill to support the Anglo-French plan of union, and thus strengthen Reynaud's hand in dealing with the growing number of advisers who insisted on an armistice.[15]

Having completed this mission, de Gaulle flew to Bordeaux in a plane provided by Churchill. There he learned from his aides that Reynaud had resigned and that President Lebrun had asked Pétain to form a new government. Knowing that this meant "certain capitulation," de Gaulle decided to leave France the next morning. Because his wife and children would be endangered when he left the country, he arranged for them to join him in England. On June 17 he arrived in London on the plane lent to him by Churchill, feeling, he said, "like a man on the shore of an ocean proposing to swim across."[16]

The view from England was grim. German armies had conquered Poland in 26 days, Norway in 28 days, Denmark in 24 hours, the Netherlands in 5 days, Belgium in 18 days, and now France in an unbelievable 42 days. Britain was expected to be the next victim, and hardly anyone believed that the British could stop the Nazi tide.

Despite these successes of the German juggernaut, de Gaulle was determined to muster what forces he could against the invaders. He conferred with Churchill, who agreed to put the BBC at his disposal. On June 18 the young general delivered his famous appeal to the French:

> Speaking in full knowledge of the facts, I ask you to believe me when I say that the cause of France is not lost. . . . This war is not limited to one unfortunate country. The outcome of the struggle has not been decided by the Battle of France. This is a world war. . . . Today we are crushed by the sheer weight of mechanized force hurled against us, but we can still look to a future in which even greater mechanized force will bring us to victory. The destiny of the world is at stake.
>
> I, General de Gaulle, now in London, call on all French officers and men who are at present on British soil, or may be in the future, with or without their arms; I call on all engineers and skilled workmen from the armament factories who are at present on British soil, or may be in the future, to get in touch with me.
>
> Whatever happens, the flame of French resistance must not and shall not die.[17]

De Gaulle wanted to set up a military force of French soldiers and sailors to continue the fight against the Germans. He wanted his compatriots to understand that even though Pétain had capitulated, the war would go on and eventually they would be victorious. Since he was the first to use the word "resistance," his speech marked the birth of the resistance outside of France and inspired many patriots within the country.

As it turned out, the French resistance was not limited to military action.

It would include all activities that violated the German and Italian armistice agreements.[18] It would also include underground action taken in defiance of enemy and Vichy decrees in France. Resistance therefore ranged from chalking "V for Victory" signs on sidewalks to fighting guerrilla actions against the Germans.

At first only a few volunteers joined de Gaulle in London, partly because he was not well known. Fully aware of this handicap, de Gaulle offered to serve under higher-ranking French army officers if they would reject the armistice and come to London. When no one accepted his offer, de Gaulle picked up the mantle and was recognized by the British government on June 28 as "leader of the Free French." This action infuriated the Vichy regime, which ordered de Gaulle to return to France to be tried for desertion. A month later a court martial condemned him to death in absentia.[19]

Few people in France heard de Gaulle's "Appeal of June 18," but many nevertheless made the perilous decision not to accept defeat. They were offended by the craven surrender and the presence of German troops in their country. They were indignant that huge swastika flags flew from the public buildings and monuments of Paris, including the Arc de Triomphe, which had been commissioned by Napoleon. They were annoyed that the clocks in occupied France were advanced to German summer time.

Feeling both angry and frustrated, some patriots met with friends to discuss what to do. They spontaneously formed small groups that responded to immediate needs. In the occupied zone they helped French and British prisoners of war and Jews to escape across the demarcation line to the south of France, and they collected military intelligence about the German armed forces. In both zones such groups provided food and shelter for fugitives, made false identity cards, collected and hid weapons, and wrote and distributed underground leaflets and newspapers. Gradually, they established contact with others to become part of a resistance *réseau* (network). By 1943 a complex web of networks extended across France.

How resistance groups evolved into networks can be illustrated by the experience of Germaine Tillion, a 33-year-old French anthropologist, who helped to organize and federate early resistance groups in occupied France. Shortly before the French capitulation, Tillion had returned to Paris from a scientific study of the Berbers in Algeria. Deciding that they must do something about the German occupation, she and some of her friends met to plan their moves. They were all amateurs and had to invent the structure of the resistance, but they quickly became effective. In August 1940 Tillion organized evasion groups by obtaining the addresses of places where the demarcation line could be crossed without the special German pass required under the new regime. She also obtained names of people who would house and feed evaders or furnish them with false papers. The first to be aided by her were French prisoners of war in temporary detention camps in France and Jews trying to flee the country.[20]

During this early effort Tillion was approached by a 74-year-old retired army colonel, Paul Hauet. A graduate of the Ecole Polytechnique and a World War I veteran, Hauet was director of the Union National des Combattants Coloniaux, an organization officially involved in providing food for French African and Asian prisoners of war held in German camps in France. He permitted Tillion to use the offices of the Union for organizing a resistance group. She recruited teams of men and women who could tell the prisoners in their own language how they might escape.[21]

Tillion and Hauet were joined by Col. Duthiel de La Rochère, also a graduate of the Ecole Polytechnique and a veteran of World War I. The two retired officers had met by accident under curious circumstances. Soon after the occupation the Germans had used sledgehammers and dynamite to destroy a statue of Gen. Charles Mangin, a World War I hero, charging that the general had provided German prostitutes for African troops during the French occupation of the Rhineland following the French victory in 1918. Drawn to the scene of the wreckage, the two colonels had fallen into conversation, and together decided that they must take action against the enemy.[22]

Since La Rochère wanted to concentrate on military intelligence, he and Hauet set up separate intelligence sections to collect and send information to England about the German armed forces. Tillion gave the two officers any items of intelligence that came to her attention, and in turn they gave her information about escape lines. It was easier to collect intelligence, however, than to send it to England, and La Rochère's next task was to look for another group that had contact with the British.[23] Tillion also aided in this project.

She was by this time involved not only with her own resistance groups and the Hauet-La Rochère groups, but also with friends at the Musée de l'Homme. This museum still occupies one of the two curving pavilions of the Palais de Chaillot, and between them lies the vast esplanade where a triumphant Hitler was photographed with the Eiffel Tower as a backdrop.

The director of the museum, Paul Rivet, had returned from an assignment in Colombia; Germaine Tillion knew that he and his close associates were fervently anti-fascist, and that they especially condemned the racial theories of the Nazis. In fact, as she found out, members of the museum staff were already taking steps against the Germans. Yvonne Oddon, the head librarian, had sent books and clothes to French prisoners of war in camps near Paris. With a friend, Mme Lucie Boutillier du Rétail, she had also helped some prisoners to escape and provided shelter, food, and information about routes across the demarcation line.[24]

Other staff members joining in the resistance efforts included Boris Vildé, a linguist, and Anatole Lewitsky, an anthropologist. The two men were Russian-born, naturalized French citizens who had served in the French army. They helped prisoners of war and Jews to escape, but they also planned to write and circulate propaganda leaflets and a newspaper opposing all collaboration with the enemy; they also hoped to send military intelligence to London. Vildé made contact with a British intelligence agent, and by the end of August the resistance group in the Musée de l'Homme was in full swing.[25]

Meanwhile Colonel de La Rochère, who was still looking for a way to transmit his intelligence and that of Hauet to London, heard of Yvonne Oddon through someone in the American embassy. He offered to give her intelligence about the German armed forces if she could dispatch it to England. She checked with Vildé and Lewitsky, and they agreed to relay the information from the colonel. Since La Rochère had served in Africa, he was made a member of the Société des Africainistes, a good cover for his trips to the library of the museum.[26] Despite their precautions, however, members of the museum group were arrested between February and April 1941. After de La Rochère and Hauet were arrested, on July 3, 1941, Germaine Tillion received the military intelligence from their agents and arranged for its transmission to England, first by the British and then by the Free French intelligence services.[27]

She knew that risks had to be taken if the German grip on France was to be loosened, and she continued to help create and federate groups. In 1941, through her friend Jacques Lecompte-Boinet, she was in touch with a resistance group led by Elisabeth Dussauze; and when the leaders of that group were arrested in February 1942, she helped Lecompte-Boinet set up a new group, Manipule. She also met with another intelligence group, SMH Gloria. It was because of her connection with Gloria that she was betrayed to the police by a double agent and arrested on August 13, 1942. After being imprisoned in France, she was deported to Ravensbrück, the notorious concentration camp for women.[28]

Because of the need for security, early resistance groups did not have names. After the war Germaine Tillion gave the name Musée de l'Homme to the loosely structured early network. Her first group, she explains, was a "patchwork" that was allied with the "patchwork Hauet" and the "patchwork La Rochère." La Rochère's group was sewed to the "patchwork Vildé," and these four groups became the *réseau* Musée de l'Homme, one of the most important of the early resistance.[29]

The Germans were too experienced as conquerors to delay letting the French know who was in charge in the occupied zone. They issued a proclamation on June 20 that followed the principle of a little carrot and a big stick. The people were to put their trust in the German army, which would guarantee their personal security. Those inhabitants who behaved peacefully would have nothing to fear. The systems supplying gas, electricity, and water, along with the railroads and national art treasures, were put under the protection of the German army. Any acts of violence and sabotage, including damage to German posters, would be punished.

A list of particular violations that would bring the accused before a military tribunal was added to the proclamation:

1. Assistance to Allied soldiers in the occupied zone
2. Aid to civilians trying to flee to unoccupied France
3. All transmission of intelligence to persons outside of the occupied territory
4. All connections with prisoners
5. All offenses against the German army and its chiefs
6. All public assemblies, demonstrations, and distribution of leaflets without the approval of the German authority
7. All work stoppages, whether in public services, the police, schools, or business enterprises.[30]

The German proclamation made it clear to everyone who refused to bow to the conqueror that acts of resistance would be dangerous. French citizens would be punished for such simple infractions as defacing German posters. But many were not cowed by Nazi threats. They believed that outwitting the police was a challenge and sometimes a game, even when the German decrees multiplied and the penalty became death or deportation.

In the occupied zone several police agencies confronted those who resisted. First there were the traditional French police, who were sometimes cooperative and sympathetic to the resistance. More dangerous were the German security agencies, such as the Abwehr of the German armed forces and the Sicherheitsdienst (SD) of the Schutzstaffel (SS). The Abwehr, under Adm. Wilhelm Canaris, had its Paris headquarters in the Hotel Lutétia on the boulevard Raspail. Its main branches were the Geheime Feldpolizei (GFP), the secret field police, whose chief function was to arrest suspects, and branch III, which was responsible for security, counterintelligence, and the liquidation of Allied agents. It had sections in the army, air force, and navy. It also placed agents in arms factories, railroad organizations, and the postal service, and it censored all domestic and foreign mail. This organization posed a special threat to resisters because it infiltrated double agents into their groups.[31]

The SD, under the notorious Heinrich Himmler, the head of the SS, had its Paris headquarters at 82-86 avenue Foch, within sight of the Arc de Triomphe. As Hitler's minister of the interior, Himmler also controlled the Geheime Staatspolizei (Gestapo), the secret state police. Its bleak headquarters were on the rue des Saussaies, in the gray building formerly occupied by the French Ministry of the Interior. The Gestapo and the SD had conflicting jurisdictions, and the responsibilities of both overlapped to some extent those of the Abwehr.[32]

As far as the French were concerned, the Abwehr, SD, and Gestapo were all lumped together and referred to with dread as the Gestapo. The men of the Gestapo were the ones who wore trench coats and drove around in black cars, and who knocked on doors at 4 A.M. to take resisters to the rue des Saussaies for harsh interrogation and imprisonment.

As long as only part of France was technically under occupation, the

German security services were not visible in the Vichy zone. They kept in the background, checking up on French gendarmes, many of whom were anti-German, and arranging the arrest of Allied agents. After the American and British landings in French North Africa in November 1942, Hitler's Axis partner, Mussolini, was permitted to occupy eight French administrative departments east of the Rhone River. Because the Italian secret police, the Organizzazione di Vigilanza e Repressione dell'Antifascismo (OVRA), did not share Hitler's enthusiasm for anti-Semitic decrees, Jews fared better in Italian-occupied France than elsewhere under the occupation, although the OVRA could also be brutal. When Mussolini fell from power in the summer of 1943, the Germans administered all of France and deported thousands of Jews and others who had taken refuge in the southeastern departments.

In January 1943 the Vichy regime set up the *milice* (militia), formed from Joseph Darnard's Service d'Ordre Légionnaire, the Veterans Legion. The *milice* was a paramilitary organization of volunteer toughs and fanatics recruited to stamp out the resistance. It was the most hated of all police forces because the men were French and worked in their home areas. They were a special threat to resisters because of their familiarity with the local community.[33]

Despite the numerous police and security forces in France and despite the German warnings against those opposing the military occupation, the resistance gradually became more visible. The "V for Victory" was chalked on sidewalks and buildings. French and British prisoners of war disappeared from camps; leaflets and newspapers appeared that blamed the Germans for many things, including the food shortages. On November 11, 1940, the anniversary of the armistice of 1918, several thousand Parisian students left their lycées and the university in the first sizable demonstration against the Germans. Assembled at the Arc de Triomphe to lay flowers at the tomb of the Unknown Soldier, they began to sing the "Marseillaise." Shots rang out and German soldiers charged the crowd, beating the students with rifle butts. More than 100 students, many of them women, were arrested, and the university was forbidden to hold classes for the remainder of the semester.

After the defeat of their armies, the British immediately became involved with resisters in France. British intelligence services had been smashed by the rapid German invasion of France, and they desperately needed information to prevent the Nazis from using France as a springboard for the invasion of England.

The British secret intelligence service was known by its initials as SIS or MI 6. Headed by Stewart Menzies, its first move was to set up new contacts and groups in France. For the French the most important man in the organization was Col. Claude Dansey, Menzies' assistant chief for operations, an impatient man who opposed letting women assume positions of leadership.[34] Under Dansey was Comdr. Kenneth Cohen, the head of the French section of MI 6, who had direct responsibility for encouraging and working with the groups in France that reported to MI 6. One of the most successful of these was the Alliance network of Marie Madeleine Fourcade.

In 1939 the British created a new intelligence organization called MI 9. Its functions included facilitating the escape of British prisoners of war, aiding the return to England of those who evaded capture in enemy-occupied territory, and interrogating the men who reached Britain. One of the escape lines given assistance by MI 9 was Comet, led by Andrée de Jongh.[35]

A third important British organization that worked with the resistance in France was the Special Operations Executive (SOE), which was independent of MI 6 and MI 9. An "irregular organization," it was instructed by Prime Minister Churchill in July 1940 "to set Europe ablaze" by encouraging revolt among the oppressed peoples under the Nazi heel. More specifically, SOE had two functions: to instigate sabotage against the enemy and to prepare secret armies to join in the liberation of their countries. In carrying out its mission SOE sent thousands of containers of arms, ammunition, and explosives by parachute drop into France.[36]

Since no one knew how much support de Gaulle had in France in the summer of 1940, SOE set up a French section called F to operate independently of the Free French in London. The British were willing to work with anyone in France who wanted to break the German stranglehold on the country, and did not want to be limited to Gaullists. Early in 1941, however, SOE became impressed with the support for de Gaulle in France, and in the spring set up a new section, RF, to work with the Free French. Its primary task was to encourage and support a unified resistance movement and a secret army in France. Not surprisingly, a virulent rivalry developed between the F and RF sections.[37]

SOE also had a West European escape section, DF. Its major responsibility was to run escape lines, some across France to the coast of Brittany and others to Spain. One of its most successful lines was Var, which transported 70 evaders and agents across the Channel to and from Brittany.[38]

Women played important roles in the various sections of SOE. Unlike the older services, this new and unorthodox organization was not bound by traditions about suitable tasks for women. It employed women not only because of the shortage of qualified men, but also because its staff saw the special advantages women could offer. Women were therefore trained in intelligence, radio communications, sabotage, paramilitary activities, and parachute jumping. Many served in England as staff officers, radio operators, and code clerks, and 39 were sent as agents to France.[39] Twelve of these were executed in German prisons or concentration camps, and one died of meningitis in the field.[40]

Free French groups were active as well. Two of these were the Deuxième Bureau (intelligence) and the Troisième Bureau (operations) of de Gaulle's headquarters, both assigned at first to Capt. André Dewavrin. The immediate task of the Deuxième Bureau was to provide the British with detailed information about German military preparations to invade England. By 1942 the two sections were combined into one London-based organization called the Bureau Central de Renseignements et d'Action (BCRA), the Central Bureau of Intelligence and Action. Dewavrin, who took the name of the metro station Passy as his pseudonym, continued as chief of the entire organization, which had its headquarters at 10 Duke Street. The intelligence section was then headed by André Manuel. It maintained liaison with the British MI 6; the operations section, concerned with sabotage and military actions, had close ties with the RF section of SOE, which supplied Gaullist networks and groups in France.[41]

Dewavrin also set up an evasion section in response to a request from MI 9. Additional escape lines were needed to rescue Allied aviators shot down over France. Dewavrin's first line, Brandy, was one of a family of Gaullist networks that took the name of French wines or liqueurs.[42]

In 1943 General de Gaulle moved his headquarters to Algiers, where he served first as co-president with Gen. Henri Giraud, and then, after a political struggle, as sole president of the new French Committee of National Liberation (CFLN).[43] Dewavrin's position was now changed. Jacques Soustelle became head in Algiers of de Gaulle's Secret Service, Direction Générale des Services Spéciaux (DGSS), with Dewavrin as his technical director. Continuity was maintained in London by the section under Manuel, the Bureau of Research and Action (BRAL), which continued to work with the RF section of SOE.[44]

Relations between the British RF section and the French BCRA were close but often strained. The British controlled the aircraft for parachute and pickup operations, the arms for sabotage actions, and radio communications; and this gave them a dominant position. There was uneasy cooperation between RF and BCRA but de Gaulle and Dewavrin deeply resented the existence of F section, believing it was a subversive rival to BCRA in France.[45]

Since BCRA was as unorthodox as SOE, it also broke tradition about the roles of women, but at a slower pace. Women served as couriers, radio operators, code clerks, and sabotage instructors. In 1944 BCRA sent 11 women agents to France, most of them by parachute. All of them survived.[46]

In contrast with Great Britain, the United States government did not become involved in the French resistance until after the Japanese attack on Pearl Harbor on December 7, 1941. When World War II began on September 1, 1939, the United States had no central intelligence organization. There was a feeling that spying was a dirty business and that gentlemen did not engage in such activities. President Franklin Roosevelt, however, realized that good intelligence was essential to sound policy, particularly regarding the war in Europe. In June 1941 he appointed a Republican Wall Street lawyer, William J. (Wild Bill) Donovan, a hero of World War I, as coordinator of information. Since Donovan believed that the United States faced a dangerous threat from the Nazis, he moved quickly to set up intelligence, special operations, counterespionage, and propaganda activities under COI.

One month before the Japanese bombed Pearl Harbor, COI set up its first overseas mission headquarters in London. Its primary purpose was to establish liaison with its British and French counterparts. In June 1942, COI became the more familiar Office of Strategic Services (OSS). As head of OSS, Donovan controlled both the intelligence and the special operations services. His Secret Intelligence section (SI) worked with MI 6 and with Dewavrin of BCRA, while the Special Operations section (SO) worked with SOE. This section concentrated on training and infiltrating sabotage teams into enemy-occupied territory.[47]

At the same time that Donovan was setting up OSS, the U.S. Army was establishing a group to work with the British MI 9. Lt. Col. W. Stull Holt, an academic historian and an Eighth Air Force intelligence officer in England, had been impressed by the early success of the British unit; and through his initiative an American P/W (prisoner of war) section was activated under his command in June 1942 and installed in Beaconsfield, the British escape and evasion center just west of London. The following February it became the P/W and X Detachment of G-2 (army intelligence) in Europe, and its X section was the American equivalent of MI 9. Its responsibilities remained the same, and included the briefing of American combat personnel about escape and evasion techniques, and the interrogation of American soldiers who had made their way back to Britain. As the escape chapters of this book will show, the interrogation reports based on these interviews are rich sources of information about what women were doing to help Allied military personnel escape from France.[48]

Since the United States was a latecomer to the European war, the inexperienced Americans learned from their British counterparts and OSS agents played the role of junior partners to MI 6 and SOE through 1943. When the Allies gained control of French North Africa in November 1942, OSS set up a headquarters in Algiers. The French desk of its intelligence section sent agents to France to obtain information about German defenses and military forces in the south of France. French and American women helped in this operation.

In preparation for D Day the activities of SOE and the Operations section (OS) of OSS were integrated in January 1944.[49] Four months later SOE/OSS was given the cover name Special Force Headquarters (SFHQ). In Algiers, in keeping with the new coordination, British SOE personnel and Americans from OSS formed the Special Projects Operations Center (SPOC). The French also became part of SPOC, and some Frenchwomen were parachuted into southern France to serve as couriers.[50] The purpose of SPOC was to support the French resistance in preparation for the American-

French invasion of southern France originally scheduled to coincide with the Allied invasion of Normandy. Because of the shortage of landing craft and the prior claims of the Italian campaign, the invasion did not take place until August 15, 1944.[51]

As soon as the Allies landed in Normandy on D Day, OSS set up teams that moved with several Allied armies. When Paris was liberated, a forward headquarters was established there that soon had contact with outposts at Lyon, Dijon, Toulouse, Marseille, Nice, and Annemasse. OSS personnel continued to provide military intelligence for the advancing armies and to arm French guerrilla groups, called the maquis, that were harassing and fighting the Germans. Beginning in January 1944, the U.S. Army Air Force (USAAF) dropped thousands of containers of weapons, ammunition, and explosives by parachute to the maquis, and the number was sharply increased after D Day.[52]

The British and Americans also contributed large sums of money to help finance the resistance. F section of SOE, for example, provided £2 million to its agents in France, some of which was obtained locally by loans from sympathetic businessmen. At the same time the British provided funds for BCRA, and from November 1943 to July 1944 RF section of SOE sent 1.33 billion francs either by agents or by parachute drops. Unfortunately some of this money did not reach the resistance because it was dropped to the wrong area or seized by the Germans.[53]

OSS also sent funds to France. The money was first dispatched from neutral Switzerland, where Allen W. Dulles served as chief of OSS in Bern under the transparent cover of "special assistant to the United States minister." Dulles sent money to Henri Frenay, chief of Combat, the largest resistance organization in the south of France, in exchange for copies of the intelligence reports that Frenay was sending to BCRA. Frenay believed that he needed more money to run Combat than he received from BCRA.[54] OSS also contributed money to other groups, including the numerous networks that its agents organized in France.[55]

As will be seen in the course of this book, the operation of underground organizations was costly. One of the big items was expense money for most of the full- and part-time workers. Those who served as organizers, couriers, guides, and liaison agents were usually compensated for their travel expenses: railroad tickets; meals in black market restaurants, which did not require ration tickets; and lodging in hotels or safehouses, where the hostess had to provide black market food purchased at exorbitant prices. Escape lines also paid the travel expenses of Allied aviators who were escorted across France to Brittany, or over the Pyrenees, where Basque guides charged heavy fees to lead them into Spain.

Thanks to the sheer determination of its members, the French resistance by 1944 had grown into a vast and highly complex structure. The country had been blanketed by more than 177 networks and subnetworks, and by 41 diversified resistance movements.[56] Together these underground workers sent reams of military intelligence to London, published several hundred clandestine newspapers with a total circulation of 2 million, helped 5,000 Allied airmen to escape from France, and furnished about 200,000 guerrilla soldiers to take part in the liberation of the country. In all of these activities, women played important roles. Though they fought without uniforms, they contributed significantly to the victory against the Germans.

What motivated these women to take the grave risk of standing up to the Germans by violating the armistice terms and by ignoring the decrees against the resistance? For many fiercely patriotic Frenchwomen the presence of any foreign troops in France would have been a sufficient motive to resist, but the fascist ideology was especially offensive to people like Yvonne Oddon and her associates at the Musée de l'Homme, who were fervently anti-Nazi. Many women remembered that German armies had destroyed their family homes or those of relatives in World War I, or even in the Franco-Prussian War of 1870. Since childhood they had heard the stories of German cruelties. Thousands of women in France had already either lost their husbands in the recent fighting or learned that their husbands, sons, or other relatives were prisoners of war. They had every reason to oppose the invaders.

Who were these women who joined the resistance in France? What were their social positions, their political and religious views? Were they all French? Women of all social classes were found in the resistance: aristocrats and peasants, middle-class housewives, and professionals like Lucie Aubrac, a teacher, and Yvonne Oddon, a librarian. The fact that so many and such diverse groups were represented in the ranks gave the resistance movement a wealth of resources for gathering and dispatching intelligence, helping to organize escapes, and sabotaging the enemy's operations.

Contrary to a common belief, women in the resistance were not all single and young. Thousands were married and mothers of families. Many had husbands who were prisoners of war. Others were divorced or widowed. All ages were represented: there were women in their seventies as well as teenagers.

Their political views, like their ages and social statuses, varied widely. Between the conservatives from aristocratic and military backgrounds and the Communist intellectuals and workers were women of all political leanings, including many with no political interests because they had not been enfranchised after World War I like women in many other countries. The Musée de l'Homme network included conservatives as well as left socialists.[57] In the escape line Shelburne, a conservative countess, although outnumbered by colleagues of the center and left, helped downed Allied airmen escape from France.[58]

In the Front National (FN) led by Communists, not only Communist women participated. After the Nazis violated the German-Soviet nonaggression pact of August 1939 and invaded the Soviet Union in June 1941, the

Communist Party abandoned its earlier opposition to the "imperialist war."
It set up a broad resistance movement encompassing people of political parties from the Communist to the conservative. Madeleine Braun, a leader of
the FN, explained that non-Communists should be part of the FN because
they all had the same goal: "To fight against the Germans and to liberate
France. After that they would see."[59]

Although France is a predominantly Roman Catholic country, both
Protestants and Jews played important roles in the resistance. Yvonne Oddon
and Elisabeth Dussauze, for example, were Protestants; Annie Kriegel, a
courier with some paramilitary groups, was one of many Jews in the resistance. The Protestants, being a small minority (1 percent of the population), had a history of "resistance" to the central government. The anti-Semitic
decrees of the German and Vichy governments gave the Jews a special motive
for resisting, even though arrest would place them in double jeopardy.

Not only were many social classes, political parties, and religions represented by the women in the resistance, but the movement embraced nationals
of different countries. Among those aiding the Frenchwomen in the resistance
were British, Belgian, and American women, as well as White Russian, Polish,
and German refugees.

During the war most women did not take into account their many differences. They were too busy dodging the police and carrying out their assignments. Genevieve Soulié, who was in charge of providing lodging in Paris for
downed Allied airmen for the escape line Burgundy, summed it up this way: "In
our network there were Catholics, atheists, Protestants, Jews, and people of different political parties and social classes. Our view was that we were still at war
against the enemy occupying our country, and that was the important thing."[60]

Notes

1. This was 13 days after the Dutch had been crushed by the Nazi steamroller.

2. Henri Michel, *The Second World War*, pp. 122–23.

3. Charles de Gaulle, *The Complete War Memoirs*, pp. 59–68.

4. Ibid., p. 77.

5. Henri Philippe Pétain, *Actes et écrits*, pp. 448–49.

6. Marie Madeleine Fourcade, *Noah's Ark*, p. 22.

7. Brigitte Robert Muller, interview, Ann Arbor, MI, April 1976.

8. Hitler insisted that the French sign a companion armistice agreement with
the Italians. English text of the German-French and the Italian-French armistice
agreements is in *New York Times*, June 26, 1940.

9. The number of men echoed the restriction placed on the German army in
the Versailles Treaty of 1919, as did a requirement to pay occupation costs.

10. Robert O. Paxton, *Vichy France*, pp. 56–57, 87.

11. Not all members of Parliament were present. On June 21, 29 deputies and a senator had sailed to North Africa on the *Massilia* in an attempt to move the government there. They had been detained by Pétain's government and called "cowardly" for leaving metropolitan France. The 70-odd Communist members had been expelled from the Chamber of Deputies after the party had denounced the war against Hitler as an imperialist war of no concern to the workers. Ibid., pp. 29–32, 39.

12. Radio addresses of June 17 and 20, 1940, in Pétain, *Actes*, pp. 448–50.

13. Mme Suzanne Borel Bidault, interview, Paris, June 1974, and her *Souvenirs de guerre et d'occupation*, p. 91. As a civil servant in Vichy she helped an intelligence chief send information to England via the diplomatic pouch to Portugal. She also assisted patriots in escaping from France. Paul Paillole, *Services spéciaux 1935–1945*, p. 266. She married the prominent resister Georges Bidault after the war.

14. De Gaulle, *Memoirs*, pp. 27, 44, 67, 71.

15. Ibid., pp. 74–77.

16. Ibid., p. 80.

17. Ibid., pp. 83–84.

18. Henri Michel, *Bibliographie critique de la résistance*, p. 9.

19. De Gaulle, *Memoirs*, pp. 85, 94.

20. Germaine Tillion, letter to author, February 15, 1980.

21. Tillion, "Précis historique sur le réseau Hauet-Vildé," p. 4, Musée de l'Homme Collection, Ellen Clarke Bertrand Library, Bucknell University, Lewisburg, PA.

22. Martin Blumenson, *The Vildé Affair*, p. 64.

23. Tillion, "Précis historique," pp. 1–4.

24. Yvonne Oddon, "Rapport sur mon activité de résistance," p. 1, Musée de l'Homme Collection, Bucknell University.

25. Ibid., pp. 1–2. The group at the Musée de l'Homme had contacts with the American embassy, an intelligence group, and a writer's group.

26. Ibid., p. 8.

27. Tillion, "Précis historique," p. 5, and letter to author, February 15, 1980. Hauet was soon released from prison because of his advanced age and because de La Rochère assumed all responsibility for their intelligence activity.

28. Ibid.

29. Tillion, letter to author, October 19, 1979.

30. Confédération Nationale de Combattants Volontaires de la Résistance, "Echo de la Résistance," no. 100, 1964.

31. Hugo Bleicher, *Colonel Henri's Story*, p. 45; Paillole, pp. 64–66.

32. In the spring of 1944, Himmler, following a series of German military defeats, won the bitter internal struggle with Canaris and took over the Abwehr.

33. M. R. D. Foot, *SOE in France*, p. 120.

34. M. R. D. Foot and J. M. Langley, *MI 9*, p. 80.

35. Ibid., pp. 34–35.

36. Foot, *SOE*, pp. 20, 474.

37. Ibid., p. 21.

38. Ibid., p. 69.

39. See material on the French BCRA, below.

40. Foot, *SOE*, pp. 46–48, 465–69.

41. André Dewavrin [Colonel Passy], *2ᵉ bureau, Londres*, p. 166; and *10 Duke Street, Londres*, pp. 29–32, 45.

42. Dewavrin, *10 Duke Street*, p. 33.

43. President Roosevelt, suspicious of General de Gaulle's aims, supported General Giraud.

44. Foot, *SOE*, pp. 22–23. To avoid confusion, I will refer to de Gaulle's secret services as BCRA. Following the liberation, DGSS was replaced by the Direction Général d'Etudes et Recherches (DGER), which had an evasion section.

45. Eric Piquet-Wicks, *Four in the Shadows*, pp. 22–30; Henri Michel, *Histoire de la résistance en France*, p. 80; Dewavrin, *10 Duke Street*, pp. 165–68.

46. Jeanne Bohec, *La plastiqueuse à bicyclette*, pp. 23, 69–73, 100; Foot, *SOE*, p. 469.

47. Ray S. Cline, *Secrets, Spies, and Scholars*, pp. 59, 65; Dewavrin, *10 Duke Street*, pp. 144–46.

48. In early May 1945, the work of the Awards Section of P/W and X Detachment was continued under the name of 6801 MIS-X Detachment. RG 332, ETO, MIS, MIS-X Section, General Correspondence 1942–47, File 314.7, "History of 6801 MIS-X Detachment"; RG 407, Records of the Adjutant General's Office, "Directive of Secretary of War," WD October 6, 1942, File 383.6, vol. 1.

49. U.S. War Department, Strategic Services Unit, History Project, *War Report of the OSS*, 2:191.

50. Mary Eddy Furman, interview, Washington, D.C., February 1980.

51. RG 165, Records of the War Department General and Special Staffs, Gen. Henry Maitland Wilson, "The Invasion of Southern France," OPD 319.1, TS-Opr, Case no. 33.

52. W. F. Craven and J. L. Cate, eds., *The Army Air Forces in World War II*, 3:503–05; Foot, *SOE*, pp. 474–75; Marcel Vigneras, *Rearming the French*, p. 305.

53. Foot, *SOE*, pp. 470–74.

54. Henri Frenay, *The Night Will End*, pp. 102, 263–64.

55. For information on OSS/Bern networks, see U.S. War Department, *War Report of the OSS*, 2:181.

56. "Liste des réseaux et des mouvements," Ministry of Defense (Paris), Office of Veterans, manuscript list. In the course of the war there were more networks, but because of the diligence of German police agencies, many were destroyed without trace. F section of SOE had a total of 93 networks, 43 of which were extinct by the time France was liberated. Foot, *SOE*, pp. 145–46.

57. Tillion, "Première résistance en zone occupé," *Revue d'histoire de la deuxième guerre mondiale*, April 1958, p. 7.

58. Genevieve de Poulpiquet, interview, Paris, October 1976.

59. Madeleine Braun, interview, Paris, October 1976.

60. Genevieve Soulié Camus, interview, Paris, October 1976. After the liberation, social and political differences reappeared in many organizations.

II WOMEN TO THE RESCUE— ESCAPE LINES

2 NOTABLE CHIEFS

When the German Panzer divisions broke through the French defenses and dashed to the English Channel in May 1940, they trapped French and British forces, which withdrew to Dunkerque. More then 338,000 Allied troops were rescued in an improvised sea operation, but many others were left behind. Forty thousand French troops were taken prisoner by the Germans, while several thousand soldiers of the British Expeditionary Force either avoided capture by hiding on farms and in towns or, like many French soldiers, escaped from temporary prisoner of war enclosures and hospitals.[1]

The German victory created an immediate need for organized operations that would help Allied soldiers and sympathizers escape to Britain. The earliest efforts by patriots wanting to do something for the Allies were feeding, sheltering, and transporting the fugitives they met more or less accidentally. For example, the first escape routes were established by Breton fishermen, who dodged German patrol boats in the Channel while taking volunteers to England to fight for the Free French. Eventually, with the assistance of British and Free French organizations, such as MI 9 and BCRA, such impromptu aid by ordinary people gradually developed into a complex structure of escape lines involving about 100,000 resisters, many of whom were women. During the course of the war they helped almost 2,000 British and Commonwealth airmen and 3,000 American fliers to escape from northwest Europe, primarily France.[2]

Assisting in the return of Allied airmen shot down over occupied territory was an especially important service, since the British suffered from a desperate shortage of fighter and bomber pilots and crewmen, and it took time and money to train them: £15,000 for a fighter pilot and £23,000 for the seven-man crew of a Lancaster bomber.[3]

When the Germans increased their coastal surveillance in order to halt further escapes by sea, land routes were organized. Some extended more than 700 miles from Brussels across occupied France to Spain. Once the soldiers arrived in Spain, they had to avoid arrest by the police, and those who succeeded were guided to British consulates that arranged their transportation to Gibraltar. The unlucky ones who were imprisoned had to wait several months before the British or American consular services could arrange their release.

Other escape lines crossed the demarcation line, the formidable barrier that separated German-occupied northern France from the unoccupied zone of the Vichy government. Headquarters for these lines were set up in cities such as Marseille, from which the soldiers were passed westward along the coast to Perpignan and the Pyrenees. Sometimes the men were evacuated by British boats at night, particularly from Mediterranean beaches such as Canet Plage near Perpignan. Later in the war Allied airmen were picked up from the northern coast of Brittany by British gunboats.

Thousands of women responded to the challenge of helping stranded Allied soldiers, and many became leaders in the escape organizations. Four women headed large escape organizations: the lines known as Comet, Françoise, Marie Claire, and Marie Odile. At least ten women were chiefs of smaller lines, and many were subchiefs or heads of regional sectors. Other women also are known to have exercised leadership in these organizations.

In addition to being leaders of escape lines, women made up a significant proportion of the membership ranks. According to Georges Broussine, chief of Burgundy, about 40 percent of the helpers in his line were women. In the Comet organization, which had members in Belgium and France, some 65 to 70 percent were women. Lists of those who were singled out for postwar awards indicate that 36 percent of the recipients in the Marie Odile line, 20 percent in the Françoise line, and 35 percent in Brandy were women. These lists, however, do not reveal the total number of people associated with the organizations because the names of those who performed only infrequent service do not appear.

The Comet line grew out of a young Belgian woman's conviction that the principal effort to assist Allied soldiers should be directed toward arranging their escape to England as rapidly as possible. In this way the Belgians could help to reduce the critical British need for airmen and lessen the danger that the patriots who gave them shelter would be arrested by the Germans. Originally called the Dédée line after its founder, Andrée (Dédée) de Jongh, it later acquired the name Postman because she referred to the escaping airmen as "packages" and her code name among the British was Postman. Later Dédée named the line Comet because it returned the airmen so quickly to their bases in Britain.

This 24-year-old Belgian was the younger daughter of Frédéric de Jongh, the headmaster of a primary school in Schaerbeek, an industrial section on the outskirts of Brussels. She had dropped out of the lycée because she did not like mathematics but had trained to be both a commercial artist and a nurse. She greatly admired Edith Cavell, the British matron of a Belgian training school for nurses, who had been shot by the Germans in 1915 for helping 200 Allied soldiers to escape. When the Germans invaded Belgium, Dédée promptly volunteered as a nurse caring for wounded Belgian and British soldiers.[4]

Because Dédée wanted to do more than help the wounded, she also worked with a small group of young people to hide and feed soldiers who were trying to avoid capture. She soon resolved to take on the even riskier business of conducting Allied soldiers to Spain, where they could embark for Britain. Her family despised the Nazis as much as she did, and her father became a staunch supporter of her plans.

Although Dédée and her father were anticlerical and liberal, they recruited many Catholics, conservatives, and aristocrats as well as members of the middle and peasant classes to work for the Comet line. Despite political, religious, and class differences, there was a camaraderie among the members of the group. They were united in their goal to help defeat the Nazis, and they did not hesitate to follow Dédée's leadership. One of her Belgian assistants, Baron Jean François Nothomb, explained:

> I was from a conservative Catholic family, and I didn't take a stand against the Nazis until they invaded Belgium. Dédée and I had some lively discussions about politics and religion. She was very sure of herself. She had rigid views without nuances, but these differences did not affect our relationship. She was the chief and we all worked together to evacuate the airmen to Spain.[5]

Despite her youth, this blonde, blue-eyed Belgian was a skillful organizer and had a knack for inspiring men and women to work for Comet in the face of the constant danger of arrest, imprisonment, or death. Under her leadership and that of her section heads, airmen and soldiers who were hiding in haystacks, barns, and houses in Belgium and northern France were brought to safehouses of patriots who wanted to assist the Allied war effort. The men were fed and provided with civilian clothes even though food and clothing were rationed. They were photographed and given false identity cards that could pass rigorous police inspection. Scores of guides were recruited to escort the men to centers such as Brussels and Paris, and to accompany them along the various segments of the line to the Pyrenees. Although Comet was a Belgian line, it had many French members.

The first group to attempt escape with the help of Dédée and her fellow volunteers consisted of ten Belgians and an Englishwoman in danger of arrest by the Nazis. Dédée's chief colleague for this venture was Arnold Deppé, who was especially helpful because he had worked for several years in Bayonne, in southwest France, the direction the escape route must take now that the 42-mile Belgian coast was under the strict control of the enemy.

In June 1941 Arnold reconnoitered the route, which would cross the Belgian-French frontier on the way to Paris and lead eventually to the Pyrenees and Franco's Spain. Soon after Arnold's return they were ready to inaugurate the line with Dédée, who had dyed her hair black, and Arnold as guides. During the long journey in the German-occupied zone, the group encountered only one complication. When they reached the Somme River, a barrier patrolled by German sentries, it was night and the dinghy in which they were to cross the river was missing. Undismayed, Dédée made skillful use of a long rope and a tire tube to help each of the party across the river. She swam the Somme 24 times that night and her main concern was how foolish she would look in her wet underwear if the German guards discovered them.[6]

The results of this initial effort were mixed. Although the evaders reached the Spanish border safely, all of them were arrested after they crossed into Spain. Discovering this later, Dédée found it intolerable that the fugitives she had helped to guide so far should be thrown into Franco's prisons. In the future, she resolved, she would accompany her charges into Spain to be sure they did not fall into the hands of the police. On the positive side, the new escape organization had acquired an important ally on this first trip: Mme Elvire de Greef, a remarkable woman who became head of the southwest region for the Comet line, working with her husband Fernand.

The de Greefs had left Brussels in the exodus after the German invasion, and had found a vacant house in Anglet, near Bayonne. Elvire immediately agreed to Dédée's request that she serve as the anchor of the line in southwest France. Fernand de Greef, who was fluent in German, took a job as chief of French services for the German occupation troops in Anglet. This work served as an excellent screen for resistance activity, and gave him access to blank identity cards and certificates of domicile required by the Germans for those in the forbidden coastal zone.[7]

Under the code name Tante Go, Mme de Greef organized the line in her sector, recruiting and supervising mountain guides, keepers of safehouses, and convoyers. She used the black market to obtain food for the aviators and as a cover for her constant bicycle travel. Four times she crossed the mountains into Spain and, when necessary, she also made trips to Paris and Brussels, returning with aviators in tow. An experienced businesswoman, she also kept detailed records of the line in her sector. She even listed the names of all the aviators, agents, and others who traveled to Spain via Comet and the dates of their crossings.[8] Fortunately, the Germans never saw her records.

Not yet knowing of the arrest of their first group of evaders, and encouraged by what they thought was the success of that trip, Dédée and Arnold organized a second group in July 1941. This time the party included only soldiers, eight Belgians and one Scot. Dédée would escort the Scot, Colin Cupar, who had avoided capture at St. Valéry en Caux in 1940, and two Belgian officers who wanted to fight against the Germans. Arnold would accompany the remaining Belgians. In preparation Dédée provided the evaders with workingmen's clothes and false identity cards that had been made by a printer in Brussels.[9]

At the end of July, Dédée and Arnold left Brussels by separate routes, planning to meet at the little French town of Corbie on the Somme River. Because Cupar could not speak French, Dédée wanted to avoid customs officials who would question the soldiers. Dédée's party took a train to a border town where they could walk across the frontier into France as the Belgian workers did. In this way they reached Corbie, but Arnold and his soldiers were not there. Fearing that he and his group had been arrested, Dédée took her charges to the house of a farmer, Renée Boulanger, in whose boat they had crossed the Somme. Assured at least temporarily of their safety, Dédée took the train to Lille, which was on Arnold's route, and learned there that the seven men had not arrived on the train from Brussels. Realizing that she faced a critical situation, she rode the train to Valenciennes in search of Charles Morelle, a French soldier whom she had helped escape from Belgium in 1940. She asked him to serve as her messenger because she had to know the fate of the other party and, if necessary, warn her family. If the evaders had been arrested and if they had answered questions of the Gestapo, her family and friends would be endangered.[10]

Dédée's fears were justified. Morelle saw the de Jonghs in Brussels and learned that Arnold Deppé and his entire group had been betrayed by a friend of his. The friend had received a handsome reward from the Gestapo for each of the seven men arrested. The traitor also gave Dédée's name to the police, who had gone immediately to her house in Schaerbeek and questioned the members of her family. From this time on, the police were on the trail of Comet.[11]

Although she knew nothing of Arnold's fate at this point, Dédée was aware of the increased risk to her own group if the Germans had been alerted to the venture. Nevertheless, she was determined to continue the journey toward Spain. From Valenciennes she returned to Boulanger's farm and took her three soldiers on the train to Paris and then on the crowded night express headed for Bayonne. Because they did not have the special cards required in the forbidden coastal zones, they left the train two stops before Bayonne to avoid the police controls. With Dédée leading the way, they set out to walk the 12 miles to the safehouse of Fernand and Elvire de Greef in Anglet.[12]

The de Greefs greeted Dédée and her companions warmly, but Elvire had to impart the disturbing news about the fate of the eleven evaders whom Dédée and Arnold had brought to her on the first trip. Until then Dédée had considered that her task would end when her charges had safely reached Spain. Now she realized that she could not be sure of success unless she obtained considerable help from British officials in that country. She would need both their financial help and their assistance in transporting escapers in Spain. She therefore resolved to accompany the men and the mountain guide hired by Tante Go across the Pyrenees, to be sure that her group did not fall into the hands of the police. Since she planned to talk to British officials about money to finance her escape line, she would take the men to the British consul in Bilbao and ask him to arrange their transportation to Gibraltar.[13]

To guide Dédée and the three soldiers across the mountains, Tante Go had hired a Basque smuggler, Tomas. Tomas was very reluctant to include Dédée in the party because he did not think a girl could keep up with the men, but when Dédée explained that she was an experienced hiker and swimmer, he relented. They set out at night to avoid the border patrols. Several hours of climbing up and down mountain slopes on which it was difficult to keep their footing in the dark, brought them to the Bidassoa River, which they crossed into Spain, pushing on until the first light of dawn appeared. They had been hiking for 12 hours before they took cover in an abandoned farmhouse and ate the slices of bread and jam that Tante Go had provided. After resting there until nightfall, they walked for eight hours to a little farm just south of San Sebastian. There, exhausted by the long journey, they climbed into the hayloft to sleep.[14]

The next day another guide took them by train to Bilbao, where Dédée led the three soldiers into the British consulate. She told the astonished vice-consul that she had brought the two Belgians and the Scottish soldier from Brussels, and planned to establish an escape line between Belgium and Spain. The British, she felt, should reimburse her for the cost of bringing the men to Spain. She emphasized that her line would remain absolutely independent of British control.

The authority of this slim young woman impressed the vice-consul, and he asked her to return the next day. Meanwhile he checked with his superiors in the embassy at Madrid, and they in turn consulted London. Although the Scottish soldier, Cupar, had vouched for the fact that Dédée had escorted them from Brussels, Col. Claude Dansey at MI 6 immediately doubted her story and denounced it as a Gestapo trap. How could she have crossed the Pyrenees at night? However, Norman Crockett, chief of MI 9, which specialized in escape operations, thought her account was credible. He learned from an intelligence check that Dédée had written letters to parents of wounded servicemen, describing visits and gifts of food she had made to their sons in the hospitals in Brussels. In the face of this evidence a stubborn Dansey grudgingly agreed that MI 9 could pursue the matter.[15]

Meanwhile, Dédée was kept waiting. After ten days, the vice-consul was instructed to pay the expenses of the journey to Spain. The British also agreed to arrange for the transfer of the evaders to Gibraltar on behalf of MI 9. In this and future missions a young diplomat, Michael Creswell, would coordinate the activities in Madrid. Under the code name Postman, Dédée would try to bring a group of aviators, particularly pilots, on her next trip.[16]

Buoyed by British support, Dédée recrossed the Pyrenees, this time with a new guide, Florentino Goicoechea, who was a tough Basque smuggler and a refugee from Franco Spain. Although he had a weakness for cognac, his detailed knowledge of the routes across the mountains made him the top guide for the line. As Dédée was to learn, an untrustworthy guide could spell disaster, but Goicoechea proved invaluable. He made 66 trips across the Pyrenees, guiding 227 escapers during the course of the war. For this service he was awarded the George Medal by the British government.[17]

Despite the advantage of a reliable guide and the promise of British support, this second effort by Dédée and her group had created a serious problem, since the arrest of Arnold meant that it was no longer safe for her to return to Belgium. Charles Morelle, however, had invited her to set up her headquarters in Valenciennes, close to the French-Belgian border, and she accepted his offer. Her father assumed the duties of head of the Brussels sector, where downed airmen were collected, and Dédée took charge in France. As chief of the line she would continue to serve as a guide and maintain personal contact with Creswell, the British official in Spain. Couriers and guides would carry information about the line to Dédée so that she could coordinate the entire operation.[18]

In the spring of 1942, Dédée transferred her headquarters from Valenciennes to Paris when her father was forced to leave Belgium one step ahead of the Geheime Feldpolizei. He assumed the responsibilities of head of the Paris section, and Baron Jean Greindl took the great risk of replacing him as the chief in Brussels.

Dédée made 20 trips back and forth across the Pyrenees, conducting 118 evaders, before she was arrested by the Gestapo on January 15, 1943. She and Goicoechea had set off with one British and two American aviators to the last safehouse before the Pyrenees, the farm of a young Basque widow, Francia Usandizga. Here they had a light supper. Because of heavy rain, however, they could not cross the mountains that night, so Goicoechea returned to his house in nearby Ciboure. Since they would not attempt the next stage by daylight, he planned to rejoin them the next evening. The following noon, after a good night's sleep, Dédée was joking with the men to break the tension of waiting for darkness when a car suddenly screeched to a stop and armed Germans stormed into the house. "Hände hoch!" they shouted. They arrested everyone, including Francia, and searched the house for the absent Goicoechea. The Germans had been tipped off by a Spanish farmhand whom Dédée had ceased to use as a guide because she did not trust him. Dédée and her friends were imprisoned in nearby St. Jean de Luz and then transferred to the filthy German prison, Villa Chagrin, in Bayonne. Meanwhile, word of her capture reached Mme de Greef and Jean François Nothomb.[19]

Baron Nothomb, who took Dédée's place as head of the Comet line, was then 24 years old. He had served as an officer candidate during the 18 days of the Belgian campaign, and had escaped from a prisoner of war camp in Germany. Since October 1942 he had assisted Dédée by escorting evaders from Paris to Bayonne and across the Pyrenees. His confusing code name, Franco, came from his chief Paris guide, Elvire, Charles Morelle's sister, who thought it suitable for a dark haired man traveling into Spain. Before his arrest in January 1944, Nothomb escorted about 100 airmen from Paris to the Bayonne area. In addition, he made 18 trips across the mountains into Spain to accompany aviators and to carry reports to the British, who in return furnished expense money for Comet and useful information from MI 9.[20]

Mme de Greef and Baron Nothomb prepared several plans to rescue Dédée from prison, but each time she was transferred before the escape could be carried out. From the Villa Chagrin in Bayonne she was driven to the Maison Blanche in Biarritz. Before the war Biarritz had been a playground for European aristocrats and millionaires, and the Maison Blanche was a huge villa which the Germans had requisitioned and converted to a prison. After a brief stay Dédée was transferred to Fresnes prison on the outskirts of Paris, where several hundred women resisters, including many mentioned in this book, were incarcerated in the course of the war. In June 1943 Dédée was moved to St. Gilles prison in Brussels, to appear as a witness at the Luftwaffe court-martial of her guide, Elvire Morelle, who had been caught in a police trap in Brussels. Many members of Comet were imprisoned in St. Gilles, including Dédée's elder sister, Mme Suzanne Wittek, and their mother and aunt, who had been arrested as hostages.

During Dédée's imprisonment she was subjected to 17 interrogations by the police of the Luftwaffe, who claimed priority in dealing with personnel of escape lines; she also was questioned twice by the Gestapo. At first she admitted only that she was a guide, but when she discovered through the questioning that the police knew about the activities of some of her friends and her father, she took the full responsibility of her position. She informed her interrogators that she was the chief of the line, but they did not believe her. How could a young woman create and direct such an organization?[21]

Dédée de Jongh was deported to Germany in August 1943. Three months later she was sent to the infamous Ravensbrück concentration camp, 50 miles north of Berlin, where she found her sister Suzanne, who had helped Comet in Brussels. After four months she and Suzanne were dispatched to Mauthausen concentration camp in Austria. There, Dédée admitted that she and Suzanne could speak German, and they became interpreters. They were finally freed with 20,000 others when the International Red Cross arrived and the American army took control of the camp in early May 1945.[22] She had been imprisoned for nearly two and a half years.

Although Nothomb served as leader of Comet for only a year before he too was arrested, the line continued to function thanks to the courage and dedication of others in the organization. Elvire de Greef and the members of her family, for example, worked so efficiently that 337 airmen passed through their hands. As chief of the southwest sector Tante Go received the American Medal of Freedom with gold palm and, like Andrée de Jongh, the George Medal from the British.[23] The recognition was well deserved. Many times when those in the line were in trouble, Tante Go proved her daring and resourcefulness. On one occasion she was traveling south on the train from Bayonne, looking for a new route across the Pyrenees. She was accompanied by Albert Johnson, a stalwart English guide with false Belgian identity papers, and Mme Yvonne Lapeyre, a safehouse keeper. The German customs police searched and interrogated the group because they suspected that Johnson was English and that the women were escorting him to Spain. They took the trio from the train and placed Johnson under arrest. Mme de Greef immediately took charge of the delicate situation. She insisted that Johnson had tuberculosis and that they were taking him to a doctor. If they did not release Johnson, she threatened, she would report their action to the Kommandant. She told them she knew the Kommandant because it was her task to buy him ham, butter, and eggs on the black market. Reference to the black market unnerved the Germans, and they let Johnson go.[24]

In the three years of its existence, workers in Comet helped to guide 356 people to Spain, of whom 288 were Allied aviators.[25] Seventy-five fugitives were transferred to other lines when Comet was broken periodically by Gestapo arrests, and after D Day 345 were hidden from the Germans. Altogether 776 people were rescued by the line, the largest number of any escape line.[26]

Comet performed a dual service in enabling soldiers to evade capture. It relieved the operators of countless safehouses who would otherwise have been caught with Allied soldiers or fugitives in their houses, and imprisoned or executed. It also boosted the morale of Allied aviators flying missions over Belgium, France, and Germany. Every downed airman who returned to his unit was proof that people in occupied Europe were helping stranded aviators return to Britain.[27]

A second escape line over the Pyrenees was anchored in Toulouse, with key posts in Paris, Marseille, and Perpignan. Much of its success was owed to 60-year-old Marie Louise Dissard, another of the remarkable women who directed escape organizations.

The line was originally founded by a Scottish captain, Ian Garrow. His division, the 51st Highland, had been overwhelmed at St. Valéry in 1940, but he had managed to lead a group of fellow soldiers across the demarcation line into unoccupied France, and thus evade capture. Although his height made him conspicuous and he spoke French with a Scottish accent, he continued to help evaders and was able to avoid arrest until October 1941. He was also fortunate enough to be kept in a French prison, from which he was later able to escape with the help of the line he had organized.

While Garrow had attempted to pass himself off as a Frenchman, his successor as head of the line was a Belgian doctor, Albert Guérisse, who had masqueraded as a British naval officer under the name of Patrick O'Leary in order to carry out a mission for the Allies on April 26, 1941. The police had caught him swimming ashore on the Mediterranean coast and had interned him at Fort St. Hippolyte. On July 4, 1941, he had escaped, and made contact with Garrow's organization. When Garrow was arrested some three months later, Guérisse took over the leadership of the line, and thereafter, until his own arrest, the organization was known by his pseudonym as the Pat O'Leary line, or simply the Pat line.

Marie Louise Dissard, code-named Françoise, began her work with the Pat line in response to a request that she rent a furnished villa for a Jewish tailor and his wife, the Ullmans, who would keep it as a safehouse for airmen on the run. Since food was rationed, she brought black market meat to the villa twice a week. She also rented an apartment for Pat.[28]

By December 1942 Françoise was an important assistant to Pat O'Leary. She was the hub of the machine in the Toulouse area, enlisting guides and keepers of safehouses, and procuring civilian clothing, food, and medical supplies. Her small, dark apartment became the headquarters of the line. Agents and guides came there for information and instructions, and there she also sheltered airmen, agents in transit, and fugitives from the police. After Ian Garrow's escape from prison, he and several leaders of the Marseille sector stayed at her apartment while waiting to cross into Spain.[29] In her spare time she canned food, which she sent to her nephew in a German prisoner of war camp. She herself lived largely on black coffee, and rarely slept.

Françoise became a familiar figure to many on the side of the Allies. Short and broad, she wore her gray hair in two braids across the top of her head and kept a Gauloise Bleu cigarette in a long, ivory holder always in her mouth. Round, metal-rimmed glasses sat firmly on her nose. When she spoke, her deep, gruff voice commanded immediate attention.

Her daring and imagination made her an ideal partner. One remarkable escape that she arranged was that of six resisters and two American aviators who were imprisoned in the Castres jail west of Toulouse. Françoise had discovered that Raymond, one of the guards, was in sympathy with the resistance and wanted to join General de Gaulle, so she and Pat gave him a bottle of doped wine for the other guards. At the appointed time a moving van drove up to the front entrance of the jail, and the men, including Raymond, who had released them from their cells, filed quietly into the van. By dawn they were in Toulouse, some of them in Françoise's apartment.[30]

Although the Gestapo had made a series of arrests primarily in the northern part of the line, guides continued to bring airmen to Toulouse. One of these, Sgt. Arthur B. Cox, an engineer on a Flying Fortress who had been shot down in northeastern France in October 1942, was able, by playing a deaf-mute for three months under the wing of the Pat line, to reach Toulouse. There he was taken to the Hotel de Paris for several hours and then assigned to an apartment, following what appeared to be a well-established routine that would take him on to Perpignan and into Spain.

Under the surface of all such organizations lay the danger of treachery from within. In this case, the traitor was the guide who had brought Cox to Toulouse, Roger Le Neuveu, called Roger Le Légionnaire. While pretending to be a staunch resistance guide, he was in fact an agent of the Gestapo, and it was on his information that Pat and a fellow patriot were arrested on March 3, 1943, leaving Marie Louise Dissard with the responsibility for running the line that was soon to be called the Françoise line, after her code name.

She did not immediately know that Roger Le Neuveu was the informer. Pat had been in Marseille but had turned up at her Toulouse apartment at three in the morning to obtain the latest news and let her know that he had returned. Since she was already hiding a New Zealand-born woman, Nancy Wake Fiocca, and Renée Nouveau of Marseille, Françoise urged Pat to get some sleep in his own apartment, and she would take any messages. The next morning she heard from Paul Ullman that he and Pat were to meet Roger at the Super Bar in the rue d'Alsace Lorraine. As she learned later, the two joined Roger at 12:30 P.M., but they had hardly time to exchange greetings before the table was surrounded by Gestapo agents. While one held a gun at Pat's head, the three men were searched, handcuffed, and taken to headquarters for questioning. There Pat discovered that Roger was the traitor. Since it appeared to onlookers in the bar that all three men had been arrested, this fact was not suspected at the time by others in the line. After the interrogations Pat and Paul were thrown into the military prison in Toulouse.[31]

Françoise was alarmed, and feared further Gestapo raids when neither Pat nor Paul returned after the cafe meeting and her inquiries disclosed that the three men had been arrested. She immediately sent Nancy Fiocca to another safehouse, and later that night took Renée Nouveau and some aviators as far north as Bergerac to throw the police off her trail.[32]

At Bergerac, Françoise promptly took command of the escape organization. She arranged for Renée Nouveau, Nancy Fiocca, four aviators, and three others to hide either at Perpignan or at Mme Lebreton's hotel in Canet Plage while awaiting a convoy across the Pyrenees. Meanwhile, there had been wholesale arrests, and it was clear that she would have to rebuild the line. Since she needed operating funds, she traveled to Annemasse on the Swiss border, hoping to reach Geneva and establish contact with Victor Farrell, the British vice-consul there who provided money for the organization. After the long trip across France she did not hesitate to climb over the barbed-wire fences and dodge border guards to reach Farrell. Being assured of weekly payments to support the line, and having so far outwitted the Gestapo, she visited the key cities of her organization, where she reimbursed the surviving guides and keepers of safehouses for their expenses and recruited new ones. Françoise was very scrupulous about the subsidy money she received, and she preferred to spend her own money if there was any question about whether the expenditure was for the line.[33]

After her return home and without the knowledge of the police, she rented the Villa Pamplemousse as a lodging for the increasing number of aviators and agents seeking refuge in Toulouse. A few months later she renewed her contact with Jean Bregi, who was to become her right-hand man. He had worked with her in the Pat line before he was imprisoned for sabotaging a factory that produced munitions for the Germans. Now he not only helped arrange the convoying of fliers to Toulouse, and from there to Perpignan, but also shared the responsibility of the weekly trips to the British representatives in Annemasse and Geneva. Françoise frequently escorted aviators from the countryside to Toulouse, where she arranged for their lodging, and from Toulouse to Perpignan, where they were turned over to the Pyrenees guides. She was once questioned by police on the Perpignan express train about escorting aviators, but with considerable sangfroid, she insisted she knew nothing about such things.

Once suspected by the police, however, she could no longer serve as an escort on that route. A new guide took her place in January 1944, but he was immediately arrested in Perpignan by the Gestapo. Contrary to all security rules he was carrying a notebook with the address of the Villa Pamplemousse. Although Françoise had learned of the arrest in time to reach the villa before the Gestapo and remove all of the incriminating evidence, she was a prime suspect, and for a time she was forced to live in attics, cellars, and garages. Finally she took refuge in her own apartment near the Gestapo headquarters, where the Germans assumed she would not dare to stay. She kept the shutters closed so that the apartment looked unoccupied.[34]

When Françoise could no longer send men across the mountains via Perpignan and her freedom of movement was limited, she worked with Gabriel Nahas, a young medical student who was an agent of the Dutch-Paris escape line. She provided the funds and Gabriel passed the evaders to his mountain guides, who led them to Spain. Gabriel, a Protestant, was in charge of the Pyrenees sector of Dutch-Paris, which specialized in assisting Jews and airmen to escape from France.[35]

Many American airmen had reason to thank the resourceful and clever Françoise. According to 2d Lt. Harold O. Freeman, she exerted great influence among fellow workers in the resistance. "In March 1944," he wrote, "she helped us get out of the Toulouse railroad station through the baggage room while the Germans were inspecting identification papers in the depot." S. Sgts. Robert Finney and Kenneth Carson were picked up at a safehouse near Toulouse by a gendarme sent by Françoise. All of these men crossed the mountains into Spain.[36]

Françoise's achievements were impressive. Through her efforts about 250 aviators were returned to England, 110 of them during the period when the Gestapo was constantly searching for her. She worked either directly or indirectly with 123 agents whom she later considered important enough to receive postwar awards. Nor was she the only woman serving this line. Some 24 other women received awards, and many others performed occasional services for the line. As its chief, Françoise received the American Medal of Freedom with gold palm and equally distinguished medals from the British and French governments.[37]

The founder of the escape organization known as the Marie Claire line presents a far different figure from that of Dédée, the young, blonde Belgian, or Françoise, the disciplined spinster of Toulouse. Outspoken and independent, Mary Lindell, the Comtesse de Milleville, seems to have aroused controversy wherever she went. Nevertheless, her exploits place her among the most noteworthy of the women in escape lines.

Born in England in 1895, she had served as a field hospital nurse with the French Red Cross in World War I, and for her care of the wounded she had received the French Croix de Guerre and the Russian Order of St. Anne in 1917.[38] She had married a Frenchman, the Comte de Milleville, and since 1919 had lived in Paris. Her eldest son, Maurice, one of her helpers in the resistance, was born in 1921; she had another son and daughter, who were in their teens when World War II began.

A handsome woman of medium height, with chestnut hair and brown eyes, Mary Lindell had a commanding personality. She liked to give orders, and she spoke with the self-confidence of an aristocrat. However, Mary was not like a traditional lady. She was sometimes ungracious and abrupt; if she thought people were phony, she told them so. At other times she was charming, a good mimic, and an amusing raconteur. She did not like humdrum routine, and enjoyed the challenge of outwitting people, particularly the Germans.[39]

Like many others, Mary responded to the urgent need to help British and French soldiers and civilians flee from France. She sent stranded British subjects by train to St. Malo in Brittany or south to Marseille in response to a request from Mrs. Elizabeth Deegan, secretary to Robert Murphy in the American embassy. But she soon realized that the best way to assist the British soldiers still wandering around Paris in khaki battle dress was to escort them on trains to southwestern France and the Pyrenees. Her sons and Michèle, a lycée friend, accompanied the escapers to Bordeaux and Sauveterre de Béarn, where a former nurse of Michèle's had a farm. There a retired British major arranged for Pyrenees guides to lead the men into Spain. Two or three Allied soldiers traveled down this impromptu line each week.[40]

Meanwhile, Mary was also driving sick children across the demarcation line for the Red Cross. This activity provided a screen for driving a captain of the Welsh Guards, James Windsor-Lewis, into the free zone. The young officer had been introduced to her by Cecil Shaw, a retired English colonel who was living at the Ritz with his American wife. Windsor-Lewis had been seriously wounded and captured at Boulogne in the debacle of 1940. Although he spoke little French, he managed to enlist the help of nurses and to evade lax frontier guards. Disguised as a Belgian worker, he had come to Paris hoping to find a way to get back to England.[41]

Mary hid him in her apartment for 13 days while she obtained the necessary documents for his evasion. Relishing the dangerous game of outwitting the Germans, she went to the office of Count von Bismarck, great-grandson of the Prussian chancellor, to obtain an *ausweis* (pass) to cross the demarcation line and gasoline coupons. She told him that the French Red Cross had learned of a child on the other side of the line who needed special care, and that they wished her to rescue the child. She would need to take a nurse and a mechanic along with her. The affable count instructed his secretary to make out the necessary papers for the Comtesse de Milleville.[42] German aristocrats were impressed by French titles.

Mary disguised Windsor-Lewis as the car mechanic and Michèle, her escape guide, as a nurse for the sick child. Starting out in the direction of Orléans, she was forced to pick up a German Luftwaffe officer who was returning to his base near Châteaudun after having bailed out of his disabled bomber. Fortunately he had not been in France very long and had little knowledge of the language. He noticed the mechanic in the back seat of the car and agreed with Mary that the man did not look very bright. The deception worked so well that at the German headquarters at Châteaudun her German hitchhiker introduced her to the Kommandant. He too was impressed by her title and manner. With a click of his heels he bowed and gave her a handful of gasoline coupons as a token of his appreciation for her kindness to one of his pilots. Mary hoped that she could now continue her journey, but the pilot insisted that she drive him to the nearby airfield, where he proudly showed her German bombers and fighters — all duly noted by Windsor-Lewis.[43]

After finally taking leave of the Luftwaffe officer, Mary and her two passengers reached Ruffec the following morning. With Count von Bismarck's pass they had no difficulty in crossing the demarcation line en route to Limoges. Once in the unoccupied zone, Mary bought Windsor-Lewis a railroad ticket for Marseille. There he could go to the Seaman's Mission, headed by a Scottish minister named Donald Caskie, who was in touch with his fellow Scot, Ian Garrow, the original founder of the Pat O'Leary line. As Mary learned long afterward, the venture succeeded. Captain Windsor-Lewis made the journey back to Britain, where he later became a brigadier general. He fought to the end of the war, and his photograph had a place of honor in Mary's living room.[44]

As more stranded British soldiers were brought to Mary, often by a friendly police inspector, she decided to establish a second escape route. This one crossed the demarcation line at Ruffec, a market town 50 miles south of Poitiers. Here she found help from two farmers whose land lay on opposite sides of the demarcation line, which was patrolled by the Germans. Farm A was in occupied France on the outskirts of Ruffec, while Farm B was in the free zone a few miles away. Simply by going from one farm to the other, the guides could lead the soldiers into unoccupied France without encountering German guards.[45]

Mary's escape activities came to an abrupt end when the vigilant Geheime Feldpolizei (GFP) of the Abwehr picked up her tracks and arrested her early in 1941 for aiding the escape of British officers. During many interrogations she was confined to the Cherche Midi prison in Paris, where she shared a room with two others. One of the women, posing as a fellow patriot, was in fact planted there to obtain Mary's real story. The other was Mrs. Etta Shiber, the widow of an American journalist, who also had been working with an escape line.[46]

The German court-martial found the spirited Mary guilty as charged, but by skillful argument she succeeded in having her sentence reduced from 30 to 9 months' solitary confinement in Fresnes prison, where she was held in cell number 119,[47] which boasted a basin with a faucet and an elementary toilet. Undismayed by the dreary surroundings and the horrible food, Mary did physical and mental exercises to keep in shape.[48]

As soon as she had served her sentence and won her release in November 1941, Mary returned to her apartment and soon went into hiding. At Ruffec she stayed at the Hotel de France, where Roger and Germaine Rouillon were the proprietors. She then crossed the demarcation line from Farm A to Farm B and headed for Lyon, where she sought out George Whittinghill, the U.S. vice-consul, and found an apartment with his help.

Whittinghill was an American foreign service officer who had volunteered to work with the British MI 6 in 1939 when he was stationed in Milan. To facilitate this work his American superiors had him transferred to Lyon in October 1940 and assigned to the British consulate with the title of American vice-consul in charge of British interests. Whittinghill's assignment was to provide funds for the 2,000 British and Commonwealth subjects in central France who could not return to their homes.[49]

While carrying out his official consular duties, Whittinghill was able to gather intelligence for MI 6, to aid agents of SOE, and to cooperate with MI 9 by assisting military personnel and agents of the resistance to escape from France. One of the groups with which he worked was the Pat O'Leary line. To escapers and agents he provided false identity papers, clothing, and shelter. He also gave official rubber stamps to Pat and sent his intelligence reports via the American diplomatic pouch to Switzerland. Victor Farrell in Geneva sent funds for the line via Whittinghill's pouch.[50] Thanks to Whittinghill, Mary Lindell obtained Spanish and Portuguese visas and an exit permit from Vichy. Posing as a stranded British governess, she left France in July 1942 and soon reached London. There she reported to Lt. James M. Langley, head of P 15, the office of MI 9 responsible for escape lines in northwest Europe. Langley, an officer in the Coldstream Guards, had lost an arm at Dunkerque, escaped from a German hospital to Vichy France, and returned to England after being repatriated because of his war wounds.

The arrival in London of a woman of her position and with her knowledge and experience in occupied France could hardly have been more timely. A month earlier, in June 1942, President Roosevelt and Prime Minister Churchill had met in Washington to deal with the awesome problems of the war. American ships were being sunk in the Atlantic at an alarming rate; Field Marshal Erwin Rommel was poised at El Alamein for a breakthrough to the Suez Canal; Joseph Stalin, suspicious of his allies, was warning that the Soviet Union might be knocked out of the war unless the British and Americans opened a second front in Western Europe.

Since the Allies had neither the necessary armed forces nor the ships and planes for a frontal assault on German-occupied France, the two wartime leaders agreed on an Anglo-American invasion of North Africa, code-named Operation Torch. If successful, this strategic move, scheduled for the fall, would trap Rommel between the British Eighth Army and the forces invading from the west, and would help to protect American shipping in the south Atlantic. A little-known American officer, Lt. Gen. Dwight D. Eisenhower, was made theater commander of the operation.

One of Eisenhower's problems was to prevent submarine and air attacks against the armada of 500 ships that would carry troops and matériel from the United States and United Kingdom to North Africa. As a top priority the Eighth Air Force was ordered to bomb the bases on the west coast of France from which most of the German Atlantic submarine fleet operated. Secondary targets included the docks at Channel ports, as well as aircraft factories, repair depots, and railroad marshaling yards.[51]

With the increased bombing raids, more American and British fliers were shot down over France. Those who survived and evaded capture created bottlenecks in escape lines undertaking to return them to England. New escape lines were a necessity.

When Mary Lindell reached Langley's apartment, she was greeted by Langley and by Airey Neave, who had escaped from the German fortress of Colditz. In her amusing but sometimes arrogant fashion, she told them the story of her resistance activities and of her court-martial. Her aim, she said, was to return to France, despite the risk, and organize another escape line. When Langley told her that she must first undergo training, she snapped, "Training for what?" Langley replied that it was P 15's job to train her. "It isn't your job to teach ducks to suck eggs!" she snorted. Nevertheless, she agreed to undergo some training as an agent. She took a crash course in coding radio messages and learned the procedures for night landing of Lysander planes. At the age of 46 she became the first woman trained by MI 9 to organize and direct an escape line.[52]

Langley and Neave were concerned about the risk of sending Lindell to France because of her previous arrest. Colonel Dansey opposed sending her back for security reasons and because he did not think a woman should be a chief, but in only one interview she persuaded him to let her return. Unfortunately, P 15 did not know that several people who had worked with Mary in 1940 had been arrested in Paris, and that she had been condemned to death in absentia by the Germans. The Gestapo was already on her trail.

Mary arrived in France by Lysander plane on October 26, 1942, landing near Ussel in the unoccupied zone, about 100 miles southeast of Ruffec. There she was greeted by an SOE reception committee and headed for Ruffec, where she planned to set up her headquarters. She then traveled to Lyon, where her 21-year-old son Maurice was living and where the American vice-consul, Whittinghill, would provide her with additional funds from British officials in Geneva. Mary did not at first assume a false identity believing that she was too well known in French hotels for any such deception to be effective. She usually worked under either her maiden or her married name, using the French Red Cross as a cover. Among resisters her code name was Marie Claire, which became the name of the new escape line she would direct.[53]

In December, Mary and a French guide set out from Lyon to find a new place to cross the demarcation line. The line was still a barrier even though the Germans had occupied all of France the preceding month, when the Allies had invaded North Africa. Mary needed an alternative route so that all the airmen would not come to one city — Ruffec, for instance — and thus alert the police. As Mary and her guide rode a tandem bicycle, reconnoitering a crossing site on the Loire River near Blois, they were hit by a German car. The Frenchman was catapulted into the air and Mary was thrown onto the hood of the car, where she lay unconscious. Patriotic helpers managed to carry them to a farmhouse from which Mary could be taken secretly to a hospital in Loches, 37 miles away. She was seriously hurt: a hand wound, five broken ribs, and injuries to an arm and a leg.[54]

Mary could not notify MI 9 headquarters of the accident because she had arrived in France without a radio operator, having been unwilling to work with Groome, the only trained operator available when she left. Until another operator was trained, she would have to send couriers to Spain and Switzerland and establish a working relationship with Whittinghill in Lyon to maintain contact with London. To complicate matters even further, two British commandos had appeared in Ruffec and asked for help in making their way back to Britain.[55] They were officers of the British marines, Maj. H. G. Hasler and Cpl. W. E. Sparks, the only survivors of a commando raid that had damaged five German ships docked at Bordeaux.[56]

According to their briefing by Langley of P 15, they were to look for an organization in Ruffec. As soon as they could change their uniforms for civilian clothes, the two marines set off for Ruffec, 105 miles to the northeast, which they reached on December 18. By good luck they made contact with the Marie Claire line in the first restaurant where they stopped to eat. They were questioned by two representatives of the line, then given good civilian clothes to replace the tattered ones they had obtained near Bordeaux, and were transferred to Armand Debreuille's Farm B, just east of the demarcation line. Debreuille sent a message to Mary requesting instructions, and learned of her accident. While waiting for a guide to pick up the men, he kept them confined to their room except to go to the privy.[57]

Shortly after Christmas, Mary was able to leave the hospital, and her son Maurice took her to Lyon to recuperate. After two weeks at the farm, the commandos were picked up by Maurice and brought to Lyon to see his mother. Mary was wearing her Red Cross uniform complete with medals, and her leg was still in a plaster cast. She looked, according to Hasler, like a typical British fox-hunting woman. She told the two marines the one rule for Englishmen going down the line was "no girls." "From past experience," she explained, "we know that once escapers meet a pretty girl, everything goes to hell." She provided the men with false identity papers and installed them in a large house outside of Lyon.[58]

Mary still did not have a radio operator, and she had to report to MI 9. She also needed more money, since she could no longer count on Whittinghill, who had been recalled to Washington in October, just before the American-British invasion of North Africa.[59] Unable to wait until she had fully recovered from the accident, Mary made the journey to Geneva to see Victor Farrell. Fortunately, she did not have to climb barbed wire, as Marie Louise Dissard of the Françoise line had done. With the help of the Swiss Intelligence Service, she took a fisherman's boat across Lake Geneva.[60] After seeing Farrell she went to Bern and gave a detailed report about her line's activities to Col. Henry Cartwright, the British military attaché. She also gave him a coded message from the two British commandos whom she had taken under her wing. This was the first message that the British Admiralty received about the Bordeaux raid.[61]

Although Mary was in pain and her injured arm was infected, she was impatient to return to France. Defying MI 9's order to remain in Switzerland until she had fully recovered, she went back to Lyon. She was determined to enlarge her organization, and she still needed to plan the evasion of Major Hasler and Corporal Sparks. Her line was not then in operation across the Pyrenees, so she arranged for guides to take the two men to Marseille, where they were put in touch with the Pat line and taken into Spain.[62]

In Ruffec, the Hotel de France let Mary reserve one room for herself and six for escaping aviators. She extended the line from Paris and northern France to Ruffec and across the Pyrenees into Andorra. She recruited and instructed guides, most of whom were women, and established many safehouses. Her son Maurice was her personal courier, and 18-year-old Ginette Favre her secretary; they both doubled as guides. Another stalwart assistant was Gaston Denivelle, a major in the French army. He and Mary worked well together, she issuing the orders and he carrying them out. "He was the brain," she admitted. "I had the intuition and the funds."[63]

For security reasons Mary did not know the names of safehouse keepers, or of restaurant and cafe proprietors who assisted the line in Paris. She did know the 20 members of the network working around Ruffec and in nearby departments, 9 of whom were women. She was also in touch with the eight male mountain guides who usually escorted evaders from Foix, southwest of Toulouse, to the steep, often snow-covered mountains of Andorra, a tiny principality on the Spanish border. It was a grueling 40-hour hike.[64]

By the middle of November 1943, a little more than a year after her landing in France, Mary had to move her headquarters. The townspeople of Ruffec knew that Allied aviators were staying at the Hotel de France and that an Englishwoman was the chief of an escape organization. Trouble between her and a new guide, the Comtesse Pauline Barre de St. Venant, known as Marie Odile, who had come to Ruffec against Mary's wishes, also made it advisable to conduct operations from another point on the line. Unfortunately, the decision came too late.

Mary chose Pau as her new headquarters. The most pressing task was to move the nine airmen there from Ruffec. Mary and her secretary, Ginette Favre, took five of the men and started them toward the Pyrenees in the usual fashion. Ginette then went back to Ruffec to escort the four other evaders who were left there waiting for their turn to travel down the line. They would be disguised as deaf-mutes coming to the Institution for the Deaf in Pau. However, Ginette forgot to include a necessary medical paper in their documents. She and the four airmen, one British and three American, were arrested on the train when their papers were checked by the police. At Biarritz, where they were taken for questioning, the police found a picture of Mary in Ginette's wallet. When Ginette claimed that she did not know the person, they became suspicious and transmitted Mary's photograph to the Sicherheitsdienst (SD).

When Ginette and her charges did not appear, Mary dressed in her Red Cross uniform and began checking the incoming trains. She was picked up by the SD at the Pau railroad station on November 24, 1943, and taken to their headquarters in Biarritz.[65]

The Germans soon discovered that they were not dealing with an ordinary person. Although they rejected Mary's pose as a Red Cross supporter of Pétain, she maintained her defiant attitude and they decided to send her to Paris. In mid-December she and Ginette were transferred from the Maison Blanche in Biarritz to a train headed for Paris. Before they reached the capital, however, Mary made a desperate attempt to escape by jumping from a moving train. A Gestapo agent shot her in the back of the head as she jumped, and she was recaptured as she lay unconscious on the ground. At the Luftwaffe hospital in Tours she was operated on by a German surgeon, who saved her life. She remained in the hospital for four weeks.[66]

At Dijon, where she was transferred on January 15, 1944, Mary demanded to be treated as a prisoner of war. Instead, she was handcuffed and her feet chained, and for eight months she was kept in solitary confinement. One of her fellow prisoners was Yvonne Baseden, a young radio operator for SOE.[67] Later that year both women were shipped to Ravensbrück. Because she was a nurse, Mary contrived to be given a job in the infirmary. Though it meant working 12–14 hours a day, it gave her a chance to keep Yvonne from being assigned to a "death column" of inmates because of a spot on her lung. Mary had done a favor for a clerk in the records office, who consented in return to remove Yvonne's name from the list, an act that undoubtedly saved the young woman's life.[68]

It is not easy to assess Mary's achievements before her second arrest. Intelligence records show that 11 soldiers and 2 marine commandos reached Gibraltar via the Marie Claire line, but the records are not complete. At the time of her arrest the British diplomat Michael Creswell notified MI 9 that Lindell had 97 men hidden in the Paris area awaiting evacuation.[69] Her exploits in defying the Germans certainly sufficed to add to the medal collection she had begun after World War I. She received the Medal of Freedom, basic, from the United States for aid to airmen.[70]

After Mary Lindell was arrested in November 1943, Marie Odile, the Countess de St. Venant, took her place. A tall, vivacious woman in her forties, she had a confident, rather domineering air. Since 1940 she had been aiding the escape of French prisoners of war and civilians from Alsace-Lorraine to the unoccupied zone. Threatened with arrest, she had fled to Lyon, where she met Mary's son Maurice. Since Mary wanted a guide with contacts in Alsace-Lorraine, Maurice agreed to pay for every airman Marie Odile delivered to the Marie Claire *réseau*. Contrary to Mary's instructions, however, Marie Odile decided to go to Ruffec herself rather than transfer her aviators to a Marie Claire guide in Lyon. The two countesses quarreled openly in the

Hotel de France, recklessly disregarding security rules. Friction between the two reached an explosive point when Marie Odile returned to Ruffec after an unsuccessful attempt to open a new escape route from Alsace-Lorraine.[71]

Further disagreement was avoided by Mary's arrest, leaving Marie Odile to arrange the evasion of aviators still in the Ruffec area. She then had to go to Paris to reorganize the network. Since she needed money, she also had to travel to Switzerland to contact the British. There she was given 500,000 francs, and immediately on her return the escape line swung into action. At this time the countess changed her pseudonym from Marie Odile to Mme Alice La Roche, although the line continued to be known as the Marie Odile organization.[72]

Under her new pseudonym Mme La Roche set up her headquarters in a Paris hotel owned and operated by Marguerite Boy, the Richelieu Hotel on the rue Molière. She recruited a new staff and persuaded Max Goldblum, a professional soldier of Polish origin who had once served in the French Foreign Legion, to become her right-hand man. He had escaped from a German prison, Stalag IIA, and had been a member of another network. She also recruited Nicole Lebon to serve as her interpreter, secretary, and guide; and in a clever move she enlisted the help of two Paris plainsclothes police inspectors to convoy Allied airmen under the protection of their official passes. They met evaders arriving in Paris by train, whisked them through the ticket barriers to safehouses, and then cleared them at the Gare d'Austerlitz for the trip to Toulouse.[73]

While the airmen were being "processed" at the Hotel Richelieu, they had to be provided with food. They often went to a black market restaurant owned by Mme Alice Challoy on the rue des Cinq Diamants, not far from the hotel. Second Lieutenant Paul A. Marriott was one of the American evaders who ate at the restaurant run by Mme Alice, as she was called. His Flying Fortress had been hit by flak over Ludwigshafen and shot down en route back to England. He and half a dozen fellow airmen were taken to the restaurant by Mme La Roche and Nicole Lebon, who carried on an animated conversation partly in English. They all had a good time, but the Americans were uneasy when English was spoken.[74] Their anxiety was justified, for Mme Alice's nephew, who acted as her helper, was arrested and deported to Buchenwald (he lived to be repatriated).

After airmen were given false papers and suitable civilian clothing, La Roche, Lebon, or others escorted them on crowded trains to Toulouse in groups of ten. On March 2, 1944, Marriott's group was led by Lebon. They were met in Toulouse by Germaine and Robert Thibout, subchiefs of the region, who greeted them like old friends for the benefit of any watching Gestapo agents. The men spent two nights with the Thibouts and then took the train to Foix, getting off at a station north of the city to avoid the police control.[75] From there they were to cross the mountains, but their departure was delayed because of deep snow ahead. It took the group 16 days to reach Spain via Andorra. The men walked 60 hours in 5 exhausting days, without proper equipment or food. Once Marriott reached Barcelona, he traveled in British consular cars to Madrid and then to Gibraltar, where he was interrogated by an officer of MI 9.[76] The escape networks not only enabled Allied airmen to return to their units; they also provided military intelligence groups in Britain with valuable current information.

Again running short of funds, La Roche made a second trip to Geneva in March 1944. During her absence aviators were passed to the Françoise line, headed by Marie Louise Dissard. This time the countess returned empty-handed and discouraged. At this critical juncture Lebon introduced her to Valentin Abeille, known as Méridien. One of the leaders of de Gaulle's Direction Militaire de la Résistance, Abeille agreed to supply the necessary money, and the aviators who were backed up in the line were gradually repatriated.[77]

Now, however, a mortal blow struck the line. La Roche and Lebon were arrested near the Madeleine in Paris, and eight others were soon swept into the police net. An unknown informer had betrayed them to the Gestapo. All were deported to Germany, where the countess who headed the Marie Odile line and several others in the group died in concentration camps.[78]

Postwar records show that, like those in many other escape lines, the members of the Marie Odile organization represented a diversified group. They included owners of chateaus and of hotels and restaurants, as well as policemen, bakers, radio specialists, railroad workers, waitresses, and taxi drivers. One was a butcher; another, a priest; and still another, a garage owner. The wife of a former French ambassador was one of the many women serving the cause. Of the 90 principal members of the network whose names were listed after the war, more than one-third were women.[79]

Despite many difficulties, the Marie Odile line arranged the escape of 71 Allied aviators: 39 Americans, 8 Canadians, and 24 British. In addition, the countess arranged the escape of an English general who used the name Wilson after he had been picked up by the line. She instructed Germaine Thibout to take him to a safehouse near Toulouse, where he was dressed as a station master and passed into Spain with the help of railroad employees.[80] Marriott believed that both the Countess de St. Venant and Nicole Lebon had been "incredibly brave and invaluable to our successful evasion."[81] In recognition of their services, both women were awarded the Medal of Freedom by the American government, Lebon with bronze palm and St. Venant posthumously with silver palm.

The women chiefs of the four escape lines—Andrée de Jongh, Marie Louise Dissard, Mary Lindell, and Pauline de St. Venant—succeeded in their efforts to rescue Allied soldiers. With little experience the women created or rebuilt lines that led 690 soldiers to Spain, the first leg of their return trip to

England. In addition Comet, the largest organization, transferred 75 soldiers to other lines and hid 345 men, mostly aviators shot down in 1944, until Allied armies could reach them. In this way 420 more soldiers, or a total of 1,110, remained out of the hands of the Germans and later returned to their units.

Other women also organized and administered escape lines smaller than Comet, Françoise, Marie Claire, and Marie Odile. One of the women who organized escape lines early in the war was Mme Berthe Fraser, a 44-year-old Frenchwomen of Arras. The wife of a British soldier who had fought in World War I, she created a *réseau* that guided some 100 Allied soldiers across the demarcation line to southern France. She also visited wounded soldiers in the military hospital in nearby Doullens. In the fall of 1941 she was caught by the police and imprisoned at Loos for 15 months. Undismayed by her prison experience, she rejoined the resistance after her release and maintained contact with several organizations, including those of BCRA and SOE. Because she not only continued her escape work, but also arranged to hide explosives for saboteurs and make false documents, she was a keystone of resistance activity in Arras.[82] Arrested a second time in February 1944, she was once more imprisoned at Loos, where she refused to betray her comrades despite harsh interrogations. In recognition of her courageous service she received the Chevalier of the Legion of Honor and the Croix de Guerre from the French, and, like Andrée de Jongh and Marie Louise Dissard, the George Medal from the British.

Among the women who established small networks to help soldiers escape from the German prisoner of war enclosures in 1940, Mme Sylvette Leleu was the only World War II widow. Her pilot husband had been shot down on the Western Front in 1939, and she was eager to avenge his death. Leaving her two young sons in the care of their grandparents, she adopted the stratagem of helping to feed prisoners of war in order to smuggle civilian clothes to those men who wished to escape. In this way she "liberated" 57 from a camp in the municipal stadium at Bethune in northeastern France.[83]

In August 1940, with the help of Sister Marie Laurence (Katherine MacCarthy), an Irish nurse, Sylvette Leleu set up a small team to provide shelter and transportation for almost 200 evaders from St. Valéry and Dunkerque. The owner of a garage, she provided the transportation to Paris, although it was sometimes difficult to cross the Somme River, which was closely patrolled by the Germans. By fall she was in contact with Boris Vildé of the Musée de l'Homme and had begun to carry not only evaders but also military intelligence to Paris for that organization. She was among those associated with the museum who were arrested in April 1941 and later tried. She was sentenced to death and deported, but the death penalty was not carried out.[84]

Some women leaders not only organized their own small groups of resisters but also served as regional or sector heads of large escape lines. Marie Madeleine Davy, known to American evaders as Mlle Bourgeois, was credited with creating a group in Paris. She did this after stumbling into escape work when asked to hide British soldiers. Before the war she had been a professor at the French Institute of Berlin. When war broke out, she returned to France and began teaching philosophy at the Sorbonne, a fertile recruiting ground for resisters. She not only led her own team but also assisted several other escape lines. For Felix the Cat she was chief of the north section; for Comet she provided false papers, clothing, and lodging for evaders in Paris; and for Burgundy she fed aviators into the organization, which operated under the joint auspices of BCRA and MI 9.[85]

Marie Madeleine was very resourceful. She obtained permission from the d'Eichtal family to use their vacant Chateau de la Fortelle, 30 miles southeast of Paris, as a "summer camp."[86] This was her cover story for the safehouse, and she sent ten Americans and numerous British and French there to get in shape for crossing the Pyrenees. A woman colleague and several students from the Sorbonne were in charge of the chateau and took turns preparing the meals for the men.[87]

Marie Madeleine also arranged shelter and guides for six more Americans and assisted others, such as F. O. Pierre Bauset, a French-Canadian bombardier. His Halifax plane was shot down in November 1943 while returning from a mission to Frankfurt. He traveled by train to Paris, where a Red Cross clerk took him to Father Michel Riquet of Comet, who turned him over to Marie Madeleine. Because of arrests she could not put the young aviator on an escape line, and therefore sent him to Jacqueline Marcus, a law student at the Sorbonne. She took him to live with her family until something could be arranged.

Bauset's evasion turned out to be unusual, for when the line was not moving to the Pyrenees, a guide took him to Switzerland. He remained there for seven months before returning to liberated Paris. He was evacuated to London and reached Montreal in time for Christmas. Like many airmen, he was impressed with the courage of Marie Madeleine and four other women who aided his evasion.[88] Because of her leadership the American MIS-X Detachment Research Section listed Marie Madeleine as a network chief.

Elisabeth Barbier organized her own group and was chief of the Paris sector of Oaktree, an MI 9 escape organization. At the same time she worked with the adjunct of Frédéric de Jongh of Comet in Paris. She recruited a group of 46 people, nearly half of whom were women. Barbier was credited with aiding approximately 150 French, Polish, British, and American evaders. Because she helped so many, she, like Davy, was listed by the Americans as a network chief. However, since neither a Davy line nor a Barbier line is listed by the French Ministry of Defense, the two women are considered to be heads of sectors.[89]

Barbier's underground activity came to an abrupt end when she and her mother were caught in the net of a 21-year-old Belgian traitor, Jacques Desoubrie, who used the name of Jean Masson. He had led the SD to Frédéric de Jongh and his Paris associates in June 1943, and soon afterward he betrayed the Barbiers. Imprisoned in Fresnes and deported to Ravensbrück in January, they survived the ordeal. After the war Elisabeth, who married an American diplomat, was awarded the Medal of Freedom with bronze palm, and the French Legion of Honor and Croix de Guerre.[90]

Numerous other women were chiefs of regions or sectors in escape lines. Two noteworthy ones were attached to BCRA's Brandy line. Mme Flore Marie Spiquel, known as Monique, organized and directed the north zone of the line until her betrayal, and Mme Gabrielle Buffet Picabia was second in command of the south zone from September 1942 until the end of 1943, when she had to flee the country.

The Brandy line had been launched by Maj. Lucien Montet, an RAF fighter pilot, in May 1942 and then turned over to his brother Maurice. The line extended from northern France and Paris, across the demarcation line to Lyon, on to Toulouse or Foix, then across the mountains via Andorra to the British consulate in Barcelona.[91]

Monique was in her early forties. In the resistance she worked first with the Organisation Civile et Militaire (OCM) and then made contact with Brandy. Dissatisfied with the lack of action in the north zone, she obtained permission from Maurice to reorganize the region, using her own experienced group of resisters. During this time she went to Toulouse to discuss an evacuation mission with Albert Guérisse, Pat O'Leary, shortly before his arrest in the Super Bar.[92]

Monique's headquarters were in Paris, where she was assisted by her second in command, Jean Brion. In a reversal of traditional roles, her husband took charge of both the guides and the food supplies for the evaders. Thirty-six people, half of whom were women, were in her section. They evacuated 22 airmen, including some who had been transferred to Monique by Comet when that line was overcrowded.[93]

Like the Barbiers, Monique was betrayed by Jacques Desoubrie, who was still using the name of Masson. She had sheltered the young Belgian, not knowing that he worked for the SD. On his information they arrested her in 1943 and interrogated her at the avenue Foch headquarters. That evening she was being taken to Fresnes prison when the car broke down near the Invalides, and she was able to escape. The risk of remaining in France was too great, however, and she and Brion decided to cross the Pyrenees in an attempt to reach London. For security reasons she had known nothing about the Brandy line in the south zone, and hence had to improvise the crossing into Spain. Eventually she arrived in London. Later she was awarded the U.S. Medal of Freedom with bronze palm.[94]

When Monique entered the south zone of the Brandy line, Mme Gabrielle Buffet Picabia was second in command of the region. A short woman with graying hair, she was the former wife of the surrealist painter Francis Picabia. As a young woman she had studied music in Germany, and after marrying Picabia in January 1909 she had taken part in the Dada movement. In addition to spending two years as a student in Germany, she had visited the country in the 1930s, and was therefore well informed about the people. She had friends among Germans who sought refuge in France for political or religious reasons.[95]

In 1940 Picabia turned her studio on the rue Chateaubriand into a safehouse for escaping British soldiers, serving as the Paris link for the Belgian-French escape line Ali-France. Her second daughter, Jeannine, was the co-chief of the intelligence network S.M.H. Gloria. Although an informer told the police about the Ali-France *réseau*, Picabia was warned in time to avoid arrest. She had already put her collection of paintings in a safe place, and was gathering some papers and food when she looked out the window and saw the SD. She was able to slip out a garden door without being seen.[96]

Jeannine had already left Paris because a Gestapo agent had infiltrated her organization.[97] When the Gestapo could find neither Jeannine nor her mother, they arrested Marie, the elder married daughter, who had two children and was not in the resistance. She was imprisoned in Fresnes. This was an added blow for Gabrielle, who was still in danger of arrest and extremely concerned about her grandchildren. They had been sent to a school in Dieulefit, a small town south of Lyon, and Picabia spent some time with them there. Maurice Montet, now in charge of Brandy, came to see her and asked her help in organizing the line in the south zone. At his headquarters in Lyon she gave specific advice about organization and provided him with contacts in Chalon-sur-Saône, where evaders could cross the demarcation line. She also warned him about security precautions, urging that the members of his headquarters staff no longer live in one apartment, but in several.[98]

Carrying out her duties in the south zone, Picabia traveled throughout the area, even giving orders to Monique Spiquel of the north zone on one occasion. She also continued to help evaders from her base in Dieulefit. Eventually the SD picked up her trail thanks to the traitor Desoubrie, who had arranged the arrest of Spiquel in the north. The police waited two weeks before descending on Lyon and arresting Montet and his colleagues there.[99]

Picabia, once more threatened with arrest, knew that she must leave the country. Crossing the Pyrenees was not a problem because she was a daring and experienced mountain climber.[100] She followed the Brandy line to Barcelona, Madrid, and Gibraltar, where she was assigned to one of several apartments maintained by MI 9 for escapers and agents waiting for passage to England. After a few days of inactivity, Picabia asked Donald Darling, known as "Sunday," MI 9's representative in Gibraltar, for a pass to get some exercise on the Upper Rock. Darling was startled by her request, but succeeded in getting the pass. He warned her that if she encountered a sentry, she must stop immediately when challenged; otherwise, she would be shot on sight.[101]

While hiking on the heights Picabia saw a knotted rope dangling below two British commandos who were climbing up the steep rock. She grabbed hold and climbed with them. When they reached the top, the commandos were indignant. They demanded to know what a woman, and a foreigner at that, was doing on their rope. Darling was summoned to identify the culprit, who was nonchalantly smoking a cigarette and innocently asking, "Qu'est-ce que j'ai fait?" (What have I done?). Darling soon found space for her on a plane to England.[102]

Documents demonstrate Picabia's contribution to the resistance during three years of the German occupation. Yet in the 1960s, when an American professor of art interviewed people in Paris about her, they told him, "Gabrielle's involvement in the resistance did not amount to much."[103] Certainly she had become better known for her part in the artistic movement of Dada than for her resistance activity. Perhaps acquaintances downgraded the World War II chapter of her life because they did not believe a middle-aged woman could have done so much.

Picabia and the nine other women highlighted in this chapter are examples of the many courageous and resourceful women who took responsibility for helping stranded servicemen. They employed heretofore unrecognized organizing and leadership talents that made their lines successful. Airey Neave of MI 9, an authority on escape and evasion, was one of the first to recognize their contribution in this regard when he wrote, "Women made admirable organizers, especially in escape work."[104]

The penalties imposed by the Nazis on these women leaders were severe. Seven were arrested and one, Pauline de St. Venant, died in a concentration camp.

Notes

1. Henri Michel, *The Second World War*, pp. 122-23. Later 190,000 troops were evacuated by the British from Normandy beaches and Bordeaux. Peter Calvocoressi and Guy Wint, *Total War*, pp. 123-24.

2. Henri Michel, *Histoire de la résistance*, p. 83; Airey Neave, *Saturday at MI 9*, p. 22.

3. Neave, *Saturday*, p. 24.

4. Gilbert Renault [Rémy], *Réseau Comète*, 1:37-42.

5. Jean François Nothomb, interview, Ann Arbor, MI, July 1977.

6. Suzanne Wittek [Cecile Jouan], *Comète, histoire d'une ligne d'évasion*, p. 10; Renault, 1:43-45; RG 332, ETO, 7707 ECIC, MIC-X, Helpers, Andrée de

Jongh, "Rapport de Andrée de Jongh," pp. 9–10, dossier. (See Guide to Frequently Cited Sources.)

    7. Elvire de Greef, "Comète, secteur sud," p. 16, dossier.

    8. Ibid., 68 pp.

    9. Renault, *Réseau Comète*, 1:55–56.

    10. Ibid., 1:57–59.

    11. Ibid., 1:56, 88–89.

    12. Wittek, *Comète*, pp. 10–11.

    13. Ibid., p. 11.

    14. Ibid.

    15. James M. Langley, *Fight Another Day*, pp. 166–67; Neave, *Saturday*, pp. 129–31.

    16. Renault, *Réseau Comète*, 1:71–72.

    17. De Greef, "Comète, secteur sud," p. 23.

    18. "Rapport de Andrée de Jongh," pp. 3–4, 10–11.

    19. De Greef, "Comète," pp. 2, 9; Neave, *Saturday*, pp. 158–59.

    20. De Greef, "Comète," pp. 2, 27. Nothomb was awarded the American Medal of Freedom with gold palm after the war; RG 420, "Belgian Master List, Medal of Freedom Cases," Grades I through IV, A48-184. (See Guide to Frequently Cited Sources.)

The six grades of American awards were the following:

Grade I — Medal of Freedom with gold palm: awarded to chiefs of evasion *réseaux* who (or whose *réseau*) passed over 100 airmen to safety.

Grade 2 — Medal of Freedom with silver palm: for chiefs or helpers who were successful in returning at least 40 to 50 evaders.

Grade 3 — Medal of Freedom with bronze palm: awarded to helpers who sheltered or convoyed from 20 to 40 evaders, heads of sections, or chiefs of small organizations.

Grade 4 — basic Medal of Freedom: for helpers who sheltered or convoyed from 8 to 20 evaders.

Grade 5 — certificate signed by General Eisenhower: for helpers who sheltered from 1 to 7 evaders.

Grade 6 — informal letter of thanks signed by a military attaché.

The requirements for each award were not always the same; they were sometimes modified, depending upon the time and circumstances. RG 332, ETO, MIS, MIS-X Section, "History of the 6801 MIS-X Detachment," Decimal 314.7, pp. 17–18.

    21. M. R. D. Foot, *Six Faces of Courage*, pp. 101–02.

    22. Renault, *Réseau Comète*, 3:409–15; International Committee of the Red Cross, *Documents Relating to the Work of the Red Cross*, pp. 112–16.

    23. Elvire de Greef, "Citation for Medal of Freedom," April 29, 1946, dossier.

    24. "Report of Mme Elvire de Greef," p. 3, dossier.

    25. Fifty-eight of the total number were Belgians and ten were French; some of these were members of Comet who were escaping from the police.

    26. De Greef, "Comète," pp. 4, 56–58; Neave, *Saturday*, pp. 237–38, 270–71.

27. Langley, *Fight*, p. 252.

28. Marie Louise Dissard, "Visite de Françoise," to Paris Awards Bureau, May 6, 1946, p. 1, dossier.

29. Marie Louise Dissard, "Recommendation for Award of Medal of Freedom, Gold Palm," February 18, 1946, AG 200.6, Dissard dossier.

30. RG 332, ETO, MIS, MIS-X Section, Research Branch, Histories and Related Records Pertaining to French Organizations and Networks, 1945–46, "Rapport de Pat O'Leary," pp. 12–13. With the exception of Andrée de Jongh and Elvire de Greef, histories and reports of escape lines in this chapter have the same citation.

31. Dissard, "Visite," p. 2; "Rapport de Pat O'Leary," p. 2.

32. Dissard, "Visite," p. 3.

33. Ibid, pp. 3–5; "Rapport de Pat O'Leary," p. 7.

34. Dissard, "Visite," p. 6.

35. Ibid., pp. 5–6; Dr. Gabriel Nahas, interview, New York City, April 1978. He later joined the staff of Columbia-Presbyterian Medical Center in New York. The chief of Dutch-Paris was John Weidner, a Dutch Seventh Day Adventist, who became a businessman in California after the war.

36. 2d Lt. Harold O. Freeman, E & E Report no. 553; S. Sgt. Robert Finney, E & E Report no. 628; S. Sgt. Kenneth Carson, E & E Report no. 632.

37. Dissard, "Recommendation for Award of Medal of Freedom," pp. 2–3; Dissard, "Visite," attached "Déclarations recueillis par Françoise pour les personnes ayant travaillé pour 'Pat' et pour Françoise," pp. 1–5. The list was incomplete.

38. Barry Wynne, *No Drums . . . No Trumpets*, p. 11.

39. Mary Lindell, interview, Paris, October 1976. Mary talked for several hours about her experiences in the resistance.

40. Ibid.

41. Ibid.

42. Neave, *Saturday*, p. 185.

43. Lindell, interview.

44. Ibid.

45. Ibid.

46. Etta Shiber, *Paris Underground*, pp. 9–10; Lindell, interview.

47. For account of her trial see Wynne, pp. 107–08.

48. Ibid., pp. 110–11; Naomi Hany-Lefèbvre, *Six mois à Fresnes*, p. 30.

49. The British consulate retained its British and French staff but no principal officers, since the Vichy government had broken relations with the United Kingdom in protest against the sinking of the French fleet at Mers-el-Kebir. George Whittinghill, letter to author, October 8, 1977.

50. "Rapport de Pat O'Leary," p. 7.

51. W. F. Craven and J. L. Cate, eds., *The Army Air Forces in World War II*, 2:237–38.

52. Lindell, interview.

53. Ibid.

54. Neave, *Saturday*, pp. 192, 196.

55. Ibid., pp. 192, 199.

56. For a full account of the raid, see Cecil Ernest Lucas Phillips, *Cockleshell Heroes*.

57. Ibid, pp. 168, 201, 207.

58. Lindell, interview; Phillips, *Cockleshell*, pp. 212, 216.

59. Whittinghill document, May 17, 1968. Operation Torch took place November 8–11, 1942.

60. Lindell had a special number with Swiss Intelligence.

61. Neave, *Saturday*, p. 201.

62. Lindell, interview.

63. Ibid.

64. Ibid.; "Marie Claire," history, pp. 1–2.

65. Wynne, *No Drums*, p. 204.

66. "Report of Mary Lindell," p. 1, dossier.

67. Ibid.

68. Lindell, interview.

69. "MI 9 Report on Marie Claire," Lindell dossier.

70. French Office, MIS-X Detachment, "France Master List, Medal of Freedom Cases," Grades I through IV, June 8, 1948. Medal of Freedom awards to French resisters are on the same list. (See Guide to Frequently Cited Sources.) Lindell's citation is in her dossier. Her medal was grade 4 (basic); it would have been a higher rank if more of her airmen had reached Spain before her arrest.

71. "Marie Claire," history, p. 4; Lindell, interview.

72. "Marie Odile," history, p. 8. This is a continuation of the "Marie Claire" history. Seven pages deal with Marie Claire and 33 with Marie Odile.

73. "Marie Odile," history, pp. 9, 14, 15, 19.

74. 2d Lt. Paul A. Marriott, E & E Report no. 548.

75. Ibid.; Maj. Leon Blythe, E & E Report no. 547.

76. Marriott, E & E no. 548.

77. "Marie Odile," history, p. 10.

78. Ibid., p. 11. Marie Odile died at Ravensbrück.

79. Ibid., pp. 8, 27–29.

80. Ibid., pp. 13, 40.

81. Marriott, letter to author, March 14, 1977.

82. *La voix du nord* (Lille), April 20, 1956, in Archives, Comité d'Histoire de la Deuxième Guerre Mondiale (CHG); *Paris soir*, July 26, 1946.

83. Sylvette Leleu, Statement, Musée de l'Homme Collection, Bucknell University.

84. Ibid. See chapter 6.

85. "Réseau Burgundy," p. 86.

86. Mme Cost (née d'Eichtal), statement to Mme Genevieve Camus, October 1984.

87. S. Sgt. William G. Howell, E & E Report no. 328; 2nd Lt. Paul H. McConnell, E & E Report no. 380.

88. Pierre Bauset, letter to author, April 5, 1983.

89. "Liste des réseaux d'évasion," p. 1; "Elisabeth Barbier," dossier; *Washington Post*, June 27, 1967, p. F5; "Liste des réseaux et des mouvements," Ministry of Defense, Office of Veterans, manuscript list.

90. Barbier's mother was in charge of lodging and received the Medal of Freedom, basic.

91. "Report on Brandy," pp. 1, 8.

92. Ibid., pp. 1–3, 17–23.

93. Ibid.

94. Ibid., p. 22.

95. Picabia, taped interview with my research assistant, Constance Greenbaum, Paris, March 6, 1979.

96. Ibid.

97. See chapter 5.

98. Picabia, interview; "Report on Brandy," pp. 1, 6, 12.

99. "Report on Brandy," p. 19; Picabia, interview.

100. Picabia, interview.

101. Donald Darling, *Sunday at Large*, pp. 145–48.

102. Ibid.

103. William A. Camfield, letter to author, April 7, 1980. He is the author of *Francis Picabia*.

104. Neave, *Saturday*, p. 194.

3 IN THE COMPANY
OF STRANGERS

The escape lines, in which women chiefs were playing such a vital role, proved even more important as the air war over Europe increased in scope and intensity. Beginning in August 1942, the U.S. Eighth Air Force, based in England, launched bombing operations independently of the RAF, setting the stage for round-the-clock assaults. The British favored night raids, whereas the Americans carried out their missions by day against German bases, shipyards, aircraft and munitions factories, railroads, and marshaling yards, the strategy being to weaken the Germans' capacity to fight.[1]

Predictably, an ever larger number of British and American airmen were shot down or forced to bail out, and needed help if they were to escape capture and imprisonment for the duration of the war. In 1942, 31 of the 1,424 heavy bombers dispatched by the Eighth Air Force against French targets were reported missing. The next year U.S. losses numbered 968 out of 26,192 planes raiding Germany as well as France. In 1944 a total of 2,727 U.S. planes failed to return out of the 183,471 sent out by the Eighth Air Force. These raids included strikes against the launch sites for the V-1 flying bombs and support for the Allied landings in France. Each of the American B-17s (Flying Fortresses) carried a crew of ten.[2]

Initially the leaders of such lines as Comet and Pat could take charge of the survivors of the failed missions by arranging for their shelter, food, and clothing, and by guiding them from Belgium into Spain, as Dédée de Jongh had done. But soon the number of fugitives demanded a vastly extended organization with more helpers and more specialization among them. In particular, native guides who knew the language and the terrain were needed to escort evaders along the route to freedom. Safehouse keepers also had to be recruited to furnish the equally vital lodgings along the way. For all their courage and ingenuity, the forceful personalities who organized and led the escape lines could not have carried on their self-imposed task without the women who willingly undertook the dangerous work of guiding and lodging evaders both in the cities that were the collection points and in farms and villages along the escape routes.

Before embarking on their missions the airmen were briefed that their duty was to try to evade capture and return to their bases. If they were caught, they should show their identity tags and claim their rights as prisoners of war under the Geneva Convention of 1929.[3] According to this agreement they could not be treated as spies, even if they were wearing civilian clothes, unless they were carrying intelligence material. Nevertheless, some of the captured airmen were subjected to brutal interrogation and threatened with death as spies. Although the briefings had stressed that those who helped them would suffer much heavier penalties than could legally be imposed on military prisoners, these terror tactics did induce a few evaders to reveal the location of houses where they had been sheltered.[4]

The dangers were indeed great for men and women helping Allied personnel to return to their units. In October 1940 the military commander in France, General Otto von Stülpnagel, had ordered that any person who sheltered escaped prisoners of war would be subject to the death penalty. A year later he issued a new decree: Any man who directly or indirectly came to the aid of Allied aviators would be shot immediately; women guilty of similar offenses would be deported to German concentration camps. Following the practice of other Nazi authorities in occupied countries, Stülpnagel offered substantial rewards to collaborators who reported parachutists and fallen planes to the police.[5]

Such rewards probably played their part in persuading traitors like Roger Le Neuveu, known as Le Légionnaire, and Jacques Desoubrie to infiltrate escape lines and betray their countrymen. The Germans also assigned their own men to pose as would-be escapers and entrap those who guided and sheltered them. When the Axis occupation was extended to all of France in 1942, the danger of discovery by the vigilant and ruthless Geheime Feldpolizei (GFP) became even greater.

Despite the risks, many individuals both lodged evaders and acted as guides along the escape lines. The separation of jobs was not rigid, since circumstances often called for last-minute changes of plan. A guide might be unable to arrive at the rendezvous, and to avoid a risky wait the hostess would act as guide. Or a guide would discover that the safehouse where she was to leave her charge was under surveillance or the people had been arrested. In many cases a guide took evaders to her own house or apartment until they could safely move on. In both roles women were especially effective.

Women working as guides were less likely than men of military age to be stopped by the police. Their household shopping and errands made them seem part of the normal scene, especially when they walked in front of their charges, looking as if they were on some routine errand, but actually were wary of what might be happening to the men behind them. Sometimes they walked with the evaders, pretending to be part of a family or social group. Deceptions of this kind were easier for guides belonging to the same age group as the fliers.

As far as possible, guides accompanied the disguised airmen on all their journeys. Most often they took their charges on only one leg of a journey, such as the one by night from Paris to Bordeaux. They would leave them at a park or similar rendezvous near a safehouse, where they would be picked up by other guides.

Guides needed to have special qualities. They had to be daring, intelligent, and quick-witted if they were to be successful in escorting English-speaking soldiers under the noses of the Germans. It took nerves of steel to cope with the police checks their charges had to submit to at railroad stations, on trains, and on the streets. It also took great endurance to walk or cycle the long distances, or travel the many hours on crowded, unheated trains. A few guides, such as Dédée de Jongh, also hiked across the Pyrenees with the professional guides. Young as she seemed in her blue fisherman's pants, she encouraged the men to keep going through the night and inspired them by the force of her example. Even hard-to-please Colonel Dansey of MI 6, who had first suspected her of being a German agent, was impressed by her "courage, tenacity and powers of physical endurance."[6]

Dédée de Jongh's Comet line furnishes some especially noteworthy examples of young women who initially helped British soldiers evade capture after Dunkerque and later guided downed airmen toward safety. One of these, Andrée Dumon of Brussels, only 17 at the time of Dunkerque, was to become one of the first Comet guides. Beginning in October 1941, Andrée, whose code name was Nadine, served as a guide and courier for Frédéric de Jongh, head of the Belgian sector of Comet. She picked up messages at his school office in Schaerbeek and took them to the Comet headquarters in Valenciennes, on the French-Belgian border. Soon she took on the additional responsibility of guiding soldiers from Brussels to Valenciennes. When, in the spring of 1942, the Germans eliminated the artificial frontier at the Somme River, Nadine took about 21 men directly to Paris.[7]

Ten months after Nadine joined Comet, she and her parents were arrested by the German secret police and imprisoned in St. Gilles. She refused to divulge any information to her interrogators until they threatened to beat her mother. Then she admitted that she had helped some evaders but claimed that her mother had taken no part in the scheme.

Andrée's older sister Micheline had escaped arrest because she was a nursing student living at the Hospital St. Pierre. The German police questioned her, but since they released her without seeming suspicious, she felt safe in keeping in touch with Comet and continuing her nurse's training.[8]

By mid-1943, because of mass arrests in Paris and Brussels, Micheline left the hospital; but instead of withdrawing from the resistance, she began working full-time for Comet. Under the code name Michou she made arrangements with a group of safehouse keepers to lodge and feed aviators in Brussels, but she became known primarily as a guide.[9]

The men whose escape Michou helped to engineer were by this time chiefly airmen, many of them Americans. Two of them reported that though she told them she was 22, they could scarcely believe she was more than 16. She was only five feet tall, and took advantage of her youthful looks to dress like a schoolgirl in order to disarm the police. She confided her real age to the escapers, however, so that they would have more confidence in her leadership. Guiding was a dangerous business, and they would have to follow her instructions carefully.[10]

Early in January 1944 the German police who had arrested and deported Michou's sister and father were on her track. Forced to flee to Paris, she hoped to work with Jean François Nothomb, chief of Comet, and Count Jacques Legrelle, head of the Paris section; but only a short time after her arrival, a new series of arrests shook the line, and both men were caught in the net. Another associate was a young Belgian officer, Baron Jean de Blommaert, who had escaped to England after the arrest of Jean Greindl of Comet. He had returned by parachute, and was now known to be on the Gestapo list of suspects. The British had ordered him back to London, and had asked Michou to accompany him and his two radio operators across the Pyrenees to Spain. He was to continue on to Britain.[11]

Setting out with her three companions, Michou made the arduous journey across the mountains under stormy winter conditions. Her action had important consequences, for de Blommaert remained in England only long enough to receive special instructions from P 15, the office of MI 9 concerned with escape in northwest Europe. He was to set up a camp for evaders in the forest of Fréteval, some 90 miles southwest of Paris.

This dense forest was selected by P 15 in preparation for D Day. Such a hiding place was considered necessary for several reasons. The massive Allied bombardment that would precede and follow the invasion of Normandy would make it almost impossible for guides to escort aviators on trains to the Pyrenees. To ask safehouse keepers to run the risk of hiding evaders until the Allied forces reached their areas would be unreasonable. Finally, the fear was widespread that the Nazis, when driven back, might treat airmen as spies rather than prisoners of war if they were caught wearing civilian clothes and carrying false papers. The best solution appeared to be to conceal the evaders in an isolated forest where they would be aided by members of the resistance. Jean be Blommaert was to be one of the organizers and key leaders of the Fréteval haven.[12]

Michou was to return to Paris and undertake special assignments for Comet.[13] She seldom waited for orders, however, when she saw the need for action. On her return from Spain she had learned that Madeleine Noël, a Paris dentist known as Martine, had been arrested by the Gestapo on March 1. Through her dental practice Mme Noël had been able to recruit ten other safehouse keepers and to shelter fugitives herself. She and her husband André were early supporters of General de Gaulle, but André had been arrested in 1942. Aware that her own position was precarious, Madeleine took the precaution of moving to another Paris apartment, where she began to lodge agents and airmen for Comet. In the course of one month she collected 13 American aviators and arranged for their shelter. In her spacious apartment near the Champs de Mars she had lodged Jacques Legrelle before his arrest, as well as Jean de Blommaert.[14] Jean François Nothomb and Michou had come to her office, posing as patients.

Unfortunately, another of her visitors was Jacques Desoubrie. Once known as Jean Masson, he now went under the name of Pierre Boulain and had again wormed his way into Comet. On March 1, 1944, shortly after his visit, Gestapo officers pounded on Madeleine's door at two o'clock in the morning. For seven hours they questioned her. Persuaded of her guilt, they took her to the rue des Saussaies headquarters and then to Fresnes prison, where she was put in solitary confinement.

This arrest, after that of Nothomb and Legrelle, convinced Michou that another Gestapo agent had penetrated the line, and she set out at once to uncover the traitor. Learning where Madeleine's cell was located, she threw caution to the winds and shouted to her friend from outside the prison, "Who betrayed you?" The answer was "Pierre Boulain." Michou promptly sounded the alarm about Boulain, saving many others from betrayal.[15]

Meanwhile Madeleine was doing her part in prison by heroically refusing to sign a deposition about her resistance work, despite being subjected to a method of torture frequently employed by the Nazis: she was stripped, tied hand and foot, and submerged in a bathtub of cold water. Three times she was ordered to reveal the names and addresses of her safehouse keepers and of agents in the southern sector, and at each refusal her head was plunged underwater until she lost consciousness. At last her tormenters gave up, fearing that she would drown and hoping to find other ways to gain their end. She was deported to Ravensbrück, where she stayed until the camp was liberated at the end of April 1945.[16]

This segment of Comet was badly damaged, however, and Michou was determined to try to mend the broken threads of the line.[17] Since the line could not function between Belgium and Spain without a Paris link, she sought out Philippe d'Albert Lake, husband of the remarkable American resister Virginia.[18] He had become the right-hand man of Jean de Blommaert before Blommaert's recall to London. Michou explained to Philippe that she knew the Comet contacts in both Belgium and Bayonne but needed him to take care of the Paris sector. She knew that MI 9 had ordered the line to stop evacuating airmen for two months, until the return of a leader from London; but, being a strong-willed young woman, she bristled at the idea that Belgians should take orders from London. In her view the work must continue as long as airmen were waiting to go down the line. Philippe agreed to help her, and the line was reestablished.[19]

Guides who, like Michou, had received nurse's training found that it stood them in good stead when they had to assist wounded aviators. One of her charges was 2nd Lt. Robert Z. Grimes, who had bailed out of his plane in October 1943, landing in Belgium with a shell fragment in his thigh. Unable to walk, he was taken by volunteer helpers to a safehouse in Brussels where Michou was staying. She dressed his wound and then reported his condition to a Dr. Rouffart, who had treated injured evaders for Comet since the beginning of the line. Using a local anesthetic, the doctor removed the shell fragment from the lieutenant's leg, then immediately drove him to the safehouse, where Michou nursed him back to health. As the wound healed, she took him for long walks after dark to strengthen his muscles for the demanding hike across the mountains. He reached Spain at the end of December.[20]

Michou continued to serve as a guide for a few more months. When the Gestapo again picked up her trail in mid-May 1944, she crossed the Pyrenees on foot for the last time and reluctantly followed the British order to go to London. Her mother had been released after a year in prison and had cautiously resumed helping Comet. Her sister Nadine, who had been deported to Ravensbrück and then to Mauthausen, was liberated at the end of the war. Their father died in Germany.[21]

Both sisters were honored by the Allies when peace was restored. Michou, like Andrée de Jongh and Elvire de Greef, was awarded the George Medal by the British and the Medal of Freedom with gold palm by the Americans for her outstanding work. Nadine received the Medal of Freedom with bronze palm.[22]

Another young Comet guide, Peggy Van Lier, deserves mention not only for her success as a guide before she was forced to escape to England, but also for the rare achievement of persuading the Germans that she was innocent of complicity when resisters were arrested in the disastrous roundup that came to be known as the Maréchal affair.

Like the Dumon sisters, Peggy was young when she began working in the resistance. At age 20 she was living with her parents in Hal, near Brussels. Her father was Belgian and her mother was Irish, and English was the first language Peggy had learned. Her knowledge of French and German as well gave her an exceptional advantage in escorting Allied soldiers and in her confrontations with the Germans.

Peggy's opportunity to serve came after she started helping with lunches for children at the Swedish canteen in Brussels, which provided food and clothing for the poor children of the city. Under the direction of Baron Jean Greindl the canteen became a cover for escape line activities, a means of furnishing food for evaders, and a source of promising recruits for Frédéric de Jongh's Brussels sector of the Comet line.[23]

Comet began using the canteen for cover in early 1942, but by April the line had encountered two serious setbacks. Frédéric de Jongh was forced to flee from Brussels to Paris, and his successor in Brussels, Henri Michelli, was arrested after only six days as the head of Comet's Belgian sector. The courier Charles Morelle was also arrested.[24]

Though every arrest was a signal that there might be more, Greindl, who had taken the code name of Nemo, volunteered to act as head of the sector, an offer that Dédée was glad to accept. She was fearful for his safety, however, and told Peggy, who had carried news of the arrests and of his offer to her in Paris, "I am afraid that he will not last more than six months."[25]

Peggy became Nemo's adjutant, and one of her responsibilities was to escort airmen from outlying collection centers to Brussels. Another important service was to recruit and help train interrogators of evaders. Any man ostensibly seeking to return to Britain could be a German agent trying to entrap resisters, and Peggy's knowledge of English was essential in questioning the men and assessing their trustworthiness.[26]

When Peggy first became a guide, she had to answer the question faced by many other young women living with their families: Should she tell her parents about what she was doing? Rather than worry them, she would lead a double life. When she had to make trips for the line, she invented excuses for her absence. To pay for extra expenses for herself and her charges, she sold her jewelry and borrowed money from her married sisters. Eventually the pain of lying to those she loved was too much, and she told them about her resistance work. She was a good Catholic, and her religious faith was a source of strength. "I was greatly helped by a jolly good prayer," she recalled later, "and I always prayed before going on a mission." She also remembered the feelings of terror and relief that accompanied her risky endeavors. "I was in an absolute sweat before an assignment and then absolutely calm the day after."[27]

Peggy needed all the spiritual help she could muster when disaster struck the line on November 19, 1942. She had recruited Elsie Maréchal, an English-speaking friend, to help interrogate evaders. On this day Elsie appeared at the canteen with word that two men with doubtful accents had come to her house claiming to be Americans in the RAF. She had brought Nemo the questionnaire she had asked them to fill out, and he noted that some of the letters resembled German script. He urged Elsie to hurry home and warn her mother that they must leave the house immediately, and report their new address as soon as they safely could.[28]

The group at the canteen, which now included Victor Michiels, waited nervously for news from the Maréchals. When none came, Victor volunteered to reconnoiter the house, but he also failed to return. Peggy thought she might find out something from Victor's family. Peggy was acquainted with Victor's sister Josée, and if the Germans were there, she could pretend to be inquiring about university courses. Before leaving, she also took the precaution of putting some pictures in her handbag that she hoped would impress any German who challenged her. They were photographs of German officers from a well-known family with whom she had spent several months while she was in Germany to learn the language.[29]

A day had passed since the disappearance of Elsie and, as Peggy had feared, the Germans were at Victor's house, questioning his parents and his sister. Frightened but undaunted, Peggy, speaking in German, gave the police her prepared excuse for calling at the house. Neither her knowledge of their language nor the photographs, which came to light when they searched her handbag, prevented the Germans from taking her away for interrogation; but they did help to impress those at the headquarters of the secret police, and she was let go. The only thing she had learned was that Victor had been shot while running from the Maréchals' house.[30]

The two Germans responsible for the Maréchal affair had infiltrated the organization in Luxembourg and been escorted along the line to Brussels in the belief that they were bona fide evaders. After the arrest of the Maréchal family the two spies went on to betray almost 100 people, including guides, safehouse keepers, and innocent relatives, who were held as hostages. Within two days all were imprisoned — a heavy price to pay for the return of 60 airmen in the previous six months. Elsie's father was executed along with many others. Elsie and her mother were deported but survived.[31]

Peggy left the German headquarters on that terrible day scarcely able to believe her good fortune. She stopped in a church to give thanks, knowing that she was one of the few to be released after being arrested by the Germans. Then she telephoned Nemo, who realized that she and any others whom the Germans had reason to suspect would be watched closely. He ordered her to contact two cousins whom she had recruited as guides for the line, counts Georges and Edouard d'Oultremont, and escape with them to England. The three young people succeeded in making the journey they had helped so many others to make. In December 1942 they arrived in England, where their plane was met by the man who was to become Peggy's husband, Lt. James Langley of MI 9.

Long after the war Peggy Langley explained the feelings that led her to engage in the resistance:

> We were in a state of despair because of the German occupation. Nothing was worse than to be occupied, humiliated — our country no longer ours. We were willing to do anything to fight the Germans and to help the English. We were in the resistance together and to be part of it gave us a buoyant feeling.[32]

These single young women serving as Comet guides were forced to leave France one step ahead of the Gestapo. Another, Michou Dumon's younger sister, Nadine, had been deported to Ravensbrück. Their stories offer a chilling indication of the danger of their work.

They were not, of course, the only women guides who had to flee or who were imprisoned. Nor were all the women guides single. Mme Madeleine de Gaulle, sister-in-law of the general, was 32 and the mother of 5 children when France was defeated. Shortly after the defeat General de Gaulle, who had escaped from France and begun to organize the Free French forces, was sentenced to death in absentia, and the whole family fell under suspicion. Pierre de Gaulle, Madeleine's husband, was able to avoid arrest for a while by remaining in unoccupied France, but in February 1943 he was taken hostage and deported.

Meanwhile, his wife had joined the resistance in Paris, where she first helped a small group of students, linked with the Musée de l'Homme, who printed underground pamphlets. This work nearly put a stop to her patriotic activities. On November 25, 1941, the Germans staged a massive roundup of suspected resisters, and Madeleine was arrested along with almost 100 others swept into the net that day. Neither her interrogation nor a search of her apartment brought to light any evidence of clandestine opposition to the German conquerors, and she was released the same evening.[33]

Nevertheless, after she left Paris, the Germans kept Madeleine under surveillance at her home in Normandy. Aware of the risks but refusing to be cowed, she made contact with the large resistance movement called Libération Nord and began escorting downed aviators to Paris. Although her charges knew her only by her code name Maud, and she was careful to take other precautions, the police learned about her activity. Warned by a friend in the prefecture of Rouen that she was about to be arrested, she took her children to Spain and then to Morocco, where she remained until the end of the war.[34]

For the evaders, it meant everything to find men and women who would help them avoid capture, and many servicemen were unstinting in expressing their gratitude in official reports. They were aware that they presented grave problems to their rescuers, but they could not know all the difficulties they created or the magnitude of the efforts required to secure their safe return to Britain. For the sake of security they often did not know the real identities of those who guided or lodged them.

Part of their training, however, was designed to make their escape easier. Among detailed instructions in evasion techniques, American fliers were told to bury their parachutes and life jackets, and be on the alert for German search parties. They were instructed to seek help from farmers, doctors, priests, and teachers if no one offered immediate assistance. They were to keep their identity tags concealed and try to find civilian clothing as soon as possible. Airmen were given two tangible aids: escape boxes and purses. The boxes, meant to provide the essentials for surviving the first two days, contained high-protein food, such as malted milk tablets, a compass, adhesive tape, Benzedrine and halazone tablets, matches, and a water bag. The purses held silk maps and French francs to reimburse helpers for at least some of their food and transportation.[35]

Once they made contact with rescuers, the main problem, of course, was how to hide their identity from the Germans, and even from the local people, some of whom might be tempted to accept financial rewards for turning the men over to the Gestapo.

The first step in disguising the evaders was to provide them with civilian clothes. This was not easy because clothing was rationed and in short supply. Many airmen were bigger than Frenchmen, and available clothes did not always fit. Shoes also were scarce and frequently too small.

Women usually collected the clothing for the evaders, and if money was available, they purchased new garments on the black market. One woman in Paris bought enough garments for Comet to set up a center to outfit the evaders. Men who reached Paris gave up the heavy clothes they were wearing so that these could be reused. In exchange they received Basque berets and sport shirts to wear on the trip south.[36]

Clothing centers were the exception, however, and airmen often feared that their identities would be discovered because of their attire. After Maj. Leon Blythe arrived in Paris from a farming area, he reported, "Our country bumpkin clothes were all wrong in the city and we were stared at by everyone as we took the subway."[37] Kenneth Woodhouse, a Canadian Spitfire pilot, was given an old jacket several sizes too big for him to take the place of his Air Force tunic. Before he went to Paris on the Shelburne line, he was given a new suit, shirt, tie, and raincoat that made him look more like the 20-year-old student described on his identity card.[38]

False papers were also an essential part of the aviators' disguise. In well-organized escape lines each man was furnished with at least three cards. The first, an identity card, stated his name, profession, date and place of birth, and nationality. It also included a physical description, photograph, and thumb print. The other two were a work permit giving his place of employment and a permit to be in a coastal or frontier zone.

At first fliers were given names that were common in France, such as Dupont or Durand. By the time 2d Lt. Ralph K. Patton bailed out of his Flying Fortress over Brittany early in 1944, a formula had evolved for making up names. When possible, the men were given French names that began with the same letters as their actual first name and surname. Middle names were added. Patton became René Yves Pailly, a salesman born in the Breton coastal town of Tréboul.[39]

Even when American airmen wore civilian clothes and carried false papers, their guides, many of whom were women, faced obstacles in trying to pass off their charges as Frenchmen. Most fliers did not speak French. Others spoke it with an American accent that even the Germans would recognize. Guides had to anticipate awkward situations and avoid the police, who were particularly likely to question the men on long-distance trains and in railroad stations. To discourage talkative passengers from addressing the men, guides gave the airmen pro-German newspapers that they could pretend to be reading when they were not feigning sleep.

To minimize the language problem for evaders and their guides, many men were given papers stating that they were deaf-mutes. Nicholas Mandell, a radio operator shot down over the Netherlands, received such papers and was taught the appropriate mannerisms by the mute son of a safehouse keeper. After reaching Belgium he outwitted a German guard who tried to trick him into following spoken directions. Later, when too many were posing as mutes, evaders were given papers stating that they were Flemish. Still others had documents identifying them as foreign workers, who could not be expected to speak French.[40]

On the other hand, S. Sgt. Joseph O. Peloquin, the top turret gunner on a B-24, believed that his evasion went smoothly because he had grown up in a French-speaking family in the state of Maine. He was rescued by Mme Charles Guilloume, the mother of four children, who found a doctor to dress his wounds and hid him from a German search party after he had parachuted from his plane near Orléans in May 1944. Following the Allied landings on D Day he was one of the first evaders to hide in the camp organized by MI 9 and the French, located in the forest of Fréteval, southwest of Paris.[41]

Guides had to teach Americans the subtle but important differences between the way ordinary Frenchmen would act in certain circumstances and the way Americans were accustomed to act, since they must avoid mannerisms that would alert the police. Their instructors found, for example, that as a rule an American removed his cigarette after every puff and often discarded it only half-smoked. Frenchmen more often let their cigarettes dangle from their lips and smoked them down to a tiny stub. Cigarettes were scarce and expensive in France, and guides urged the Americans to copy the French style of smoking. They also warned them not to stare like tourists at public monuments and buildings.

They could never, of course, prepare evaders for all eventualities. S. Sgt. Robert Sweatt, a Texan, was traveling with nine other evaders in a crowded car of a small local train in Brittany. According to a Canadian companion, Kenneth Woodhouse, the two were standing surrounded by German soldiers when one of the Germans put a cigarette in his mouth and then, after searching through his pockets, turned and spoke to Sweatt. The young American could not fail to see what was wanted and, anxious only to appear obliging, pulled out his Zippo lighter. Too late he realized that his lighter was obviously American, but the German failed to notice either his sudden pallor or the unusual lighter.[42]

The same problems that made the work of guides hazardous affected the women who kept safehouses for the escape lines. The accomplishments of guides have received more recognition than those of safehouse keepers, partly because of the drama inherent in publicly flouting German authority and partly, perhaps, because many of the guides were attractive young women. Safehouse keepers' responsibilities were as a rule more mundane, involving the day-to-day chores of finding food, watching for strange faces in the neighborhood, and maintaining an air of normalcy despite the presence of fugitives sharing their frequently cramped quarters.

Moreover, the circumstances of sheltering escapers entailed special risks. A saboteur could disappear after attaching explosives to railway tracks or a bridge; an intelligence agent could change addresses after completing an assignment; but a safehouse keeper had a fixed base, and the police might knock on the door at any hour. Like the guides, not only those sheltering aviators but other members of the family could be arrested and subjected to harsh interrogations, ending too often in imprisonment and deportation to a concentration camp. Despite the risks, however, they accepted strangers into their houses and apartments because they wanted to help them return to their bases and continue the fight against the Germans.

One of the early safehouse keepers was Renée Nouveau, who, with her husband, Louis, provided the first safehouse for the Pat line in Marseille. They were the owners of a small import-export business and lived comfortably in a spacious apartment overlooking the Old Port. After the defeat of 1940, Louis planned to join the Free French in London, but Renée convinced him that it was more courageous to remain in France and do what they could to thwart the Germans. They learned how they could help from Ian Garrow, who was forming the escape organization later known as the Pat O'Leary line.[43]

The tall Scot accepted the Nouveaus' invitation to dinner at their flat and listened while Louis and Renée explained their desire to help the Allies and restore French autonomy. Then he outlined his own plans, describing the work of his fledgling escape line and the need for money and safehouses. Louis immediately arranged to advance 40,000 francs for the cause, and Renée volunteered to provide hospitality for evaders and agents. For two years their apartment was the operational headquarters of the line and a key safehouse. Renée lodged 161 men, one of whom was Airey Neave, who later served in MI 9. Louis Nouveau kept a record of the names, military affiliations, and nationalities of most of the guests, and hid the list in volume 44 of *Oeuvres complètes de Voltaire*. He noted that the one woman on the list was an American, Virginia Hall, an agent of SOE.[44]

Life was busy and tense for Renée as she carried out her many responsibilities. She had to cope with language difficulties because 145 of her guests were not French. Sometimes she had to use sign language to ask the escapers to wear slippers instead of shoes and to refrain from loud conversation that would reveal to the people in the apartment below that others were staying with the Nouveaus. She had to obtain food on the black market and, as part of the game, she stole bread ration tickets at the Red Cross canteen where she worked one night a week, hiding them under the cape of her uniform.[45]

Despite its difficulties the couple kept up this work until the German occupation of southern France made it too dangerous to remain in Marseille. At this time Renée set out for London, where she would work for the Free French. At Toulouse she was delayed, but used the time to help Marie Louise Dissard until the trip across the Pyrenees could be attempted. Even after Renée's departure Louis refused to leave the country—a costly sacrifice. Working in Paris as a leader of the Pat line, he was one of those betrayed by Roger Le Neuveu.[46]

Unlike the Nouveaus, who had their own funds, most safehouse keepers could not afford to lodge and feed evaders without some reimbursement. Guides needed money to pay their own travel expenses and those of the men they were escorting. The leaders of large escape lines obtained funding for their operations from the British and French escape headquarters, through consuls in Spain and Switzerland, and by parachute drops. They allocated money for hostesses, who at first received between 70 and 100 francs a day for each evader they sheltered. As prices soared, they received about 175 francs for partial reimbursement. Because of the clandestine nature of the resistance, many safehouse keepers received little or no expense money.

Women who were heads of lodging in towns and cities distributed reimbursement to their safehouse keepers. One who served in Paris was Mme Gabrielle Wiame, the wife of a policeman and the mother of a teenage son. She had both the nerve necessary to carry out the risky assignments and the ability to enjoy the work. "It was a nice trade," she said, "and I loved it." Wiame's pleasure did not make her incautious, however, for she escaped arrest despite the fact that many of her associates were caught by the Germans at one time or another.[47]

Wiame's first connection was with Comet. She lived on the rue Poliveau near the Gare d'Austerlitz and the Jardin des Plantes, a strategic location for a safehouse keeper, since both the station and the gardens were places where airmen could be passed from one guide to another without attracting notice. She also helped the people in the Oaktree, Burgundy, and Shelburne lines.[48]

In June 1943 Wiame's immediate superior in Comet, Robert Aylé, was arrested. So was another associate, Val Williams, the chief of Oaktree.[49] The arrests came at a particularly bad time for Wiame and the radio operator of Oaktree, Labrosse; they were left with 17 evaders on their hands. In their search for another line they met Georges Broussine, the chief of Burgundy, who had traveled to England by way of the Pat line early in 1942, and had then volunteered to train as an agent and return under the auspices of BCRA and MI 9. After landing in France by parachute in February 1943, his first mission was to work with the Brandy line, but he soon mistrusted its security procedures and decided to organize his own network, which was named Burgundy.[50]

The meeting of Wiame and Broussine proved fruitful. He asked her to assume responsibility for lodging evaders in the Paris section of Burgundy. Toward the end of the year, Broussine learned that a key woman in his organization had been arrested and that Wiame had been present. It was all too likely that she would be the next victim, and in line with standard security procedures, Broussine told her to break connections with Burgundy. She had already taken the precaution of warning her safehouse keepers, but she was too determined to give up altogether. Working with Oaktree and then with Shelburne, she continued to help airmen in their search for a line that could arrange their escape. In all, Wiame personally lodged 19 fliers, not counting those who stayed with her only during the day. Fifty-four safehouse keepers assisted her, three-fourths of them women. After the war she was credited with helping 100 airmen, including 69 Americans, return to England. For her work with several escape organizations she was awarded the Medal of Freedom with gold palm.[51]

After Wiame severed her contacts with Burgundy, 21-year-old Genevieve Soulié took over as head of lodging in Paris. She had started working for the line after meeting Broussine. She depended on her salary as an assistant in a bookstore to provide for herself and her English-born mother, who was seriously ill with tuberculosis. She was therefore glad when she was asked to take care of a man who was boarding in the apartment of one of her mother's friends. The friend, Mme Marie Elvire Flament, was active in the resistance, and the man was Broussine, who had set up the temporary headquarters of his Burgundy line in Mme Flament's apartment.[52]

Before long Broussine asked Genevieve to join his group and she was "thrilled to help the resistance." She would receive enough expense money to take care of her own needs as well as her mother's. In that way, she could give up her job and devote her time to keeping house for Broussine and other leaders of the organization when they were in Paris. Genevieve, moreover, spoke fluent English, and her help was invaluable in communicating with Allied fliers. Broussine soon put her in charge of lodging.[53]

She found that her new job was a multifaceted one. She was responsible for the men from the time of their arrival in Paris until their departure. She not only arranged for their shelter, but also dealt with questions of morale and security. Many of the aviators became discouraged when snags delayed their progress along the line, and depression was hard to overcome when they had to be isolated in apartments.

Soulié made innumerable visits to the safehouses under her supervision to make sure of her lodgers' well-being and to bring them cigarettes and books, chatting with them in English to keep up their spirits. When possible she took them out for walks to give them a change of scene, although she felt conspicuous accompanying the men, particularly during blackouts, when there were few people and few cars on the streets.[54]

During these visits Soulié checked on security as well. Were the men cooperating with their hostesses by remaining reasonably quiet? Did the neighbors know they were there? If security measures had been breached, she saw to it that the aviators were transferred to other safehouses. In this role Soulié helped in the escape of some 136 Allied airmen, of whom 84 were American. According to Yves Allain, the assistant chief of Burgundy, she carried out the "dangerous and tiring work with complete disregard for her own comfort and safety."[55]

Mme Anne Brusselmans, a 30-year-old Belgian, also had an English-born mother and was fluent in English. She was recruited in September 1940 by her pastor, Mathieu Schyns of the Protestant Eglise Evangélique du Musée in Brussels, who knew of some British soldiers hiding in the city and asked her help in finding civilian clothes and ration cards for them until they could make their way home.[56]

The appeal to be of service to some of her mother's countrymen had to be weighed against the risks to her family; but once she made the decision, she went farther than searching out food and clothing, and began to lodge evaders at her apartment on the chaussée d'Ixelles. Soon she made contact with Comet, hiding military guests and several civilians sought by the police. She also questioned evaders seeking help from escape groups to ascertain whether they were bona fide soldiers or German agents. Among the 20 soldiers she sheltered during the course of the war, some for as long as 6 weeks, was 2d Lt. Henry P. Sarnow, a bombardier on a Flying Fortress who had parachuted into Belgium. He stayed with her for a month and came to appreciate her as a "very intelligent and sincere person with a wonderful sense of humor." It took Sarnow 12 weeks in all to cross France from Belgium and then make the journey over the Pyrenees and back to England via Spain.[57] But Mme Brusselman's work was not finished. When the Allied forces reached Brussels in early September 1944, she brought 54 evaders, who had been hidden in safehouses, to the Hotel Metropole and turned them over to astonished American officers.[58]

Safehouse keepers with other special qualifications such as being nurses, were also invaluable to escape lines. As the air war intensified, about one-third of the men who parachuted or crash-landed in France needed medical care. Some had been wounded in aerial combat, some were hurt when they hit the ground or burned when their planes caught fire. Still others suffered frostbite from bailing out at high altitudes.[59]

Nurses often took care of seriously injured fliers in their own homes or apartments because it was dangerous to put them in hospitals. One who played a key role in the escape of several airmen was Germaine Royannez. The story of how she helped 1st Lt. James S. Munday after his B-17 bomber was shot down by German fighters southwest of Paris is typical of how survivors of aerial combat were cared for and passed along the escape lines.

After bailing out on July 14, 1943, Munday found himself alone and hamstrung by a wound in the back of his leg. Another hit had blown his boot off and penetrated his foot, but he was able to bandage his wounds with strips from his parachute. Soon two of his sergeants joined him. They helped him into the shelter of the woods a few miles from their landing place, and there they all agreed that they would have to ask for help.[60]

Using his college French, Munday hailed a farmer working in the fields; he proved sympathetic and sent the fliers to the cottage of a farm couple nearby. By this time Munday was running a fever. While the wife bathed his wounds with kerosene, the only disinfectant she had, her husband notified an underground group. Three days later the crewmen half-carried Munday to a secluded spot along the road, where they were told they would be picked up by a gazogene coke-burning ambulance from Paris.[61]

The ambulance brought Germaine Royannez armed with false papers authorizing Munday's transportation to a Paris hospital for an appendectomy. Riding with the driver was a member of a sabotage group who would escort the two crewmen, Sgts. Edward T. Ruby and Francis M. Green, to Paris by train. The ambulance set off for Paris but was soon stopped at a bridge by a German guard, who examined the papers and asked several questions but was content to let the party proceed. At Paris they were stopped by a second roadblock, and the nurse again presented the papers. This time the guards searched the ambulance but did not disturb Munday. Finally the party was waved through and arrived at Royannez's apartment on avenue Niel, after making a victorious circuit around the Arc de Triomphe. At the apartment entrance, to Munday's dismay, a group of young Luftwaffe officers were standing and chatting; the nurse coolly asked the soldiers to let them pass, and she and her patient were allowed to reach the safety of her apartment.[62]

Royannez treated Munday's wounds with scarce sulfa powder, bandaged his head and jaw so that he could not speak if the police stopped him, and transferred him to the care of a trusted doctor, who lodged him for ten days until a maid in the building discovered his presence and he was forced to return to Royannez's apartment. There he spent two weeks with his sergeants, whom she was also lodging, before they could undertake the journey to Spain.

All three airmen eventually crossed the Pyrenees and returned to England. Munday hiked seven hours over the mountains but had to stop because his wounds were not yet fully healed. His guide arranged for him to stay in a cottage to rest, and after several days he joined a party of Frenchmen traveling on foot to Spain via Andorra. Following the usual pattern, Munday received help at British consulates. When he reached Britain, he had been a fugitive for a little over two months.[63]

When evaders were suffering from wounds or other injuries, their situation and that of those helping them became more complicated because it was dangerous to keep them for very long in any one place, but painful and sometimes medically inadvisable to move them. Their rescuers' first job was to hide them from the Germans. Then they treated their wounds, using whatever skill and supplies they possessed until a doctor or nurse could take over.

Second Lieutenant Donald M. Lewis never learned the name of the owner of a chateau who discovered him in her garden somewhere southwest of Versailles in April 1944. His fighter plane had caught fire and he had been severely burned, but had managed to bail out. He remembered that she gave him rum to ease his pain before trying, with the help of her nine-year-old daughter, to carry him into the chateau, where she hid him in a loft. The next day a doctor arrived to take Lewis in an ambulance to a hospital where his burns could be treated. Because Germans were also in the hospital, Lewis was placed in an isolated back room where he could escape into the fields outside the building if a search was ordered. After a week he was well enough to be moved to the house of a nurseryman, whose wife and two daughters cared for him for three weeks under the supervision of the doctor.[64]

His presence became so well known, however, and so many friendly neighbors came to visit him, that Lewis had to be transferred once again, this time to the farm of a woman he knew only as Mme Madeleine, where he spent a month recuperating. Finally, on June 14, to avoid any further risk to those who had saved his life, he was escorted to the camp in the forest of Fréteval.[65]

In cities and towns along the escape routes and in the ports from which escapers might be picked up, accommodations were often provided by owners and managers of hotels, many of them women. Thanks to the poor economic conditions, they nearly always had rooms available. They needed guests, but to house Allied soldiers entailed special risks because of the regulations imposed on hotel keepers. The police routinely checked hotel registrations and sometimes extended their inspection to the rooms. If guests stayed without registering, it was a violation of the law. Even if the men were registered, they had to produce identity papers and possibly submit to questioning.

Mme Lebreton, of the Hôtel du Tennis in the resort of Canet Plage, had all the characteristics of a typical hotel manager as she provided lodging for agents of the Pat line. In the summer and early fall of 1942, many British soldiers broke out of Vichy internment camps with the help of O'Leary's organization, and Pat had worked out a scheme for mass evacuations from Canet Plage. Mme Lebreton provided one of her vacant holiday bungalows as a hiding place for the 30 to 40 men in each party. She also prepared food for them and had it smuggled into the crowded bungalow late at night. In three separate operations of this kind, despite delays and complications, a total of 95 people left the beach by dinghy and boarded the British armed trawler *Tarana*, which took them to Gibraltar. One of those on board was Paula Spriewald, the anti-Nazi daughter of a German socialist, who had been O'Leary's secretary in Marseille. Two of the men were Val Williams and the Canadian Lucien Dumais, who would return to France as chiefs of the escape lines Oaktree and Shelburne.[66]

Other places where the comings and goings of different people offered some protection for evaders were public institutions. Marguerite Gronier was the director of the Vichy-sponsored Secours National in Senlis, north of Paris, whose headquarters were in a large, secluded house. Here she and her staff carried on the work of assisting war widows, wives of prisoners of war, and victims of the bombing raids. Here also she lodged 12 Allied soldiers, 7 of them Americans.

Only two young women on her staff, Paulette Thomas and Jacqueline Cabre, knew that the soldiers were hiding in the building.[67] During working hours the men were confined to an isolated room, but after six o'clock they were free to walk around the house and gardens. Jacqueline and Paulette took charge of obtaining and preparing food for the men, who had their meals after the rest of the staff went home. The young women also provided a change of routine for the young airmen, staying on some evenings to dance with them. They also arranged for the men to go to the public baths, where the Americans had to stand in line with Germans while they waited their turn.[68]

For two of the Americans the waiting was worth the risk, for it was their first real bath since they bailed out of their disabled bomber in March 1944, two months earlier. They had slept in haystacks for several nights, eating only frozen potatoes, until a friendly Frenchman offered them a ride in his garbage truck and drove them to his house in Senlis. Here his wife took charge of them for two months until they were transferred to the Secours National. There another month passed before they could move on toward Britain.[69]

On June 3, just before D Day, they set out for Paris and soon reached the forest of Fréteval. On July 31, less than a month before the liberation of Paris, they were joined by another of Gronier's protégés, 2d Lt. Heyward C. Spinks, the pilot of a P-51 Mustang fighter, who had been forced down near Senlis when his engine failed. Spinks's first hosts were a Polish couple whose family had migrated to France after World War I. They cared for him until a sympathetic policeman took him to Senlis by bicycle five days later and turned him over to Gronier, who hid him for five weeks.[70]

Not all of those who gave refuge to airmen were regularly associated with escape lines. Notable among the independent sympathizers who took in fugitives were women in religious communities, who were well aware that membership in a religious order would not guarantee protection against deportation and perhaps death. An outstanding example was Mother Yvonne Aimée de Jesus (Yvonne Beauvais), the mother superior of a convent of Augustinian sisters in Malestroit, Brittany. She hid wounded resisters and Allied airmen in the clinic of the convent. On one occasion she was told that 2d Lt. Robert E. Kylius of Yankton, South Dakota, was hiding in the area and that the Germans were looking for him. She immediately arranged for him to be brought to the convent, where she hid him in the bishop's suite of the clinic. In his report to his superiors, Kylius wrote:

> I remained hidden there for four days and was allowed in the garden only for a half-hour during the afternoons. The Mother Superior told me that six of my crew members had been killed, but that the French had misled the Germans by making coffins for eight.[71]

In the course of such rescues the mother superior became skilled in throwing the Gestapo off the scent. Once when they came to the convent looking for two Allied aviators she was sheltering, she had the airmen dress as nuns and sent them to the chapel to pray. Rumors continued to reach the Gestapo, however, that resisters were finding refuge in the clinic. They brought Mother Yvonne to their headquarters for interrogation, but she adroitly sidestepped their questions and was permitted to return to the convent.[72]

The mother superior of another convent provided refuge for Lt. John J. Bradley, navigator of a Flying Fortress, who had bailed out of his burning plane over the Netherlands on November 5, 1943. Although he was able to find a safehouse near Lanklaar, Belgium, just west of the Dutch border, its keeper was arrested shortly afterward. He managed to avoid capture and was taken in at the convent of the Sisters of Providence. Here he spent nearly a week among the nuns; most of them were Belgian, but several were French and one was Dutch. One of them, Sister Thérèse, had studied English and served as an interpreter, with Bradley helping her to correct her accent. She also tried to teach him Flemish, some knowledge of which might be useful to him.

For his sake the convent rules were relaxed so that the nuns could play cards with him, using candy, cookies, and nuts for forfeits, before going to the chapel at nine o'clock to pray. Normally they did not play cards and the earlier hour was spent in prayer, with bedtime at nine o'clock.[73]

When Bradley tried to reach France, his luck ran out. He was arrested at the border by German secret police and turned over to the Luftwaffe police, who told him that he would be shot because he was wearing civilian clothes. Instead he was imprisoned at St. Gilles, the Brussels prison where so many members of Comet had been taken. When the advancing Allies neared the capital, the Germans hastily crowded Bradley and 42 other men into a boxcar destined for Germany, but the men were able to escape and rejoin their American companions.[74]

The stories of women guides and safehouse keepers provide a glimpse of their escape activities. Along with women chiefs and subchiefs they played a major role in the lines that assisted about 3,000 downed U.S. airmen and 2,000 British and Commonwealth fliers to return to their bases, chiefly from France. They also aided some 500 American and 1,100 British combat soldiers to escape or evade and return to their units. It was a remarkable record.[75]

Notes

1. W. F. Craven and J. L. Cates, eds., *The Army Air Forces in World War II*, 2: 215–16.

2. Ibid., pp. 841–43. Data cited include all planes dispatched on bombing missions. A significant number returned to base, for one reason or another, without attacking their targets. The crew of a B-17 consisted of pilot, copilot, navigator, bombardier, radio operator, top and ball turret gunners, one tail gunner, and two waist gunners. "Heavy Bombers Dispatched and Missing 1944–45," Research Division, Albert F. Simpson Historical Research Center, USAF, Maxwell Air Force Base, AL.

3. The Geneva Convention was the first formal codification of international law concerned solely with the treatment and status of prisoners of war. It was signed by 47 countries, including Germany.

4. RG 332, ETO, MIS, MIS-X Section, MIS Manual on Escape, Evasion, and Survival, February 1944, pp. 4–13.

5. Raphaël Lemkin, *Axis Rule in Occupied Europe*, p. 395; Archives, Comité d'Histoire de la Deuxième Guerre Mondiale, document 232-15R 139, from Roger Huguen, *Par les nuits les plus longues*, forepage. Comité will be abbreviated in future citations to CHG.

6. Jean François Nothomb, interview, Ann Arbor, MI, July 1977; James M. Langley, *Fight Another Day*, p. 171.

7. Mme Andrée Dumon Antoine, interview, Brussels, October 1976; RG 332, ETO, 7707 ECIC, MIS-X, Helpers, Andrée de Jongh, "Rapport de Andrée de Jongh," p. 13, dossier. All dossiers in this chapter have the same citation.

8. Mme Micheline Dumon Ugeux, interview, Brussels, October 1976; Michou Dumon, "Statement About Comète," September 24, 1944, dossier.

9. M. Dumon, "Statement."

10. 2d Lts. Martin G. Minnich and Henry P. Sarnow, E & E Report nos. 229–230; Sarnow, letter to author, April 10, 1978.

11. Jean de Blommaert, interview, Orlando, FL, October 1980.

12. Airey Neave, *Saturday at MI 9*, pp. 250–52; *L'extraordinaire aventure de la forêt de Fréteval*, pp. 3, 4, 7.

13. "Report of Mme Elvire de Greef," p. 4; Mme de Greef, "Comète, secteur sud," pp. 45, 68, dossier.

14. "Rapport de Madame Madeleine Noël," July 24, 1945, pp. 1–5, dossier.

15. Suzanne Wittek [Cecile Jouan], *Comète, histoire d'une ligne d'évasion,* pp. 151–52; Micheline Dumon Ugeux, interview.

16. "Rapport de Mme Noël." She received the Medal of Freedom with silver palm from the American government.

17. "Report of Mme Elvire de Greef," p. 4.

18. For the story of Virginia d'Albert Lake, see chapter 8.

19. "Report from Philippe d'Albert Lake," p. 1, dossier.

20. 2d Lt. Robert Z. Grimes, E & E Report no. 361; Grimes, telephone interview, November 1978, Fairfax, VA.

21. Mme Elvire de Greef, "Comète, secteur sud," pp. 45, 68.

22. "Report of Mme Elvire de Greef," p. 4. Now Mme Pierre Ugeux, Michou is the secretary and prime mover of the Comet Society, which keeps in touch with surviving helpers and holds annual reunions in Brussels, one of which the author was invited to attend in October 1976.

23. Peggy Van Lier Langley, interview, Woodbridge, England, October 1976; Baronne Bernadette Greindl, interview, Brussels, October 1976.

24. "Rapport de Andrée de Jongh," dossier, pp. 6, 15.

25. Peggy Langley, interview.

26. Ibid.; "Rapport de Andrée de Jongh," p. 21.

27. Peggy Langley, interview.

28. Ibid.

29. Ibid.

30. Ibid.

31. Wittek, *Comète*, p. 56.

32. Peggy Langley, interview.

33. Germaine Tillion, "Déclaration," n.d., Musée de l'Homme Collection, Ellen Clarke Bertrand Library, Bucknell University, Lewisburg, PA.

34. Mme Madeleine de Gaulle, French questionnaire, November 19, 1945, dossier. She received a certificate of appreciation signed by General Eisenhower.

35. MIS Manual on Escape, Evasion, and Survival, pp. 4–13.

36. Jacques Le Grelle, "Report of Agent Jacques Le Grelle," personal archives, pp. 8–9.

37. Maj. Leon Blythe, E & E Report no. 547.

38. Kenneth Woodhouse, "My Escape," personal archives, pp. 7, 13.

39. Ralph K. Patton, personal archives.

40. Nicholas Mandell, letter to author, August 31, 1977.

41. Peloquin was the only member of the Air Forces Escape and Evasion Society (AFEES) from a French-speaking family. (See Guide to Frequently Cited Sources.) Joseph Peloquin, letters to author, February 13, 1977, and June 14, 1979; Peloquin, E & E Report no. 1054.

42. Woodhouse, "My Escape," p. 31.

43. Louis H. Nouveau, *Des capitaines par milliers*, pp. 17–18, 92–96.

44. Ibid., pp. 18–28, 97–100. For more on Virginia Hall, see chapter 8.

45. Nouveau, *Des capitaines*, pp. 14, 18, 146, 193, 293, 311.

46. Ibid., pp. 146, 338–40; "Rapport de Pat O'Leary," pp. 9, 11. Nouveau was deported to a concentration camp but survived.

47. Mme Gabrielle Wiame, "Rapport au sujet de l'activité des personnes qui ont collaboré avec Madame Wiame," January 10, 1945, dossier.

48. "History of Mme Marie Wiame," February 8, 1946, Colonel Vendeu, interrogating officer, Fourth Section, Mme Wiame dossier. The Shelburne line is discussed in chapter 4.

49. The code name was taken by Vladimir Bouryschkine.

50. RG 332, ETO, MIS, MIS-X Section, Research Branch, Histories and Related Records Pertaining to French Organizations and Networks, 1945–1946, "Réseau Burgundy," p. 5; Georges Broussine, interview, Paris, October 1976.

51. "History of Mme Marie Wiame"; Wiame, "Rapport."

52. Mme Genevieve Soulié Camus, interview, Paris, 1976.

53. Ibid.

54. Ibid.

55. Statement of Yves Allain in "Réseau Burgundy," p. 181; Genevieve Soulié Camus, interview; "History of Mlle Genevieve Germaine Soulié"; "Déclaration," September 26, 1944, dossier; "Liste d'aviateurs, reséau Bourgogne," personal archives of Mme Camus. She received the Croix de Guerre, Order of the British Empire, and the Medal of Freedom with silver palm.

56. Mme Anne Brusselmans, interview, Cincinnati, OH, October 1982; "Rapport activité Madame Anne Brusselmans," Service Rapatriément Aviateurs Alliés, Brussels, September 16, 1944, dossier.

57. "Rapport activité Madame Anne Brusselmans"; Anne Brusselmans, *Rendezvous 127*, pp. 50, 62, 69, 83, 84, 94, 101, 105; Brusselmans, letter to author, April 25, 1978; Henry P. Sarnow, letter to author, April 10, 1978; 2d Lts. Martin C. Minnich and Henry P. Sarnow, E & E Reports nos. 229–230.

58. Anne received the Medal of Freedom with silver palm, and 200 of her compatriots also received the Medal of Freedom for their assistance to evaders. Brusselmans, letter to author.

59. Air Forces Escape and Evasion Society, questionnaires.

60. Lt. Col. James S. Munday, interview, Savannah, GA, April 1978.

61. Ibid.

62. Ibid.; 1st Lt. James S. Munday and S. Sgt. Francis M. Green, E & E Reports nos. 104–105; T. Sgt. Edward T. Ruby, E & E Report no. 108.

63. Munday, interview; Munday and Green, E & E Reports nos. 104–105.

64. 2d Lt. Donald M. Lewis, questionnaire, AFEES. (See Guide to Frequently Cited Sources.)

65. Ibid.

66. "Rapport de Pat O'Leary," pp. 7–8; Langley, *Fight Another Day*, pp. 173–77.

67. Now Mesdames Declercq and Leroy.

68. Mme Paulette Declercq, interview, Orlando, FL, October 1980. Mme Declercq was a guest at the reunion of the Eighth Air Force and AFEES in Orlando, FL, October 29–November 2, 1980.

69. 2d Lt. Jonathan Pearson, questionnaire; Pearson and Cpl. Thomas L. Yankus, E & E Reports nos. 1063–1064; Pearson, interview, Orlando, FL, October 1980.

70. Heyward C. Spinks, letter to author, February 16, 1977; Spinks, E & E Report no. 963.

71. 2d Lt. Robert E. Kylius, E & E Report no. 45.

72. She was awarded the Legion of Honor, the Medal of the Resistance, and the Medal of Freedom.

73. John J. Bradley, "Diary," 1945, pp. 10–12; Bradley, E & E Report no. 1590.

74. Bradley, "Diary," pp. 18–30.

75. The E & E reports of American airmen in the Washington National Records Center run to number 2968 with some omissions. (For details see Guide to Frequently Cited Sources.) M. R. D. Foot and J. M. Langley, *MI 9*, pp. 310–11.

4 THE CROSS-CHANNEL FERRY

Among the networks organizing escapes for airmen and others in danger of imprisonment by the Germans, the Shelburne line, set up by MI 9 in late 1943, operated for only a short time but posted an impressive record. On eight occasions between January and August 1944, motor gunboats (MGBs) of the Royal Navy slipped past the formidable German coastal batteries and waited within a mile and a half of a closely patrolled beach in Brittany while sailors who had volunteered for this hazardous duty rowed to the shore, picked up escaping aviators, and brought them back on board. Nor was that the whole task. The gunboats had brought matériel for resistance groups that had to be loaded onto skiffs, then unloaded on the beach before the airmen could be taken aboard. The success of these eight missions testifies not merely to the daring and the naval skill of those manning the MGBs and the small boats but also to the heroism of French civilians in the intricate network, many of them women who risked their lives in this endeavor.

The Shelburne story is important because the work of the women serving the line can be told from the viewpoint of the airmen.[1] The young men who were forced to land in occupied territory found it a strange and unnerving experience to be fugitives after having been almost universally envied and often favored among the armed forces. Now their distinctive uniforms were a menace, and to make themselves understood they had to resort to gestures or childish phrases. Particularly strange, perhaps, was accepting guidance and instructions from women, sometimes girls still in their teens, who had to remind them that many people could win privileges from the enemy by betraying them, and that the aid they received could cost their helpers deportation if not death. It is no wonder that so many of the men escaping via the Shelburne line still vividly remember how much the women members did to make possible their return to England.

Until Shelburne began operations in Brittany, most evaders en route to Britain had relied on lines, such as Comet and Burgundy, that could convey them south across the mountains into Spain and eventually to Gibraltar. But as D Day approached, it became urgent to find a more direct route and, if possible, a way of handling larger numbers of evaders in one trip than the few who could be led over the Pyrenees at one time.

The shortest line from France to England was, of course, across the Channel, and the need for escape lines from Brittany to England had been recognized as early as 1941. After the French defeat, fishing boats had been used by Frenchmen willing to risk German patrols and rough seas to reach their countrymen training in England. The same means had been used to carry French and British agents and weapons across the Channel. By 1942 the hardpressed British Admiralty occasionally permitted an MGB to carry important BCRA and SOE personages to and from France.[2] They also had at their disposal three 28-knot motor torpedo boats (MTBs). SOE set up its own escape lines under the DF section, including the sea escape organization Var, which later carried Virginia Hall to Brittany.

The first plan called for a line code-named Oaktree to be set up by two men: Val Williams and his radio operator, Raymond Labrosse. Williams had been sought by the Vichy police for his participation in the Pat line but was among the many who escaped to England aboard the trawler *Tarana*. Labrosse, a radio operator of the Canadian Signal Corps, had been recruited from the Canadian Military Headquarters in London.[3]

In February 1943 the two men parachuted into France, but their mission met with bad luck from the start. Labrosse's radio would not function, and in June, while they were still waiting for a new one, Val Williams was arrested; Labrosse escaped through Spain. The two men left one important accomplishment behind them, however. They had made several contacts that were to prove useful in the next attempt to establish a cross-Channel ferry to England. One of the most helpful was Paul François Campinchi, a Paris lawyer in the Préfecture de la Seine. With his wife Thérèse, a nurse, he would prove an invaluable ally at a critical point in the beginning of Shelburne.[4]

Another was Countess Genevieve de Poulpiquet, a safehouse keeper, who had been forced into hiding after the Germans raided her chateau during her absence, and arrested her husband and others in the household. Although a strong supporter of Marshal Pétain and his regime, she bitterly disliked the Germans and had already helped airmen to escape before meeting Williams and volunteering for Oaktree.[5]

After she was able to join the fledgling Oaktree line and the more successful Shelburne, Genevieve worked principally as a guide escorting airmen to Brittany. She was especially useful in that role because she knew a railway official and was able to reserve compartments in the overcrowded trains. If the Channel route could not be used, she guided the men to Pau.[6]

Thanks to these contacts, it was clear that despite its failure, Oaktree had left willing helpers both in Paris and in the coastal area, and MI 9 renewed preparations to set up a line across the Channel. Chief of the new line, to be called Shelburne, was Sgt. Maj. Lucien Dumais of the Fusiliers Mont Royal, Second Canadian Division. A tough, stocky professional soldier, Dumais had taken part in the Dieppe raid and been captured by the Germans, but had made his escape by jumping off the train en route to a prisoner of war camp. Like Val Williams, he had been evacuated from Canet Plage in the fall of 1942. His fellow Canadian Labrosse volunteered to return with him to France and serve as his radio operator and second in command.[7]

Although MI 9 saw the urgent need for evacuation lines to be strengthened before the invasion, scheduled for the spring of 1944, it was October 1943 before Dumais and Labrosse landed by Lysander plane near Compiègne. Each carried a set of codes so that they could communicate directly with London by radio if necessary. They also carried 750,000 French francs to cover expenses of the line. Both had undergone special training in sea evacuations.[8]

According to the Shelburne plan, aviators would be collected and sheltered in Paris before traveling by train to Brittany, where they would be lodged briefly until a British gunboat could come on a moonless night and pick them up. To increase the airmen's opportunities to reach Britain, Dumais was instructed to organize an additional escape route over the Pyrenees into Spain.

The tasks faced by Dumais and Labrosse were complicated. They would have to find subchiefs in Paris and Brittany who in turn would select heads of lodging. They would also need people in Brittany to help with transporting and concealing weapons and supplies brought up from the beach after each evacuation. On one occasion they would hide 4 million francs sent by London for the expenses of the line.[9]

The strip of beach considered most suitable for Operation Bonaparte, as the evacuation came to be called, lay within a tiny cove on the northern coast of the Breton peninsula, a three-and-a-half-mile walk from the village of Plouha. The nearest towns of any size were St. Brieuc and Guingamp, both on the Paris-Brest railway line. Plouha was served by a small local line running from St. Brieuc. The rail service would be of great use, because the men would have to be dispersed for safety's sake while they waited to embark; and bad weather conditions, German troop movements, and any number of other factors would make delays inevitable.

If all went well, the men would travel by rail from Paris to St. Brieuc, a distance of about 250 miles. At St. Brieuc they would change trains for

Plouha, only 18 miles up the coast. The Germans suspended the passenger service on the local train soon after the second evacuation of airmen from Bonaparte Beach, and it became necessary to transport the men along the final leg of the journey by truck.[10]

Once the site of the evacuation was approved, Dumais, Labrosse, and their top associates were able to recruit a remarkable corps of helpers, not only in the vicinity of Plouha but also in the other key towns along the escape route. While it was possible, and sometimes advantageous, to have safehouses in scattered locations, members of the beach party would have to live close to the embarkation point, since the BBC signal that the gunboats were on their way could come only at the last moment, leaving little time for men and helpers to assemble. To head the beach party Dumais recruited François Le Cornec, ostensibly the proprietor of a cafe in Plouha, but secretly the chief of a resistance group affiliated with the Front National, Défense de la France and Libération Nord. He selected three other people who were to serve as members of the party in all eight of the successful operations from Bonaparte Beach.[11]

One of the regular members of the beach party was Marie Thérèse Le Calvez, an 18-year-old who became an almost legendary figure in the memory of the airmen who met her, not only for her beauty but also for the serene courage she showed when guiding the men along the rough cliffs to the exposed beach and waiting with them during the last anxious moments before they heard the sound of oars in the darkness.[12]

Even before Le Cornec chose her as his liaison agent and member of the beach party, her widowed mother, Mme Léonie Le Calvez, had been one of the first two safehouse keepers recruited in the area.[13] Madame Le Calvez enlisted the help of her friend Germaine Couffon, who employed four women as seamstresses in the dressmaking shop that was also her home.[14]

Serving along with Le Cornec and Marie Thérèse Le Calvez in all of the operations were Pierre Huet, a former pilot with the air arm of the French fleet, and Joseph Mainguy, a captain in the merchant marine. Ordinarily they were able to rely for help on three other families who became key supporters of the line and rendered outstanding service in its operations: Georges Ropers and his wife and daughter, Jean and Marie Tréhiou, and Jean Guiquel and his wife.

The Ropers lodged airmen on the last stage of their journey to the beach, and helped to guide the men down the cliffs and unload cargo. Marie Tréhiou and her brother Jean carried out a variety of tasks. After the death of their parents, they had taken charge of their younger brothers and the isolated family farm near Plouha. Soon after the French defeat, Jean and Marie had begun to serve the resistance, providing shelter for young men seeking to avoid forced labor in Germany. Now Jean worked with Le Cornec and participated in the evacuations as a member of the beach party. Marie also lodged escapers and, when necessary, used her horse and cart to carry contraband material, including supplies brought from England by the gunboats. She allayed suspicion by putting straw and potatoes in the front of the cart and hiding such things as radio transmitters, and money, clothes, and food for the evaders in the back. "I was not afraid," she said later, "because no one knew we were in the resistance, not even our neighbors. Sometimes when the aviators were at our farm the Germans came to our door asking for eggs, milk, and cider. I would give them cider with a big smile and they were pleased."[15]

In setting up the Paris end of the line, the first contacts of Dumais and Labrosse were two women who had been helping aviators escape to Spain via the Samson line. They welcomed the arrival of Dumais and Labrosse but, unfortunately, were arrested the next day.[16]

As soon as he learned of this setback, Labrosse considered approaching Paul Campinchi, whom he had known during the brief time that Oaktree operated and who had also had connections with Louis Nouveau of the Pat line. The instructions given Labrosse had contained specific warnings against communicating with former members of Oaktree, but he had no choice. As it turned out, Campinchi had escaped capture after the failure of Oaktree. He agreed to recruit some key people for the Paris sector. First, however, he wished to be assured that the leaders of the new line would insist on tight security. Labrosse must have been able to satisfy Campinchi's doubts, because the lawyer agreed to take on the work of organizing the corps of helpers needed in the Paris area.[17]

Campinchi began his duties by recruiting Marie Rose Zerling as his assistant. By education and previous experience in the resistance she was well suited for the tasks she undertook. During 1927–28 she had been a student at Wellesley College, and was familiar with the language and customs of Americans. Before the war she had taught at Strasbourg, where she knew Professor Jean Cavaillès, who later became chief of the Cohors intelligence *réseau*.[18] Zerling had started her resistance work by distributing the clandestine newspaper *Libération*, but after obtaining the post of professor at the lycée of Valenciennes in October 1942, she agreed to help Cavaillès, then a professor at the Sorbonne. He put her in touch with a French army intelligence officer in Valenciennes, Gilbert Bostsarron. Each weekend she carried correspondence between Bostsarron and Cavaillès in Paris. After the arrest of Bostsarron in December 1943, Zerling took a leave of absence from her teaching duties and moved to Paris, where her parents lived. By the time she joined Shelburne, she had already used her command of English to help Oaktree and other lines giving aid to Allied aviators in hiding after parachuting into northern France.[19]

In the role of Campinchi's assistant, Zerling soon became the most important woman member of the Paris section of the Sherlburne line. She was chief of lodging and enlisted the help of more than a dozen women and couples to shelter and feed the men. Zerling also had the responsibility of interrogating evaders in Paris to make sure the men were actually Allied soldiers and not German agents who had infiltrated the line. Following well-known security procedures, she sounded out the men's knowledge of the United States and had them answer questionnaires prepared by MI 9. Typical questions dealt with baseball rules, sports figures, film stars, and rationing at home. Zerling performed her tasks so skillfully that some airmen believed she was the best organization worker they had encountered.[20]

While the Paris sector of Shelburne was being organized, Raymond Labrosse made arrangements there for communicating with London by radio. The station master at the freight depot of Batignolles, at Pajol in northern Paris, a man named Jean Dorré, had assisted him during the Oaktree operation. Now Dorré permitted him to set up his radio transmitter in the Dorrés' dining room, putting the aerial around the walls. The radio functioned well, and he could now communicate regularly with MI 9 from either Paris or Plouha, using his own code. To transmit from two different places, however, Labrosse had to carry radio parts with him. Despite the risk, Dorré's daughter Ginette sometimes accompanied the young radio operator and concealed the telltale crystals in her purse.[21]

Within two months of their arrival, Dumais and Labrosse had a sufficiently reliable organization in place to handle the first group of evaders from Bonaparte Beach. All of the men assembled in Paris would be escorted to Brittany by guides. Those who had bailed out over Normandy and Brittany could be transferred directly to Plouha or some nearby town, often by people who were not in the organized resistance or were members of other networks. But Paris was the principal collecting point.

Even to get that far was a harrowing experience for 2d Lt. Sidney Casden.[22] He had been shot down near Paris and given shelter for more than six months by various people, most of whom had no contacts with resistance groups and therefore could not put him in touch with escape lines. Finally, however, he and another American, Sgt. Andrew F. Hathaway, were escorted by a young woman to the safehouse of Madame Schmitt, a hostess for Zerling, who was already sheltering three other evaders: S. Sgt. Walter E. Dickerman, S. Sgt. Paul R. Saunders, and P. O. Norman of the Royal Canadian Air Force. All five would soon set out for Bonaparte Beach, but only three would escape arrest on the way.[23]

It was dangerous to assemble the men near the beach where they would embark for Britain, and it was also risky to escort more than a few at a time on the Paris-Brest train. During the next few weeks Zerling visited Casden and his companions several times, explaining the delay. Finally, on the evening of January 18, the men underwent one more interrogation, this time by Dumais, and were given false identity papers to present to guards at the stations and on the train. Zerling took them to the Gare Montparnasse, where a younger woman took over as guide until they arrived at St. Brieuc.

Here the luck of Saunders and Norman ran out. The gendarme inspecting their papers became suspicious of their true identity and promptly arrested them. Eventually they were sent to a prisoner of war camp. Casden, Hathaway, and Dickerman passed through the control successfully.

Zerling also took Lt. Richard M. Smith and 2d Lt. Morton Shapiro to the Gare Montparnasse, from which they would leave for Plouha. She gave Smith, who had bailed out of his Flying Fortress at St. Just less than a month earlier, a pro-German newspaper that he could seem to be reading and pointed out the guide who would accompany them on the train. Two staff sergeants, Walter J. Sentkowski and James A. King, were also in the party. Among the instructions Zerling gave them was to hand the conductor their tickets when he asked for them but to avoid looking at him, and especially to avoid meeting the glances of the police guard who would be at his side.[24]

Two of the group waiting to be the first evaders from Bonaparte Beach were former prisoners, one well known to resisters in the area. Val Williams of Oaktree, whose arrest had brought that operation to a halt, had been imprisoned in Rennes but had managed to escape on December 20, 1943, with a fellow prisoner of war, a towering Russian officer named Bougaiev. Although Williams had broken his leg in jumping from the outer wall of the prison, Bougaiev had carried him to a safehouse where his leg could be set and where they could send a message to Campinchi and Zerling in Paris. These two arranged for the fugitives to travel safely to Paris, but the police were looking for them and it was urgent to get them out of France. No one could predict how much torture it might take before a prisoner reached the breaking point, and Williams knew a great deal about the resistance.[25]

Still on crutches when two guides brought him and Bougaiev from Paris to Plouha by train, Williams found a safe shelter at the farmhouse of Françoise Montjarret. She not only cared for the injured man and his companion for 15 days, but also called on a relative in nearby Paimpol who was a doctor and could treat Williams' injured leg.[26]

Despite the difficulties of getting the men to the staging point and keeping them in hiding during the delay caused by the stormy weather, the first cross-Channel ferrying operation from Bonaparte Beach was a success. Thirteen American airmen, the pilot of a British Typhoon, and the pilot and radio operator from a Halifax bomber were picked up, along with Val Williams and his Russian companion.

On the night of January 28, 1944, three rowboats carried them without incident from the beach to the gunboat lying offshore. One man, Lt. Casden, had spent eight months in hiding, thanks to the help of countless French patriots. In contrast, Lt. Smith returned to England after only 32 days as a fugitive.[27]

Before another group could be evacuated from Bonaparte Beach, however, tragedy struck the new line. Marie Rose Zerling and her parents were arrested on February 5, little more than a week after the triumphant embarkation at Plouha.[28]

In Fresnes prison Marie Rose, known only as Claudette to the many who had relied on her, was told that she had been condemned to death. The sentence was never carried out, however. A few days before the liberation of Paris, the Germans deported her and her parents to Auschwitz. There her father died, but she and her mother were among the barely surviving prisoners rescued by the arrival of Allied troops.

After Marie Rose Zerling's arrest her place was taken by Marcel Cola, personnel manager of Ford of France. He was already an experienced resister, using his work with Ford to sabotage trucks destined for Germany. Another advantage was that he had lived for 12 years in Canada and 2 years in the United States, and was therefore well qualified to interrogate men claiming to be evaders. Anita Lemonnier, who was born in France but had been educated at St. Joseph's, a convent near London, became his assistant. Some of her work entailed escorting men in Paris and nearby towns, and she and her mother also sheltered evaders in their Paris apartment at 2, rue Ernest Renan.[29]

The second operation from Bonaparte Beach was successful, though the arrest of two airmen in the group could have brought disaster. As in the earlier operation, the party of escapers included a mixed group, though this was a slightly larger one. Eighteen Allied pilots and crewmen made up the bulk of the party. In addition one Belgian soldier and two young French volunteers boarded the British gunboat. Of the 16 American fliers, 8 had been downed as recently as January 5; in contrast, S. Sgt. Lee C. Gordon had spent four months as a fugitive after his escape from Stalag VIIA in Moosburg. He was probably the only American airman to escape from a German prisoner of war camp and return to Britain.[30]

With two successful evacuations behind them, Airey Neave and James Langley of MI 9 shared the elation of Dumais and Labrosse and their fellow workers in Shelburne. Every one of the 34 airmen who returned offered reassuring evidence to other fliers that they could count on assistance from the French if they were forced down. Many also brought valuable intelligence about troop concentrations and military installations. As experienced evaders, their tips on how to deceive the police in tight situations could help at least some of their comrades to avoid capture.

The chief concern now was to make preparations for a third operation as quickly as possible. Roughly a month had intervened between the first and second pickups from Bonaparte. This time they hoped to cut the interval and also to take more men aboard, since the aim was to make as many trips as possible before D Day.

A detailed account of this third evacuation has come from 2d Lt. Ralph

K. Patton. On January 5, 1944, as copilot of a relatively new B-17G bomber, he took off on his ninth bombing mission and his first night formation. More than half of the 521 planes headed for Germany, primarily Kiel. The others, including Patton's, flew south to attack either Tours or the Bordeaux Marignac Luftwaffe base. Fighter escort was provided by P-47s, but only as far as La Pallice, about 90 miles north of Bordeaux, which was the limit of the fighters' range. Of the 117 bombers dispatched to the Bordeaux base, 11 were lost and 110 crew members were listed as missing.[31]

Patton's plane met only moderate flak from ground installations near the big air base, but after the bombardier unleashed his load over the target, the plane was attacked by several FW 190s stationed 60 miles south of Bordeaux. The fighters succeeded in damaging the tail assembly, but the crew fended off the attack and headed the plane north at reduced speed. By the time they had passed the Breton coast, they were ten miles behind the flight formation, a tempting target to the two German fighters that suddenly closed in. This time the crippled plane suffered more severe damage. It could no longer be controlled, and the only recourse was to bail out.[32]

As Patton drifted down, he counted six other parachutes; but when he landed among a group of peasants, he was joined only by the bombardier, 2d Lt. Jack McGough, and the pilot, 1st Lt. Glenn B. Johnson. A pillar of black smoke less than a mile away marked the spot where the plane had crashed and burned. It was a grim warning that the area would soon be searched for survivors.[33]

Patton opened his escape kit and found the standard items, including 2,000 francs, a silk map of France, and a compass. After studying the map the men decided that they must be near the Breton village of Kergrist-Moëlou, in the central part of the peninsula. Since the onlookers surrounding them made no move either to help or to hinder them, the fliers started to walk away. Ultimately they hoped to reach Spain, but meanwhile they needed temporary cover until they could obtain civilian clothes to replace their flying gear. To avoid any further encounters during the day, they walked across fields. Eventually they came upon a big, isolated farmhouse where the farmer and his wife gave them food and shelter for the night.

After breakfast they again set out cross-country, and in late afternoon were lucky enough to meet a friendly young Frenchman. He told them they were just outside the village of Gouarec, about 30 miles southwest of St. Brieuc. For the time being, he said, he knew of a small farm where they could hide. There the farmer seemed pleased to see them; he brought them food and promised that they could stay in a haystack overnight. At dawn their young guide returned and led them toward Gouarec, saying that they could surely pass through the town because the German guards would not be at their stations so early.

So far they had seen no others from the plane, but suddenly two men jumped out of a ditch alongside the road and greeted them joyfully. One was

S. Sgt. Isadore C. Viola, the waist gunner from their plane. The other was 2d Lt. Norman R. King, a navigator from another plane that had been shot down the same day.

Glad as they were to know that others had survived, the men recognized the hazards of having five aviators, all in uniform, in one group. Their guide took them across the bridge and hid them on a hillside just beyond it. After dark he came back with food and led them five miles along a road to the southwest. There he stopped and gave the airmen a sketch map, pointing out that they were not far from the abbey of Langonnet, where the monks would help them. He warned them not to travel at night because of the curfew and the German patrols in the area.

The night was cold, and the men could not sleep on their makeshift bed of pine boughs. At 5:30 in the morning they gave up the attempt and resumed walking. By noon they reached Plouray, about four miles northeast of the abbey. To avoid being seen, they took to the fields. A villager, Louis Caoueder, soon approached them and invited them into his house. Word of their arrival had already been spread by a nine-year-old boy who had spotted them and reported their presence to his surprised teacher, Mme Marie Antoinette Piriou. Turning the class over to her assistant, Pierre Daniel, she set out with the boy and her friend Josephine Le Vely to help the Americans.[34]

Meanwhile, about 20 men of the town, hearing the news, had gathered at the Caoueder house to share in a festive welcome for the strangers, which included food, wine, and the promise of civilian clothes. The wine and friendly company made the fugitives forget the danger they and their hosts were incurring. "For a while," Patton said later, "we didn't much care whether there was a war or not."[35]

Soon, however, Marie Antoinette and Josephine arrived. Marie Antoinette told them in good English that she had earlier helped an aviator to get back to England. His name was Frank Greene, and as it happened, McGough knew a man by that name. The fliers had already been prepared to trust themselves to her care after learning that her husband was a prisoner of war in Germany and her brother was in hiding from the Germans.

That evening Marie Antoinette came back with three villagers to take the fliers to the schoolhouse. Josephine Le Vely was also with the group, accompanied by her fiancé, Marcel Pasco. Their help was needed because the long journey on foot had left S. Sgt. Viola's feet so blistered that two of the men had to support him as they made their way through the village. To the men it seemed like a parade, with scouts at every corner to give the all-clear signal and almost half the village waiting to greet their arrival at the schoolhouse.

The building also served as Marie Antoinette's living quarters, with a classroom on either side of her apartment and an attic above where the men could take refuge in case of unwanted visitors. Frank Greene, they were told, had fashioned a hiding place up there by taking out part of the floor. The presence of Marie Antoinette's brother Alain made six evaders in all, too many to be accommodated in the schoolhouse itself. Johnson and Viola would sleep at Josephine Le Vely's house, which was only a few steps from the school, and King would stay with Pasco across the street, but all would spend the daylight hours together in the schoolhouse.[36]

Marie Antoinette, whom the Americans soon came to call Toni, proved to be an excellent leader and Josephine, nicknamed Jo, an able adjutant. While Toni taught her classes as usual, Jo prepared meals for their charges, keeping them in good spirits by her own cheerfulness. Though she knew no English, she managed to communicate with them by resorting to the French-English dictionary in the school's stock of reference books. Games of chess, cards, and checkers helped to pass the time, and occasionally there were small parties, enlivened by gifts of wine and cider sent by the villagers.

They were never able to forget for long the risks they were under. One day some Germans came to inquire about places where they could lodge troops. While the men hid in the attic, Jo told the visitors that the teacher was absent but would be back shortly. Eventually the Germans tired of waiting and drove away. Another time Johnson, who was six feet four, left such giant footprints in the snow that a farmer asked Pasco what kind of stranger could have passed through the village.

Johnson's size added to the problem of finding suitable clothing for the men. Toni's older brother Jean brought some civilian clothes, and Jo obtained a few ration tickets for clothes from her cousin the mayor. But they were not enough, and nothing was big enough for Glenn Johnson. Even his bed had to have an added plank at the end; and because he shared it with Isadore Viola, a much shorter man, they had trouble with the covers. "Isadore's face would be hidden," Jo recalled, "and Glenn only partly covered, so they fussed about this."

Providing food for the airmen also was difficult. Farmers who had children in school sent gifts of food with them. Jo's parents contributed grain for bread. Generously, the evaders' hosts subsisted on potatoes and carrots, giving the bread, butter, and sugar to their guests. It was important to keep them well because it was unsafe to take them to a doctor.

Two weeks or so after their arrival, Toni's contacts brought results in the person of the mayor of Gourin and a retired professor, who arrived in Plouray with word that they were arranging for the airmen's return to England by boat. They would have to photograph the men first, however, so that false papers could be made for them. Meanwhile, the men were to remain in Plouray. The promise of rescue raised their hopes immensely, but for a month nothing happened. The waiting was all the harder because they knew that every day in the care of their French friends increased the danger to themselves and was even more of a threat to those sheltering them.[37]

At last, however, the five airmen were able to leave Plouray on February 20, 1944, under the guidance of the organized resistance. By this time all of them had civilian clothes and forged identity papers. Patton was to pass as Yves Pailly, a commercial traveler born June 5, 1915, at Tréboul in western Brittany. He was also given an *identité titulaire*, a work certificate showing that he was employed, and a card authorizing him to be in the forbidden coastal zone.[38]

He and King were first taken to a bistro about two miles along the road to Lorient, where they spent ten uncomfortable days confined to one room. Waiting under such conditions was trying, but they knew that every effort was being made to move them along the line as fast as security would allow. Their next stop was at the Hotel Tournebride, opposite the abbey of Langonnet, to which they had been directed shortly after they landed. Here their host was a young Frenchman who had been a sailor in the French navy. At the two airmen's next safehouse, a farm outside of Langonnet, they were reunited with Johnson and Viola. This refuge, provided by Madame Lanour and her two sons, Baptiste and Louis, was a welcome change because they could move freely out of doors when the coast was clear, and find release from tension through physical activity.[39] Madame Lanour spoke only Breton, so conversation was limited, but they found amusement in the evenings by playing touch football with a rolled-up newspaper.

At the end of their third week after leaving Plouray, a barber from Gourin, M. Lecren, and a companion arrived at the farm in Lecren's small truck. With a hurried "Allez vite!" they were bundled into the truck, where, to their surprise, they found their fellow escaper McGough, whom they had last seen in Plouray. The plan had been to drive them to Gourin, where they could board a train to Guingamp, but at Gourin they found they had missed connections and would have to stay overnight with Lecren, who used part of the time to give them much-needed haircuts.[40]

From here on, there would be no more long delays. The next afternoon a young English-speaking Frenchman took the party onto the train for Guingamp. Although it was crowded with German troops, no one bothered them, nor were their papers checked at the station. For this last stage the group was split up, Patton and McGough being escorted to the home of Mme Francine Laurent, who was among Shelburne's most valuable hostesses. For two days the men spent the daylight hours uneasily watching the Germans from a nearby machine gun company going through their daily drill, though Mme Laurent assured them that superficially they could pass for Frenchmen. "You do not have 'Americans' written across your forehead," she told them.[41]

Their approaching evacuation, the third from Bonaparte Beach, would differ from the first two in one important respect. On the earlier occasions it had been possible to transport the fliers from St. Brieuc to Plouha by train, but recently the Germans had restricted the line to freight for the Atlantic

Wall. To take its place a garage owner, François Kerambrun, agreed to pick up the men at Guingamp and drive them to Plouha in his small, charcoal-burning Citroën truck. In the daytime he had to rent it to the Germans, but he still had a permit to drive it at times when they did not commandeer it. Most of his trips with airmen as passengers were at night, but because of the curfew he sometimes took the men, disguised as workmen, during the day. He carried as many men as he could pack into the vehicle, explaining later that the penalty was the same for one as for 20. Gendarmes once stopped him and began to question him about his passengers. Since there was no hope of deceiving the two policemen about the American aviators, Kerambrun told them the truth, guessing rightly that they would not report the incident. Like many gendarmes in Brittany and elsewhere in France, they were sympathetic to the resistance.[42]

Nevertheless, the risks were great both for the driver and his passengers, who eventually totaled about 100. Cars running on charcoal could not go very fast. Kerambrun claimed after the war, "Even the motorbikes passed us." But risks did not seem to deter this slight man with bushy eyebrows; and on the night scheduled for the third operation, he and Mathurin Branchoux, a leader of the resistance in Guingamp, arrived at the Laurent home to wait with the fliers for the BBC signal. It would come after the 7:30 program "Les français parlent aux français," along with other coded messages to the French underground. "Bonjour, tout le monde à la maison d'Alphonse" (Good afternoon, everyone at the house of Alphonse) would mean that the mission was on for that night. A postponement would be signaled by "Yvonne pense toujours à l'heureuse occasion" (Yvonne always thinks of the happy occasion).[43]

That night the message was "Bonjour, tout le monde." Quickly the two Frenchmen hustled Patton and McGough into the truck, picking up six more Americans before leaving town. On the return journey the space might be used for weapons brought in by the British. Kerambrun drove the 15 miles to the outskirts of Plouha, using the secondary roads because they were in the coastal defense zone, where the Germans were especially vigilant. While they were still in the countryside, the truck stopped and the Frenchmen told them they were near the farmhouse of Françoise Montjarret. From there they would have to walk a mile to the Giquels' house, code-named Maison d'Alphonse.[44]

Meanwhile, other airmen were converging on the Maison d'Alphonse after similarly memorable, often grim, experiences. It had taken 2d Lt. William H. Spinning only 35 days to reach the final rendezvous after bailing out. His was the shortest time. The longest was that of 2d Lt. Joseph A. Birdwell, who had spent seven months dodging the Germans, including a stay of three weeks with Marie Rose Zerling before her arrest. For the entire group the average time on the run had been 71 days.[45]

Lieutenant Spinning and 2d Lt. Manuel Rogoff had found shelter for several weeks with Maurice Cavalier and his wife at the old and famous Lycée St. Louis on the boulevard St. Michel, where Maurice was the bursar. At the end of their stay they were joined by two of Rogoff's crewmates, 2d Lts. Shirley D. Berry and Russell L. Paquin, the latter recovering from surgery. Technical Sgt. Harold Vines, who later joined the group, had stood with resistance workers attending the burial of five American airmen who had crashed near Pithiviers. Each grave was marked with a flier's helmet and an American flag. Three headboards carried the names of the men who had been identified. The other two bore only the words "Aviateur Américain." A priest was there for the burial, and many people in the crowd left flowers on the new graves.[46]

The Maison d'Alphonse was becoming more and more crowded as the time approached for the party to leave for the beach. The Giquels' cottage was a typical Breton fisherman's dwelling of stone, with two rooms and an attic used as a hayloft. It was only three-fourths of a mile from Bonaparte Beach. Some of the men had been led there by Marie Thérèse Le Calvez, who would also serve in the beach party, as she had done twice before and would eventually do five more times. Fourteen men in the group had traveled to the staging area by truck from the railroad station at Châtelaudren, about eight miles east of Guingamp on the Paris-Brest line, and had been met by her in the darkness near the house she shared with her mother. After hearing the signal from the BBC, she and the men had worked their way cautiously across the fields to avoid patrols, skirting a church and traversing a cemetery on the way.[47]

Thirty aviators, 23 of them American, were now assembled. They were a strange-looking group in their ill-matching, badly fitting civilian clothes, eked out with miscellaneous items of military dress. The fortunate ones were those with GI shoes. For some it had been a joyful reunion with crewmates. Others, like Patton, had learned that some of their crews had already reached England by way of Shelburne's earlier operations.[48]

Now they were chiefly aware that a brusque stranger, calling himself Captain Harrison of British Military Intelligence, had taken charge. He was in fact Lucien Dumais, the chief of Shelburne, fulfilling his duty of making sure once more that all the men were bona fide evaders and that they understood the necessity of obeying instructions to the letter. He was a tough man; and when he checked his list and found that Patton and McGough were not included, he held them at gunpoint and began barking questions at them: "When do you wear epaulets? What was your last stop before you shipped out from the States? Where were you stationed in England?"[49]

At this moment a man shouted to the airmen, "You don't have to tell him anything but your name, rank, and serial number."

"Shut up!" Dumais commanded. "It's my job to get you back to England. Some of you may have a hole in your belly, but you'll get back."

Only when he was convinced that Patton and McGough were not spies did he issue his final warnings and instructions. This would be the most dangerous part of their escape, he told them. The curfew was in effect, and they would have to dodge German sentries and patrols.

"Do exactly as you're told. When you leave here, follow the man in front of you very closely. When you get to the cliff, sit down and dig in tightly with your heels and hands. Don't slip, or you might take the whole line with you. Above all, keep your mouths shut."[50]

By this time it was midnight, time to set out. Silently the men walked in Indian file to the steep cliff overlooking Bonaparte Beach. It was hard enough to climb down a cliff like that in daylight. It would be very dangerous on a black night when the slightest noise would betray them; but by following Dumais's instructions they were able to ease their way down the 100 feet to the beach, passing Joseph Mainguy, the merchant marine captain who was one of Dumais's chief helpers. His job was to remain halfway up the cliff long enough to signal the incoming MGB, using a flashlight masked by a cardboard tube.[51]

As the party reached the end of the descent, he began to flash the letter B in Morse code, repeating it at two-minute intervals. At the foot of the cliff, in a small grotto, Marie Thérèse Le Calvez held a flashlight, screened with blue plastic, that she kept constantly lighted.

For nearly an hour the men waited apprehensively on the cold, dark beach, well aware that a German blockhouse manned by about 50 white Russian and German soldiers, and equipped with heavy artillery and machine guns, was only about 1,300 yards to their left and that another German post lay to their right. An even more serious threat was the German installation near Paimpol, ten miles north of the beach, where there was radar as well as artillery.[52]

Finally Dumais gave the signal that he had heard the password "Dinan" over his walkie-talkie, indicating that the gunboat was offshore. Using his own password "St. Brieuc," he answered that his party was ready, but warned that the Germans were under an alert. As if to confirm the threat, the German batteries on the coast near Paimpol immediately opened fire. Each of the five blasts lit up the beach, and the gunboat signaled that it would have to withdraw but would return. Two hours passed while those waiting grew fearful that dawn would break before they could get away. But once more the signal came, and soon five small skiffs appeared, each manned by two British sailors rowing with muffled oars. The tide was out, and the aviators had to cross more than 300 yards of wet sand, fully exposed to the guns at the Pointe de la Tour on their left. As soon as the beach party had unloaded the supplies brought in from Britain, the men hurriedly climbed into the boats. In the confusion some had to run up and down the beach trying to find seats, but eventually all were accommodated. The incoming tide would soon cover their footprints.[53]

To their great relief the airmen reached the waiting MGB 502 without incident. Early in the journey to Dartmouth, a sailor came below to warn them that German E boats had been sighted, and for a long time they could see the German searchlights. Nevertheless, they docked safely at Dartmouth at 9:00 A.M. Very shortly afterward they left for London to report to U.S. intelligence units. There they were asked for details about their evasion, and particularly about the people who had helped them to escape.[54]

After the evaders' departure from Plouha, there was little rest for workers in the Shelburne line, since the fourth group was to be evacuated only three days later. Patton's crewmates, Johnson the pilot and Viola the waist gunner, had missed being part of the third group but were among those assembling at the Maison d'Alphonse on March 19. This party comprised 25 airmen, 16 of whom were American, and a French agent.[55]

Experience with the previous evacuations helped to make the fourth run smoothly. It took only five or six minutes for the beach party, moving into the frigid water, to unload the heavy packages brought in by the rowboats and for the aviators to climb aboard. Once more the MGB avoided the coastal guns and German E boats. Too many men were waiting to return to England, however, for the line to rest, and Dumais moved quickly to set up a fifth operation for March 23.

The fifth group to be evacuated would be made up principally of noncommissioned crewmen from downed planes, since first priority had been given in earlier operations to the officers and pilots with longer training, who were more difficult to replace. Most of the men in the new group were collected in Paris. Among them were three Canadians: F. O. Kenneth Woodhouse, pilot of a Spitfire, who had parachuted near Beauvais, and two men from a Lancaster bomber on its first mission.[56]

Woodhouse and other evaders in the fifth group reached the staging point for the cross-Channel ferry with the help of a young woman, still unidentified, who led the men to a reserved coach on the Paris-Brest express. Fighting their way through the crowd, the airmen finally reached their compartment but found it jammed with people and luggage. Their young guide scolded the passengers who had usurped the places of her charges but could not make them move. Fortunately, there was time to lodge a protest with the station officials, so she signaled the men to retrace their steps and wait on the platform while she sought help. With a conductor in tow she was soon leading them once more through the train, and this time the passengers in their compartment moved reluctantly out of the way. The incident gave Woodhouse a particularly bad moment because one of the disgruntled passengers asked him in French to lower the window and hand him his suitcase when he reached the platform. Woodhouse, who knew no French, attempted to show by a gesture toward his throat that he could not talk. Fortunately the Frenchman became impatient and lowered the window himself, throwing his suitcase disgustedly onto the platform. He evidently took the party to be German civilians who could command space for themselves at the expense of ordinary Frenchmen.[57]

Among the 21 Americans assembled at the Giquels' Maison d'Alphonse in anticipation of the fifth beach operation, the two who had traveled the farthest after landing were 1st Lt. William B. Lock of Colorado and his engineer, S. Sgt. Charles H. Mullins of New Mexico, who had bailed out over the Netherlands 71 days earlier. Others in the group had been on the same raid but in different planes.[58]

In addition to the fliers, the fifth group of evaders would include Jean Tréhiou, a member of the original beach party, whose sister Marie was also a stalwart helper of the line. While she continued as the manager of their farm, Jean would undergo training in Britain in preparation for an MI 9 mission before D Day, which all knew could not be far away.[59]

Once again the evacuation met with the success the leaders of Shelburne had come to expect. This operation at Bonaparte would be the last evacuation before the invasion in June, though there would be three more in the months following D Day. Both Dumais and Airey Neave, his chief in MI 9, grasped the necessity of avoiding incidents that would give the Germans any reason to strengthen their defenses in that area before the Allied landings, and they agreed to postpone further evacuations until after D Day.

In fact, the Germans had already become sufficiently alarmed to inspect the Breton area in February, under orders from Field Marshal Rommel, and to lay minefields along the coast. At the end of April several members of the beach team, including Marie Thérèse Le Calvez, observed that the work had begun. The minefield at Bonaparte Beach was 350 yards wide and would make the last leg of the sea route extremely hazardous, if not impassable.[60]

The test of whether boats could safely approach the beach at this point came on June 16, ten days after the Normandy landings, when Jean Tréhiou and two fellow commandos were returning from England by MGB to establish a new evacuation beach for fliers farther west along the Breton coast. Although they were unaware that they were crossing a minefield, they reached safe ground without mishap and were later picked up by Marie Tréhiou, who had brought her horse and cart to transport the men and their heavy valises to the farm. Soon after their arrival, lodgings had to be found for three more men from MGB 502. Ens. Guy Hamilton and the two sailors, who had rowed Jean and his companions to the beach, set out to sea again but were unable to find the gunboat. In desperation they rowed back to shore and succeeded in crossing the minefield. A patriot hid them temporarily in a deep hollow in the edge of his farm, but they had to be moved. Dumais and Le Cornec, apprehensive that the sailors might be a Gestapo plant, asked Marie Thérèse Le Calvez to question them. She knew the area, and after working as a secretary at the Agricultural Trade Association, she rode her bicycle to the farm.

She found the men and Ensign Hamilton recounted their unusual story in French. Marie Thérèse was reassured because he had heard her name in England, and later that night she escorted the men to her house, the first stop on their return trip.[61]

Shortly before these events, on June 7, Dumais and Labrosse, who had left Brittany suddenly after the fifth evacuation, were ordered to return to Plouha from Paris. Accompanying the two was a young Breton woman named Louisette Lorré, whom Dumais had recruited to be his liaison agent and who was proving to be invaluable to Shelburne. Among her assets were her good looks and intelligence. She was also reported to be "fearless to the point of rashness," particularly in showing her contempt for the Germans.[62]

The Allied landings made it urgent to continue the evacuations, even though the German defenses were being strengthened. Dumais insisted that the sixth operation be scheduled for July, and instructed Mainguy and Huet of the beach party to map a path to the beach by marking each mine along the route. With his scrappy temperament, the prospect of doing even more for France was making him restive. He thought he and his companions should recruit more Frenchmen for the maquis in their area while he, Louisette Lorré, and the beach crew continued to plan and carry out the evacuations.[63]

Although the gunboats had brought weapons on each of their operations, there were still not enough to arm more than 50 men. Dumais therefore asked London to send in weapons by parachute, along with two mine detectors. These arrived at the end of June. Madame Mainguy and Albert Le Marchand, a helper for Shelburne, transferred the mine detectors, hidden under alfalfa in a farm cart, to her mother's house, three miles from the beach. There they lay hidden under a pile of potatoes until the evening set for the sixth evacuation.[64]

Fearing the Germans had learned the meaning of the earlier "Bonjour, tout le monde," Dumais changed the messages to be relayed by the BBC. "The class warmly salutes its friends" would mean that the MGB was on its way. A 24-hour delay would be signaled by "Louis Philippe was a good king." On July 12 the listeners heard the signal to start moving. This time they could not stand by until it was dark, because the mines had to be marked. At dusk, Huet and Mainguy moved out to begin their dangerous job of locating the explosives with detectors and then marking the sites with white cloths that they would remove when the evaders were safely aboard the boats. When the job was done, 17 bits of white were in place, grim reminders that a misstep could mean death or crippling wounds.[65]

Eleven airmen, four of them Americans, were waiting at the Giquels' small house. Four other men brought the group to 15: a British parachute captain, Ens. Guy Hamilton, and the two sailors. Two of the Americans, 2d Lts. William C. Hawkins and Joseph Lilly, had found shelter in Brest with Mme Yvonne de la Marnière and Mme Jeanne Marie Callarec, both of whom worked primarily for the Bordeaux-Loupiac and Burgundy lines, but also co-operated with Shelburne.[66] The other two American lieutenants, Richard J. Gordon and Frank L. Lee, Jr., had bailed out of their disabled bomber on June 17 near Lamballe, only 30 miles southeast of Plouha. They had found shelter with Mme Lucienne de Ponfilly, whose husband had died fighting for France in 1940, leaving her with two young sons.[67]

Luck held once more for Operation Bonaparte. Thanks to the skilled guidance of the beach party, which this time included two women, the evaders crossed the minefield safely before boarding the skiffs that would take them to the gunboat and land them at Dartmouth the next morning.[68]

With the seventh and eighth evacuations, the nature of Shelburne's mission changed. Instead of being primarily for escaping airmen, it was used mainly to enable the swift return to Britain of officers on military missions and Allied secret agents.

The seventh evacuation turned out to be more eventful than anyone had anticipated. At this time Le Cornec and Dumais still used the Giquels' Maison d'Alphonse as the final assembly point. On July 23, the night before the scheduled departure, Dumais and Le Cornec brought five men to the Giquel house, among them a British officer, Maj. Oswald Elwes, and his batman, Sgt. E. Mills of the Special Air Services (SAS), who had parachuted into Brittany on June 21. Elwes was on the last leg of his mission to observe and report on the progress of the maquis and the parachute troops fighting against the Germans in Brittany. Another SAS officer, Major Smith, had joined Elwes in Plouha after working with the parachute troops who formed units with the FFI and FTP. Two fighter pilots completed the group waiting at the Giquels' house: F. Sgt. T. P. Fargher of the RAF and an American officer, Maj. William A. Jones, who had been shot down on May 24 in an attack on the St. Brieuc airfield.[69]

Dumais and Le Cornec left the assembled men at the Giquel house and set out for their headquarters. Ten minutes after their departure a Russian patrol arrived. According to Mainguy, things had been worse for the line since the German troops in the area had been bolstered by Russians, whose commander, General Vlassov, had expressed his opposition to Stalin's ruthlessness by choosing to cooperate with the Germans after his army was surrounded at Leningrad. Of these troops, who wore white armbands with a blue cross, Mainguy said that they were more aggressive than the Germans. "They saw terrorists everywhere. They behaved like ruffians, demanding something to drink at all hours of the night, and their unpredictability had made everyone uneasy since their arrival."[70]

True to form, these Russians burst into the Giquel house, firing wildly into the stairway and ceiling, shouting "Terroristes ici! Tous kapout." Fortunately the evaders had already retreated to the loft where they escaped injury, but the shots had wounded one of the Russians' comrades. After Marie Giquel treated the man's wound and the Russians had left for Pointe de la

Tour, Giquel swiftly hid his five charges in a field nearby. Then he went with his wife and baby to the home of friends, knowing that the house would no longer be safe. He was right. The Russians returned the next morning, this time with German troops. Although they could not find the Giquels, they ransacked the house, set fire to it, and ignited an explosive charge that toppled several of the stone walls. They did not find the arms and ammunition that had been hidden under the woodpile ever since the sixth evacuation.[71]

Although the entire operation had been endangered by the raid, Dumais was reluctant to give it up. Instead, he arranged for 20 men from the maquis, armed with Bren guns, to support the scheduled embarkation. At his signal Marie Thérèse Le Calvez, who had also joined the maquis, took her place at the head of the procession. Dumais, accompanied by Giquel, the maquis fighters, and the five evaders, followed. Barking dogs told of German patrols as they walked cautiously toward the beach. Then a skiff appeared out of the darkness and was hastily unloaded so that the escaping men could climb aboard. While they set off for the gunboat and the night voyage to England, the beach party would accomplish the less glamorous task of carrying the heavy arms, packed in valises, from the beach to a safe hiding place. They had one less helper, for Giquel had come under too much suspicion to remain in the area; for his own and his family's safety, he was persuaded to join the men in the boats bound for England. The seventh operation succeeded without further setbacks.[72]

The eighth and last evacuation took place slightly more than two weeks later. The Allies had by this time broken through the Normandy defenses, forcing German withdrawals from points along the coast, including Plouha and Pointe de la Tour. Initially the maquis, led by Le Cornec, Dumais, and Labrosse, took control of the town; on August 6 three American tanks arrived, and the maquis became the supporting infantry.[73]

This last evacuation differed from the others in almost every respect except the outcome. There were only three men going aboard, one British and two French agents, since British and U.S. bases now existed in France to receive downed airmen. For the first time Marie Thérèse Le Calvez and her companions did not need the cover of darkness, and could see the silhouette of the waiting gunboat in the predawn light. For the last time they heard the sailors warmly thanking them for their help in the dangerous missions of the previous months. On this day the Shelburne workers could return to their homes without fear, but they would not forget how courageously the British crews had braved heavy seas and enemy artillery to do their part in ferrying evaders across the Channel. MGB 403 probably should be credited with carrying out the largest number of evacuations from Bonaparte. It later hit a mine in the North Sea and sank with all aboard.[74]

Operation Bonaparte was a triumph. In the 8 evacuations from January 20 through August 8, 1944, 128 Allied aviators, plus 19 others, including secret agents and commandos, reached England by way of Shelburne's cross-Channel ferry. Of this number, 94 were American. Except for the arrests at St. Brieuc, all the airmen dispatched from Paris to Plouha reached England safely, an outstanding record, thanks to good organization, tight security, discipline, and the courage of the participants.[75]

Approximately 200 members of the Shelburne network were directly responsible for Operation Bonaparte. About half of these were based in or near Paris. They included 50 safehouse keepers, 30 guides, several couriers, 2 forgers of documents, and various others who purchased food and clothing on the black market, and procured other necessary supplies and services. In Brittany about 75 men and women worked for Shelburne. In addition, several hundred in other organized networks, as well as people not connected with any group, gave aid to the airmen until Shelburne could take charge. Such large numbers of helpers inevitably meant that some would be arrested and deported. As Labrosse said later, "An escape line was very vulnerable." The 23 deaths among Shelburne members in Brittany before the liberation bear him out.[76]

The leaders of Shelburne and MI 9 recognized the important contributions made by the women who worked for the line. Scores served as safehouse keepers and guides, and others as couriers. The airmen were impressed by their courage and perseverance, and they believed that without the assistance of the women, they would not have escaped from France. It was the women who took a keen interest in helping them return to their bases, while many Frenchmen were involved with sabotage and guerrilla operations.[77]

Flight Officer Kenneth Woodhouse, for example, who set a record for the group by returning to England only a week after he was forced to bail out of his Spitfire north of Paris on March 16, 1944, reported that ten different women had helped him along his route to Brittany.[78] Second Lieutenant Robert V. Laux was shot down only 45 miles from where Woodhouse parachuted, and during his 41-day escape he was assisted by 19 women, including 9 safehouse keepers. He reported later that "neither I nor any of us could have evaded or escaped without the women helpers."[79]

A number of valiant women who aided Shelburne were able to greet the liberation of Paris in August 1944 with a sense of achievement, though none would want to repeat those days. Among the successful ones was Countess Bertranne d'Hespel, the eldest daughter of Countess Elisabeth de la Bourdonnaye, who was arrested in the Musée de l'Homme disaster of 1941.[80] Bertranne was a young widow whose husband, a test pilot, was killed while on duty in 1939. She was also a medical student who spent much of her time working in the hospital Hôtel Dieu. She lived alone in a small apartment at 7, rue Maspero in the 16th arrondissement. Although extremely busy, she found time to shelter not only Frenchmen sought by the police, but also 17 Allied airmen, 14 of whom were American. She also guided six to Brittany.[81]

Like other young women living alone, Bertranne had to answer questions about whether it was suitable for her to house military men. Her in-laws did not approve of what she was doing, and sent her brother-in-law to persuade her to quit the dangerous activity. He explained to Bertranne that they did not want her to be arrested and shot by the Germans, and added, "It isn't proper for a young woman, a widow, to shelter men in her home." The self-confident Bertranne smiled and replied, "Concern about what is appropriate is of secondary importance at this difficult time. Since I am the widow of an aviator, isn't it a normal thing for me to help Allied aviators?" She continued to work for Shelburne.[82]

Finally, when Paris was liberated by General Leclerc's Second Armored Division, Bertranne joined her mother in welcoming her brother, a tank officer, who had escaped to England to join the Free French forces.[83]

Among those who had sheltered Lt. Patton and his companions at the schoolhouse in Plouray, Marie Antoinette Piriou had continued to help escapers until she learned that the Gestapo was on her trail. Since she knew it would be hazardous to remain at the school, she joined other women serving as guides and couriers in the maquis. Major Jones had stayed with her on his way to Plouha for the seventh evacuation from Bonaparte Beach. He last saw her at a maquis camp, nursing a wounded soldier.[84]

Her young friend Josephine Le Vely was also in the maquis, becoming a liaison agent for them and carrying messages to her group from her cousin, the mayor of Plouray. An example of the weakening German will occurred when a nervous German soldier confronted Josephine one day in July 1944, gave her his pistol, and told her he wanted to change sides. Holding the pistol at his back, she made the ten-mile journey to the maquis camp and turned him over to her fiancé, Marcel Pasco. Six months later the two French patriots were married.[85]

The airmen rescued by Shelburne were very touched by the assistance given to them by the uncounted number of women and men in France. Patton and some associates were determined to show their appreciation to the helpers "for laying their lives on the line for them" by organizing the Air Forces Escape and Evasion Society in 1964. The nongovernmental organization has sponsored helpers' visits to the United States and members' tours of France, Belgium, and the Netherlands to retrace their evasion routes. Their motto is "We shall never forget."[86]

Notes

1. Specific Information about how women helped aviators was obtained from questionnaires sent by the author to the members of the Air Forces Escape and Evasion Society (AFEES), an American, nongovernmental organization (see preface). Additional information was obtained from Escape and Evasion Reports.

2. An MGB was 117 feet long, carried a crew of 36, and was powered by 3

silenced, high-speed diesel engines. It cruised at 21 knots. The boat was armed with a two-pounder cannon forward, a six-pounder aft, and twin turrets on either side and aft of the bridge. M. R. D. Foot, *SOE in France*, p. 64; Airey Neave, *Saturday at MI 9*, p. 229.

3. Neave, *Saturday*, p. 220.

4. Raymond Labrosse, interview, Birmingham, MI, October 1976.

5. Countess Genevieve de Poulpiquet, interview, Paris, October 1976.

6. Ibid.

7. Lucien Dumais, *The Man Who Went Back*, pp. 5–6, 21.

8. Labrosse, interview.

9. Dumais, *The Man*, p. 152.

10. Joseph Mainguy, "Le réseau d'évasion Shelburn, plage Bonaparte," pp. 5–7, 12.

11. Ibid., pp. 2–4.

12. Sgt. David Warner reported in his questionnaire that Marie Thérèse "led us to the beach as if going on a Sunday picnic. She appeared to be very cool and fearless." S. Sgt. George P. Buckner in his questionnaire called her "fantastically brave." She was awarded the Legion of Honor, the Croix de Guerre, the Medal of the Resistance, the (British) King's Medal for Courage in the Cause of Freedom, and the American Medal of Freedom with silver palm. Dominique Martin Le Trividic, *Une femme du réseau Shelburn*, pp. 103–06.

13. Madame Le Calvez sheltered 32 men in her home during the operation from Bonaparte Beach. She received decorations similar to those of her daughter except for the Croix de Guerre.

14. Labrosse, interview.

15. Mme Marie Tréhiou Cosse, interview, Birmingham, MI, October 1976. She was awarded the Medal of Freedom, basic, by the U.S. government.

16. Labrosse, interview.

17. Ibid.

18. See chapter 5.

19. Marie Granet, *Cohors-Asturies*, pp. 11, 52; 2d Lt. Joseph A. Birdwell, E & E Report no. 471.

20. Birdwell, E & E Report no. 471.

21. Labrosse, interview. Raymond and Ginette were married in 1945.

22. 2d Lt. Sidney Casden, E & E Report no. 355.

23. Mme Schmitt was later arrested. 2d Lts. Louis Feingold and Warren C. Tarkington, E & E Reports nos. 419–20.

24. Richard M. Smith, E & E Report no. 349.

25. Neave, *Saturday*, p. 233.

26. Mainguy, "Le Réseau . . . Shelburn," p. 7.

27. Casden, E & E Report no. 355; Richard M. Smith, E & E Report no. 349. The following Americans were in the first evacuation from Bonaparte Beach: 1st Lts. Donald J. Heskett, Richard M. Smith; 2d Lts. William R. Booher, Sidney Casden, Morton B. Shapiro; T. Sgts. Andrew F. Hathaway, Alphonse M. Mele; S. Sgts. Walter E. Dickerman, Jerry Eshuis, James A. King, Walter J. Sentkoski; Sgts. Fred T. Schmitt and John L. Sullivan, Jr. Ralph K. Patton, "List of Americans Evacuated from Bonaparte Beach," n.d.

28. Birdwell, E & E Report no. 471.

29. Anita Lemonnier Hartman, interview, New York City, March 1979.

30. Ralph K. Patton, president, Air Forces Escape and Evasion Society. The 16 Americans were 2d Lts. Milton L. Church, Louis Feingold, Ernest H. Hugonnet, James A. Schneider, Warren C. Tarkington; T. Sgts. Kenneth Blye, James N. Quinn; S. Sgts. Lee C. Gordon, Donald D. McLeod, Harry L. Minor, Mike Olynik, John Semach; Sgts. Harold O. Gilley, Marion A. Hall, Robert A. Schwartzburg, and Robert C. Southers. S. Sgt. Gordon received help from the French Arbeitskommando workers in the railroad yards at Munich.

31. RG 18, Records of the Army Air Forces, Combat Operations Reports 1939–47, VIII Bomber Command, Narrative of Operations, 176th Operation, January 5, 1944. 325 bombers were sent to Germany and 79 to Tours.

32. Ralph K. Patton, interview, Pittsburgh, PA, November 1978.

33. Ralph K. Patton, "Notes on My Evasion," 1965, pp. 2–4.

34. The aviators called Pierre Daniel "Mr. Chips." He later died for his resistance work.

35. Patton, interview.

36. Josephine Le Vely Pasco, interview, Birmingham, MI, October 1976.

37. Patton, interview.

38. Patton, "Notes on My Evasion," p. 5.

39. Ibid.

40. Lecren's son René, who had a lame knee, helped to lodge aviators and later became a chef at the Plaza Hotel in New York. His brother Désiré, an agent for Turma Vengeance network, later joined the Forces Françaises de l'Intérieur (FFI). Désiré Lecren also moved to the New York City area. Letter to author, February 18, 1980.

41. Patton, interview.

42. François Kerambrun, interview, Birmingham, MI, October 1976.

43. Ibid.; Mainguy, "Le réseau . . . Shelburn," p. 7.

44. Mainguy, "Le réseau . . . Shelburn," pp. 7–8.

45. William H. Spinning, interview, Birmingham, MI, October 1976, and E & E Report no. 477; Birdwell, E & E Report no. 471.

46. Spinning, E & E Report no. 477; 2d Lt. Manuel M. Rogoff, E & E Report no. 455; T. Sgt. Harold R. Vines, E & E Report no. 457.

47. Patton, interview; 2d Lt. Earl J. Wolf, Jr., questionnaire.

48. Ralph K. Patton, "Operation Bonaparte," *94th Bomb Group Nostalgic Notes*, December 1976, pp. 2–3. On the third Bonaparte mission 23 Americans were evacuated: 2d Lts. Shirley D. Berry, Joseph A. Birdwell, William T. Campbell, Philip A. Capo, Edward J. Donaldson, Jack McGough, Ralph K. Patton, Manuel M. Rogoff, William H. Spinning, Dean W. Tate, Charles B. Winkelman; T. Sgts. John T. Amery, Kenneth P. Christian, William C. Lessig, Harold R. Vines; S. Sgts. Robert K. Fruth, Frank J. Moast, Russell L. Paquin, Everett E. Stump; Sgts. Charles W. Cregger, Carl W. Mielke, Neelan B. Parker, Carlyle A. Van Selus.

49. Ibid.

50. Ibid.

51. Patton, "Notes on My Evasion," p. 7.

52. Mainguy, "Le réseau . . . Shelburn," pp. 9, 15; map drawn by Mainguy.

53. Mainguy, "Le réseau . . . Shelburn," p. 14; Patton, interview.

54. The German E boats that frequently patrolled the Channel coast of France could cruise at 35 knots.

55. The 16 Americans were: 1st Lts. Francis P. Hennessy, Glenn B. Johnson, Earl J. Wolf, Jr.; 2d Lts. Robert L. Costello, Norman R. King, Robert O. Lorenzi, John A. McGlynn, Paul R. Packer, Clyde C. Richardson, Richard F. Schafer; T. Sgt. Elmer D. Risch; S. Sgts. Leonard F. Bergeron, Paul F. Dicken, William J. Scanlon, Edward J. Sweeney, Isadore C. Viola.

56. Kenneth Woodhouse, "Escape Account," pp. 3–4.

57. Ibid., pp. 28–30.

58. On the fifth Bonaparte Beach mission 21 Americans were evacuated: 1st Lts. William B. Lock, Milton L. Rosenblatt, Milton V. Shevchik; 2d Lts. Shirley V. Casey, William A. Hoffman III, Robert V. Laux, James M. Thorson, Phlemon T. Wright; T. Sgt. Robert J. Rujawitz; S. Sgts. John F. Bernier, George P. Buckner, David G. Helsel, Charles H. Mullins, Keith W. Sutor, Robert H. Sweatt; Sgts. Rudolph Cutino, Thomas J. Glennan, Richard C. Hamilton, Abe A. Helfgott, Francis C. Wall, David Warner.

59. Marie Tréhiou, interview.

60. Mainguy, "Le réseau . . . Shelburn," p. 24.

61. Marie Tréhiou, interview; Dominique Le Trividic, Une femme, pp. 57–65.

62. The departmental train resumed running between St. Brieuc and Plouha in April 1944. Mainguy, "Le réseau . . . Shelburn," p. 27.

63. Dumais, The Man, pp. 158–59.

64. Mainguy, "Le réseau . . . Shelburn," p. 34.

65. Ibid., pp. 38–39.

66. Both women were honored by the United States with the Medal of Freedom. Yvonne de la Marnière, "Recommendation for Award of Medal of Freedom," dossier; Mme Jeanne Marie Callarec, "Déclaration," December 15, 1944. The dossiers in this chapter are in RG 332, ETO, 7707 ECIC, MIS-X Section. 2d Lt. William C. Hawkins, E & E Report no. 832; 2d Lt. Joseph A. Lilly, E & E Report no. 833.

67. 1st Lts. Richard J. Gordon and Frank L. Lee, Jr., E & E Reports nos. 830–831.

68. The second woman was Marguerite Le Saux of Plouha. Raymond Labrosse, memorandum, n.d.

69. Maj. William A. Jones, E & E Report no. 834.

70. Mainguy, "Le réseau . . . Shelburn," p. 42.

71. Ibid., pp. 43–44, 47.

72. Ibid.

73. Ibid., pp. 48–50.

74. Ibid., pp. 51–52.

75. Ibid., p. 54; Roger Huguen, "Les débuts et le fonctionnement d'un réseau d'évasion; Le réseau Shelburne," Revue d'histoire de la deuxième guerre mondiale, January 1972, p. 49.

76. Labrosse, interview.

77. Patton, interview and numerous questionnaires.

78. Woodhouse, "Escape Account," pp. 8–42.

79. 2d Lt. Robert V. Laux, questionnaire.

80. See chapter 6.

81. Dr. Bertranne d'Hespel Auvert, "Mémoires 1940–1945," pp. 3–21.

82. Ibid., p. 19.

83. Ibid., pp. 26–29. After the war Bertranne remarried, had nine children, and was an eye surgeon.

84. Maj. William A. Jones, E & E Report no. 834; Piriou, "Questionnaire pour les personnes qui ont aidé les aviateurs alliés pendant l'occupation," n.d., dossier.

85. Josephine Le Vly Pasco, interview.

86. Patton, interview. The Royal Air Forces Escaping Society and the RAF Escaping Society, Canadian Branch, also sponsor helpers' visits and members' tours.

U.S. General Lewis decorating Marie Louise Dissard with the Medal of Freedom with gold palm while Andrée de Jongh awaits her turn, August 16, 1946. (Courtesy of Alfred Satterthwaite.)

Genevieve Soulié about 1944. She is now Mme Camus. (Courtesy of Genevieve Soulié Camus.)

Marie Thérèse Le Calvez, 1944.

Mme Léonie Le Calvez about 1944. She was the mother of Marie Thérèse and a heroine in her own right. (Courtesy of Victor Le Calvez.)

Second Lieutenant Ralph K. Patton and four fellow evaders from France. Three were from his crew. England, March 1944. Left to right: S. Sgt. Isadore Viola, 2d Lt. Norman King (different crew), 1st Lt. Glenn Johnson, 2d Lt. Jack McGough, and Patton. They were all helped by Josephine Le Vely (now Mme Pasco) and Mme Marie Antoinette Piriou in Plouray. (Courtesy of Ralph Patton.)

Countess Bertranne d'Hespel with group outside her apartment, Paris, 1944. On her left is a friend and resistance colleague Bernard d'Havrincourt. Back of them are three American airmen: Ted Krol behind Bertranne, Alfred Hickman behind Bernard, and Bill Bender at the top. Bertranne was then a young widow. She is now Mme Bertranne Auvert. (Courtesy of Bertranne Auvert.)

Mme Suzanne Tony Robert, 1944.
(Courtesy of Suzanne Tony Robert.)

Hélène Viannay, 1944.
(Courtesy of Génia Gemahling.)

Denise Jacob in Nice, 1942. She is now Madame Vernay.
(Courtesy of Denise Vernay.)

Mme Génia Deschamps, about 1943, on
bicycle. She is now Madame Gemahling.
(Courtesy of Génia Gemahling.)

Virginia Hall, Venice, April 5, 1936. She was in the U.S. Consulate there. (She is deceased.) (Courtesy of Lorna H. Catling.)

Virginia and Philippe d'Albert Lake, 1940. (Above picture courtesy of Virginia d'Albert Lake.)

Drue Tartière, about 1939. She was an actress, and this is a publicity picture. Her professional name was Drue Leyton. (Courtesy of Drue Parsons.)

Rosemary Wright Maeght, Pau 1942. (Courtesy of Rosemary W. Maeght.)

III SERVICE IN OTHER SPHERES

5 CLOAK AND DAGGER

When the Germans swept into France in 1940, they badly damaged the French and British intelligence services. Although they did not seize the archives of the famed Deuxième Bureau (Intelligence Bureau) of the French army, as has often been reported, they did capture the documents of the General Headquarters.[1] This important coup affected the British Secret Intelligence Service, known as SIS or MI 6, since SIS had maintained close relations with its French counterpart and depended on it for much of the military intelligence obtained from that country.[2] Before the French surrender the liaison had been so effective that SIS in Paris considered it unnecessary to have its own sources during the war. Six days after the armistice, however, the radio that provided the intelligence to the British ceased to function.[3] SIS also lost its network of "honorable correspondents" who had reported through the British embassy and consulates, since most of these were closed after the surrender.

At this critical time the British feared that Germany might invade England, and they were desperate for military intelligence about the intentions of the Wehrmacht. To meet this urgent need, some intelligence networks were set up spontaneously by patriots in France; others were organized by the intelligence sections of de Gaulle's BCRA, the British SIS, and, much later, the Secret Intelligence section of the American OSS (SI/OSS). By 1943 BCRA had 60 intelligence *réseaux* with 30,000 men and women involved in its operations.[4] SIS supported about a dozen networks, but the rebuilding took time.[5] It revived its contacts with the French in Vichy, setting up its own Vichy network, but only in the spring of 1941 did it have an intelligence organization reporting from the French Atlantic ports. A year later it replaced the irregular fishing boat service to Brittany with regular motor torpedo boats, which became part of the cross-Channel ferry.[6]

113

The Alliance *réseau* was one of the largest and earliest intelligence organizations originating in France. Another was the intelligence section of Combat, with Henri Frenay as its head. Frenay, a military officer, maintained contact with the Deuxième Bureau in Vichy, whose counterespionage unit under Col. Paul Paillole had saved all 30 tons of its archives.[7] Although these agencies were banned by the Germans, their structure remained virtually intact.[8]

OSS was a latecomer to the field and did not work with or establish intelligence networks in France until 1943–44. Then, however, OSS agents were sent into the country from Switzerland, Spain, Algiers, and London. Bern had eight networks under its control, with some 100 agents in France. By the fall of 1943, SI/OSS chiefs in Barcelona and Bilbao had sparked the formation of 10 intelligence chains from France into Spain, and by D Day 15 were furnishing intelligence to Allied Forces Headquarters in London.[9] SI/OSS in Algiers organized a dozen *réseaux* in southern France to provide military intelligence for Operation Dragoon, the Allied invasion of the Riviera.

British leaders, including Claude Dansey, deputy chief of SIS, had doubts about amateur American sleuths and opposed the formation by OSS of independent intelligence units in France. He feared that inexperienced agents, usually speaking with an American accent, would blow the cover of British agents and endanger established networks. Eventually, however, joint SIS/OSS intelligence operations were carried out with the dispatching of two-man teams, code-named Sussex, from England to France; 26 were sent by SIS and the same number by the Americans.[10]

Intelligence *réseaux* were responsible for providing military information about the German war machine to their respective headquarters.[11] This included reports about movements of German troops and supply trains, the arrivals and departures of Axis submarines and ships, the disposition of German airfields and aircraft, and the location of factories making war matériel for the enemy. Later in the war, detailed plans of German defenses along the Channel and the Riviera, and information about rocket sites, became of prime importance. Intelligence about the enemy's order of battle was also vital: the locations, names, strength, composition, and armament of the various formations and units would yield valuable clues about the Germans' intentions.[12]

In all of this work of collecting, coding, and dispatching military intelligence to headquarters in London and elsewhere, women served well. Although intelligence reporting had none of the glamour or instant results of sabotage and guerrilla warfare, several thousand women offered to help. Some could only volunteer to report bits of information that came their way at home or on their jobs; others filled the demanding roles of organizers and chiefs of networks, couriers, radio operators, and coding specialists.

Housewives kept track of Axis ships in ports and on French canals. They counted the number of cars in German troop trains. They took note of the colored pipings on soldiers' shoulder straps because the German army distinguished the main arms of its service in this way.

Many women obtained information at their jobs. Jeanne Berthomier, a civil servant in the Ministry of Public Works in Paris, delivered top-secret information, typed on gossamer-thin sheets of paper, to the Alliance chief, Marie Madeleine Fourcade.[13] Mme Paule Letty-Mouroux of the marine section of the Polish-French intelligence network F2, which shared its information with SIS and the Deuxième Bureau, took a job as a secretary and writer in the Marine de Toulon so that she could report on the repair of Axis ships and their equipment.[14]

Mme Marguerite Claeys, the leader of a small unit, collected information for the BCRA Mithridates intelligence *réseau* at the wholesale milk company that she and her husband owned in Paris. Agents posing as customers came to see her at the office, and she also made "business calls" on them. She was assisted by her teenage son and sympathetic friends, but had to hide her underground activity from her husband, who did not share her strong anti-German and pro-American sentiments.[15]

Women working in the Postal, Telegraph, and Telephone Service (PTT) had particularly good opportunities to obtain intelligence about the Germans. Simone Michel Lévy, an editor at a PTT technical research center, obtained valuable information that she sent to London through the BCRA intelligence *réseau* Confrérie Notre Dame (CND), headed by Rémy, the code name of Gilbert Renault. Under the name of Emma she helped organize resistance activities within the central telephone exchange and other units in Paris. She also managed to have the radio transmitters and funds of CND carried in mail bags in PTT trucks, which were permitted to circulate at all hours.

In November 1943, however, Simone and many others of the *réseau* were betrayed by the chief radio operator in the Paris central exchange, who had been arrested by the German police.[16] Four months after her arrest she was deported to Ravensbrück and assigned to a munitions factory in Holleischen. Bitterly resentful of the German practice of forcing concentration camp inmates to make arms to be used against their countrymen, she organized two work stoppages. For these acts her German captors condemned Simone to death, and in April 1945 she was hanged. Her sacrifice was recognized after the war when she became one of only six women to be awarded the Cross of the Liberation created by General de Gaulle in 1940, and one of the few to be portrayed in the series of postage stamps honoring heroes of the resistance.[17]

The help of women who used their jobs to add to the flow of intelligence to Allied headquarters was invaluable, but women were also needed as full-time, trained agents who could take on the heavy duties of gathering intelligence, coding and transmitting messages, acting as couriers, and helping to organize and administer networks to fill the growing demand for information as D Day approached.

Late in 1943, Sussex teams were being organized to supply the strategic and tactical information that would be needed after the landings. Before they were flown to France, however, it was thought necessary to send in a Pathfinder team of four, which could select landing sites, organize reception committees, locate safehouses, and enlist radio operators and local agents.[18] The suggestion came from Rémy, who had returned to London after the betrayal of his network in November 1943. He also offered to provide the members of such a team. Among those chosen was Jeanne Guyot, who would be one of only two women to receive the Distinguished Service Cross from the U.S. government.

A young Burgundian living in Paris on the rue Verniquet, Jeanne had become a member of Rémy's CND in January 1942, serving as a liaison agent under the name of Jeannette. Six months later she was threatened with arrest, and Rémy had ordered her and a colleague, Felix Svagrovsky, known as César, to cross the demarcation line into the unoccupied zone, where they set up their base near Chalon-sur-Saône. There Jeannette provided liaison for CND, sometimes traveling to Lyon.

Jeannette could usually outwit the Germans, but on one crossing of the demarcation line she was stopped by an SS officer who examined her false identity card and ordered her to report to Gestapo headquarters the next day to retrieve it. Since she would probably now be under surveillance, especially in view of the betrayal of other CND members, Jeannette was ordered to London.[19]

At first she worked with César, who also had escaped to London, in his "Section of Military Mail" on Palace Street. This agency specialized in the prompt distribution of military intelligence to the Free French and Allied services. During each month it provided 200,000 mimeographed sheets, 60,000 printed sheets, and 10,000 photographs detailing intelligence.[20]

Despite the importance of this work, the appeal to be one of the Pathfinder team found Jeannette ready to return to France. With a radio operator and two other men whom Rémy had enlisted, she spent a week in parachute school before the four boarded a British bomber on February 8, 1944.[21]

Their first base was to be in Paris. Jeannette was the only team member with previous experience in occupied France, and under her leadership they set up headquarters at 8, rue Tournefort, near the Pantheon, in a cafe owned by Mme Andrée Goubillon. She was the wife of a prisoner of war, and in the course of the occupation she allowed her place to be a letter drop for secret messages as well as a restaurant and safehouse for some 21 OSS agents.[22]

Jeannette and her team faced difficulties from the start. Most of their supplies were not dropped with them, and the radio operator could not transmit to London. Jeannette solved this difficulty with the help of a network with which she had formerly worked in Lyon. Then the first three Sussex teams arrived in her area, and when she met them at the station in Chateauroux, she was furious to see that they were all wearing clothes of the same cut, with Tyrolean knapsacks on their backs to make them even more conspicuous. The worst event was the arrest of her radio operator, but he did not reveal the names of his colleagues.[23]

There is little doubt that Jeannette risked being deported or summarily shot, judging from the fate of Evelyne Clopet, the only woman Sussex agent, who was captured and shot in the course of her work. She was born in 1922 in Pornic, near the mouth of the Loire, but her father was an industrialist in Casablanca, and she had worked as a stenographer in North Africa before the war. After the armistice she joined the Free French Corps Féminin before undertaking the rigorous training required of Sussex volunteers. Her training and that of her 51 male comrades was carried on under the wing of the Americans in the joint SI/OSS and SIS school in England. It lasted from 9 to 16 weeks, depending on the student's aptitude, and included physical conditioning, elementary radio training, map reading, and close combat.[24]

After finishing the course, Evelyne, now a radio operator and second lieutenant, and Roger Fosset, a master sergeant in the Free French forces, were dispatched to France on July 3, 1944, along with two other teams. By mistake the five men were dropped to a reception committee that was expecting arms but not men, and they extinguished their lights before Evelyne could jump. Her disappointment at having to return to England was brief, however, for she was able to fly in with another team four days later and join her comrades, temporarily established in the village of Château l'Hermitage, ten miles south of Le Mans.[25]

Things were not going well with the teams. One safehouse had been bombed, another was under surveillance, and Roger had not found a safehouse in Angers, where they had been assigned. Despite these strains Evelyne remained cheerful and raised the spirits of her colleagues.[26]

Meanwhile, the military front was changing rapidly, and a month after their arrival her group faced the possibility of being encircled by the Germans. The local resistance committee provided them with a small German truck, in which they could load their radio equipment, luggage, and several bicycles. Their first stop was to be Vendôme, en route to Paris, but ten miles west of the town they were stopped by retreating Germans, who requisitioned the truck and bicycles, and ordered them to dismount with their belongings. Hurrying to comply with the orders, one of them dropped a suitcase, which fell open and revealed a radio transmitter. Immediately the agents were bundled back into the truck; and with guards mounted on top and on the running boards, they were driven to the gendarmerie in Vendôme.

A few hours later, at dawn, a laborer found their cruelly beaten bodies in a quarry outside of town. Townspeople took them to the Church of St.

Ouen, where they lay in state for two days before being buried in a simple ceremony attended by many. They were the only Sussex agents killed by the enemy.[27]

Hélène Deschamps was typical of the intelligence agents working in France under OSS in Algiers. The daughter of an officer in the French colonial army, she was born in 1923 in the French concession at Tientsin, north China, and was later sent to the school of the Convent of the Sacred Heart in Avignon.[28]

In 1940 Hélène was living with her widowed mother and adopted sister Jackie in Aix-en-Provence. After the French surrender her two brothers joined the Free French forces, and she became a courier for a military intelligence network carrying messages from Aix to cities along the Riviera. Some months later Jackie joined her in the resistance, and the two often worked as a team. By the end of 1943, however, Hélène had grown to dislike the political infighting of the French groups, and she and her sister volunteered as agents with the OSS network known to the French as OSS Jacques and to the Americans as Penny Farthing. It was the most successful network run by the chief of the SI section of OSS in Algiers, the redoubtable Henry Hyde.

Although the sisters had no special training in espionage, once they were on the job, they learned the skills needed to collect information about German troop movements, coastal defenses, and camouflaged antiaircraft batteries. On August 15, 1944, when the Allies were landing on the Mediterranean coast, the sisters were working at Apt. Since they could furnish valuable information about their sector, they were ordered to report to St. Tropez, some 72 miles away, but before they could reach their destination, Jackie was killed by a sniper's bullet. Hélène carried on alone, eventually being assigned to the Seventh Army's Strategic Services section, a special unit that supplemented the intelligence chains of OSS and provided tactical intelligence.[29]

Some women went through the German lines to obtain the needed information. They volunteered for these dangerous missions because they attracted less attention than able-bodied young men and were less likely to be challenged and searched by the Germans.[30] Hélène worked on such assignments. According to Henry Hyde, "Hélène was a very gutsy young woman. She went through the lines for us, observing German defense installations and order of battle. She took many risks and was a genuinely good operator."[31]

Annie Thinesse was another young Frenchwoman who penetrated the enemy lines to bring back useful intelligence to the Seventh Army. At her home in Epinal in the Vosges she was active in the resistance after the Germans occupied the town, but her chance to perform extraordinary service came when she volunteered to obtain tactical intelligence for the 45th Infantry Division of the Seventh Army, which was planning to drive the Germans from Epinal and secure the area. The Americans knew that most of the city's bridges across the Moselle had been blown up, but bad weather prevented them from photographing the site from the air.[32] According to the official report, Annie walked through the German lines carrying "a detailed map of Epinal showing not only complete bridge information but also locating all the enemy defensive positions and indicating the number and type of enemy personnel defending them. This intelligence proved to be of the highest value to the 45th Division in its attack and subsequent advance."[33] After the 45th had advanced northeast toward the Meurthe River, Annie again penetrated the enemy lines and explored the defenses along ten miles of the river, returning with detailed information about conditions in St. Die and enemy artillery positions. The mission took five days, during which she was at terrible risk, but it undoubtedly helped the 45th and three other divisions to clear the area.[34]

These field agents for OSS could not have functioned without the support of a headquarters staff, and women helped to see that their information reached the right hands. In Algiers, Rachel Griese, a WAC warrant officer, provided information for the French, Spanish, and Italian desks of OSS. A former teacher at Columbia University, she sifted through thousands of intelligence items to compile detailed reports about German troops and defenses in southern France and other countries.[35] She received the Legion of Merit for her work and was among the few women in OSS to receive a decoration. Although OSS employed some 2,000 women out of a total of 16,000 (12.5 percent), it awarded decorations to only 36 women out of some 2,428 recipients (1.5 percent).[36]

Another young woman was Ann Willets, who had arrived in Algiers in September 1943, in the first contingent of OSS women. Like many OSS volunteers she was from a wealthy, well-traveled family. Her parents had taken her to France many times, and when she joined OSS in 1942, she had the advantage of being fluent in French and knowledgeable about the country.[37]

When she reached Algiers, it was clear that the men resented the addition of civilian women to the staff. Soon, however, the women earned their acceptance. Ann served for a while as secretary to Col. William A. Eddy; the commanding officer of OSS in North Africa; after he left Algiers, she transferred to the French intelligence desk under Henry Hyde, and soon became his chief assistant and office administrator.[38]

Ann enjoyed working for Hyde, who was bright, witty, and creative.[39] He was also hard-working and kept his staff on their toes. Ann was on the job at all hours when missions—sometimes as many as ten during a full moon—were being prepared and dispatched. On these days the atmosphere was tense and the work hectic. The agents, called Joes, who were getting ready to parachute into France were understandably nervous, and Ann accompanied them to Blida Airport. In a recent interview Hyde explained, "We discovered that no man wants to act afraid in front of a woman. If a woman is present at the airfield, the agents will put on a good bluff. They may be peeing in their pants literally with apprehension, but they won't show it."[40]

The work called for stamina in the face of discomfort as well as danger. After OSS moved its headquarters to Caserta, Italy, Ann and her colleague Cynthia Jacobsen, a Vassar graduate who had arrived in Algiers in July 1944, were transferred to Hyde's forward headquarters outside of Lyon. They lived and worked in the Chateau Glaizol, formerly a residence of Pétain. Now, however, the once luxurious rooms were unheated and the Renoir paintings looked down on an untidy collection of parachutes and supplies. Ann took charge of the office and had to answer cables, talk with the army liaison officer, and deal with transient agents who stayed at a nearby "Joehouse." Some agents were German prisoners of war opposed to the Nazis who had volunteered to parachute 50 or 60 miles behind the German lines to obtain tactical intelligence for the Americans. Several others were young women recruited around Strasbourg because they were fluent in German. One had been the mistress of an SS officer and wanted to redeem herself. She gathered a good deal of information for the Americans.[41]

Ann and others administering intelligence for military units, as well as for resistance networks, depended on couriers to pick up information from the field agents. Most of the couriers were women, since men of military age were more suspect. When possible they wrote or typed the information on very thin paper and carried it in the hem of a coat or a skirt or hidden in the false bottom of a toilet kit, briefcase, or suitcase. For security reasons they sometimes took the material to a letter drop—a safe address such as a cafe, apartment, or doctor's office—where another courier or the chief could pick up the "mail," as it was called, by giving the correct password. In large *réseaux* still another courier might transfer the information to the national chief of the organization.

Mme Nicole de Hautecloque, who became a prominent Gaullist deputy in the French National Assembly after the war, was an early courier for Rémy's *réseau* CND. Her family had strong military connections; her father was a colonel and her brother, Marc Saint Denis, was a marine officer with General de Gaulle. Her husband, Pierre, also a Free French officer, was a cousin of Jacques Philippe de Hautecloque, the future General Leclerc, who had changed his name to protect his family from enemy reprisals. Nicole was living with her six-year-old daughter Brigitte at her parents' apartment in Nantes when she joined Rémy's CND in October 1940, at the age of 27. As a courier she carried intelligence reports about German activity in the ports of St. Nazaire and Lorient. She also recruited couriers and a doctor for the network's headquarters.[42]

In June 1942, Nicole went to Paris, where Rémy had moved his headquarters. Assuming her brother's name, Marc, she worked as a courier in the radio section of CND, and also coded and decoded radio messages.[43] Although the work was clearly dangerous, security measures were sometimes neglected. For instance, soon after her arrival Rémy invited her and a chief radio operator to have dinner with him in the lively Schubert restaurant. He warned them that another chief radio operator with whom he had dined there two nights earlier had just been arrested, and it was quite possible that the place would be under surveillance. If they escaped this time, he promised, they should return soon for an even bigger party.[44] Many members of Nicole's group in Paris were arrested, and in June 1943 she left Paris for the south of France. There she put Brigitte in a boarding school and continued her intelligence work in the Turma *réseau*.[45]

The dangerous circumstances under which intelligence networks operated and the changing military situation after the tide began to turn in favor of the Allies made fixed organizations and systematic procedures almost impossible. As one *réseau* became vulnerable because of arrests, members were ordered to London or went underground, often joining another group. The nature of the information needed by the leaders also changed with the increase in bombing missions and the firmer prospect of Allied assaults on the ground. Still later, military commanders urgently needed local information that would enable them to advance with the least cost in lives.

The career of Dr. Aimée Batier during the war illustrates these changing patterns of leadership and activities. When her father refused to let her study medicine, considering it unsuitable for a woman, she settled for a degree as doctor of pharmacy; but as soon as she gained her independence, she went back to the university and eventually took her degree in medicine. In the fall of 1940, although the mother of one child and pregnant with another, she volunteered to act as a courier for her cousin Henri Gorce, whose pseudonym was Franklin.[46] The two had widely divergent political views: she was a conservative, like many in the medical profession, and he was a militant of the Left and had fought in Spain against Franco. They overlooked their differences and worked closely together.

Henri Gorce was responsible for the intelligence *réseau* named Famille of the network Interallié, which in turn was a sub*réseau* of F2.[47] The Paris chief of Interallié was Roman Czerniawski, a Polish intelligence officer. Unfortunately, a woman who proved untrustworthy served as adjunct to the chief and had access not only to the intelligence the group acquired but also to the names and addresses of personnel. She was known as La Chatte (the Cat) because of the way she walked. Her real name was Mathilde Carré, and she had been trained by a French agent in intelligence gathering techniques. She and Roman therefore shared their intelligence with the French Deuxième Bureau while working in a *réseau* financed by SIS.[48] Unlike many women arrested and interrogated by the German security services, who refused even under torture to betray their comrades, La Chatte was unwilling to endure imprisonment. She not only became the mistress of Hugo Bleicher of the

Abwehr but also betrayed about 100 members of her network and sent false information by radio to MI 6 in London.[49]

Henri Gorce was one of those known to the Cat, but he escaped arrest and joined the Free French in England in October 1942. Four months later he returned to France as chief of the BCRA mission Gallia, with headquarters in Lyon. This *réseau* was charged with coordinating and transmitting intelligence collected by the Mouvements Unis de Résistance (MUR), a federation of three major resistance movements in the south of France: Combat, Libération, and Franc Tireur.[50] These organizational changes were not always accomplished without friction. Frenay, the organizer of Combat's large intelligence service, resented the fact that an emissary from BCRA in London was sent to take over the direction of intelligence work in MUR.[51]

Throughout this critical time Dr. Batier, known as Janine, had continued working as a courier and liaison agent in Paris, but she was careful to take her information only to the CND. After Franklin's return, she was asked to become chief of a branch of Gallia in Paris that would assure liaison with key civil servants in such organizations as the post office (PTT) and the railroads (SNCF). For 14 months she not only fulfilled this responsibility but also continued to carry on her medical duties and run a household that now included her husband and two children.

With the Allied landings almost at hand, the Paris unit of Gallia became the *réseau* Darius and was put under the orders of a military officer; Janine was made chief of its headquarters staff. A month later a series of arrests hit the network, and she was forced to abandon her home and her practice, leaving her younger child with her husband and her older daughter with her mother. Although now in hiding, Janine worked periodically at headquarters, but the odds were against anyone with so long a record of service to the resistance. On July 4, 1944, she was arrested and tortured in a vain effort to make her reveal the names of her co-workers. When she refused, she was deported to Ravensbrück, from which she returned at the end of the war with her health seriously impaired.[52]

The names of countless other couriers are unknown today. To foil the police, the young women were called only by their first names, instead of being given pseudonyms that would have included them in the membership lists of resistance groups. According to a French officer assigned to help provide intelligence to American and French units advancing from the south in the fall of 1944, they had no trouble finding women for this hazardous undertaking: "We looked for suitable women whom we could use as couriers. It was quite easy to find several young girls who volunteered to help us." None of these "young girls" were identified, even after the war.[53]

As soon as possible after couriers brought their information to the headquarters of the various networks or military units, the material had to be read and sifted for distribution. Tactical intelligence often could be easily included in field orders or briefing sessions, but messages dispatched to London or Algiers had to be in code. A common code grouped letters in fives. The chief or assistant selected a key that changed with every message. Many women took on the tedious assignment of encoding, a task that resembled setting up a crossword puzzle on a grid. And although the work was time-consuming—messages could range from 80 to 120 groups of letters—they also served in many cases as couriers and helped to find safehouses for agents.

In some large networks coding was a full-time job. Young Christiane de Renty, working for the Alliance network in Paris, sometimes spent entire nights coding and decoding urgent telegrams in five-letter code. At the same time her apartment was a letter drop, where she received telephone calls and intelligence reports. She also met agents at metro stations, cafes, or other places to pick up verbal or written messages and to distribute money.[54]

At the Lyon headquarters of Gallia, Edith, the wife of Henri Gorce, was in charge of the coding section, which consisted of seven women and one man. In 1940, while still teaching, she had helped Henri at night and on weekends with his work for the Famille section of F2. After Henri's escape to London she stayed with his mother in Ville d'Avray, a suburb of Paris. By June 1943 Henri was back in Lyon, and Edith left their daughter, born on the same day in November 1941 that the Cat betrayed the *réseau*, with Mme Gorce and joined him.

The coding section in her charge had to process a great deal of material because Gallia was one of the largest BCRA organizations, with a monthly budget between 4 and 5 million francs and more than 1,757 agents: 655 were clandestine, full-time agents classified as P2, 10 percent of these being women; 752 others retained the cover of a job and were classified as P1; and 350 were occasional workers. The latter, mostly women, provided meeting places or letter drops, and also served as part-time couriers.[55]

In addition to being coded, some messages had to be translated into either French or English, a responsibility that women assumed in many instances. One of the well-qualified translators was an OSS volunteer, the Marquise Claire de Forbin. She had been active in the resistance in the Alpes Maritimes before the Allies landed in southern France, working with her good friend Isabel Townsend Pell, an American who had chosen to remain in France out of loyalty to her French friends. After the landings Claire helped to establish the Headquarters Base Section of OSS in Grasse and then in Nice.[56] Later, as chief of the section under Capt. M. T. Jones of OSS, she took charge of processing the intelligence reports of over 100 field agents. The reports were in French, Italian, or German, and she was the official translator, with five women assistants. Since Isabel knew many people in the vicinity, she was able to advise Jones about local conditions and furnish the names of prospective staff members.[57]

Isabel Pell was an unconventional, energetic woman from a socially prominent New York family. When the war broke out, she raised sizable sums of money to provide vehicles for the Anglo-American Ambulance Corps in Nice.[58] Later she joined the resistance, was arrested and imprisoned for a while in the Puget Thenier prison north of Nice, and escaped in September 1943. Working underground and using the pseudonym Fredericka, she led 16 American paratroopers to safety after they had been dropped ten miles from their destination, in an area surrounded by Germans. She was one of the few American women to be awarded the Medal of the Resistance by the French government.[59]

Translating and coding were preliminaries to the actual dispatching of intelligence to the military leaders. Early in the war intelligence networks sent information to London via Vichy or American diplomatic pouches to Spain and Switzerland, or by couriers to these countries. Reports useful for long-range planning, such as information about enemy installations, defenses, and armament factories, could be taken by couriers, but details about troop movements and the arrivals and departures of ships and submarines had to be sent by radio.[60]

To speed transmission and to facilitate prompt military responses, the British first used a shortwave radio transmitter and receiver weighing some 60 pounds. Later the British and Americans developed sets weighing only half as much, which could be carried in a suitcase two feet long. Some of these early sets were sent in by diplomatic pouch, but most were dropped by parachute to reception committees.[61]

Radio operators were called "pianists." At first only men already qualified as radio operators in the navy, merchant marine, or army were used, but later some French and British women were trained in England for this work. Mlles Jeanne Garnier and Charlotte Huneau and Mme Heym received such training, then parachuted into France to work for the *réseau* Cohors. All three were arrested at the end of 1943: the two single women were deported to Germany, and Mme Heym was imprisoned.[62]

Radio operators served in the front line of the resistance, transmitting for several hours each day on regular schedules, knowing that camouflaged German detection vans could be close at hand. Each van was equipped with a rotating direction-finder antenna. If only one van was operating, it moved quickly along the base of a triangle, took another reading, and headed for the point where the two lines intersected to pinpoint the block where the clandestine operator was at work. Most of the early operators were caught by the Germans. Later they were able to reduce the length of their messages and to broadcast at irregular intervals and on different wavelengths. They also moved their posts more frequently, but the risks were always great.

The young women volunteering for this work knew that it was vital to the Allied cause. In the occupied port of La Rochelle, Odette Lioret, a post office employee, was recruited by the head of an OSS mission code-named

Aquitaine to transmit information needed for an assault to clear that part of the coast. By that time, April 1945, the Germans' situation was hopeless; but 90,000 German troops were still holding six pockets along the Atlantic coast that General de Gaulle was determined to attack — he asserted later, "I would not permit German units to remain intact until the war's end upon French soil jeering at us behind their ramparts."[63] Odette accepted the assignment. Surrounded by enemy troops, she transmitted 48 intelligence messages from station Marsouin in 3 weeks, giving detailed information about enemy positions, units, troop movements, and maritime traffic.[64] She was awarded the Medal of Freedom, becoming, like Jeanne Guyot, Evelyne Clopet, Rachel Griese, and Claire de Forbin, one of the few OSS women to receive such awards.

Although radio operators took many precautions, the Germans arrested a higher percentage of them than any other workers in the resistance. In addition to the vans the Gestapo adopted other techniques. For example, after picking up a clandestine broadcast, they would cut off the electricity to the various sections of a city in turn and note when the illicit broadcasting ceased. In this way they learned the general location of the transmission. Operators could avoid this danger by using storage batteries for power, but these were heavy, conspicuous to transport, and had to be recharged.[65]

To spare the overworked and endangered operators who transmitted urgent intelligence by radio, strategic information was often carried by clandestine planes taking passengers and supplies into France on moonlit nights. The first such planes were small Westland Lysanders, which could carry only the daring pilot and three passengers (four in an emergency). Space was so limited that they could not wear parachutes.[66]

The Lysanders needed only 600 yards of clear, firm ground to land and take off. Reception committees formed a large L pointed to windward and lit it with their flashlights. At the sound of the plane's engines, their leader flashed a prearranged signal in Morse code; if all went well, the pilot landed on target and took off as soon as his cargo was unloaded. When Marie Madeleine Fourcade of Alliance went to London by Lysander in July 1943, she was impressed by the smooth operation. In less than seven minutes the plane landed, disgorged three agents, intelligence bags, and other cargo, then took on three other agents as well as parcels of documents, and finally soared off safely, only 25 miles from occupied Paris.[67] In the same summer twin-engine Lockheed Hudson light bombers also transported agents in and out of France. They were much more difficult to land, requiring a 1,600-yard runway, but they could carry ten passengers.

Intelligence organizations in England made significant use of the BBC to communicate with their groups in France. Following the nightly news, listeners could hear enigmatic messages like "The rabbit has eaten his soup." These could confirm the dispatch of a Lysander, the arrival of agents and bags of intelligence in London, or impending Allied assaults. On the eve of the Allied North African landings on November 7, 1942, the BBC insistently warned, "Léda ne joue plus avec son cygne" (Leda no longer plays with her swan). The message, based on a Greek myth, was typical of those that made the German counterespionage service waste fruitless hours trying to discover a code or pattern in the wording—a pattern that, of course, did not exist.

Correlating the work of radio operators, couriers, and agents were the chiefs, subchiefs, and heads of sectors in the various networks. Many of these were women. One of the most notable leaders was Marie Madeleine Fourcade, chief of Alliance. Under her direction this network was to become one of the largest and earliest intelligence *réseaux*, whose members over the course of the war numbered 3,000.

She was born at Marseille in 1909, into a largely military family. Marie Madeleine spent much of her childhood in the Far East, and her formal education was concluded at the Ecole Normale de Musique in Paris. She ignored as much as possible a physical handicap—a congenital dislocation of a hip that made it difficult for her to run and sometimes gave her a pronounced limp. In 1929 she married an army officer; but after eight years the marriage failed, and to support herself and her two children, Marie Madeleine became the general secretary for a publishing company headed by Commandant Georges Loustaunau-Lacau. A specialist in military intelligence, he edited the company's right-wing journal *L'ordre national*. After the general mobilization she took charge of *L'ordre* until the enterprise was shut down because of the war.[68]

After the French debacle Loustaunau-Lacau played two roles. Under the pseudonym Navarre he set about organizing the underground activities of an intelligence network. Meanwhile he remained above reproach by directing the Légion des Combattants, a veterans' organization, for the Vichy government. It was a fortuitous combination, since his official job brought him into contact with former soldiers who wanted to continue the fight against the Germans.

As Navarre he had discussed his aims in 1941 with the British SIS in Lisbon. Through the head of its French section, Kenneth Cohen, he was immediately promised funds for the fledgling network, the first installment amounting to 5 million francs. He also received a radio transmitter, a code book, and questionnaires covering the information that the British needed about ports and ships, airfields, and troop movements.[69]

Navarre asked Marie Madeleine to organize the underground work so that he could maintain his cover by directing the veterans' organization. She was startled by his request, doubting that a woman could effectively direct the army officers he was likely to recruit, but he insisted that he could not trust anyone else. In 1941 she set up a center in Pau, ready to receive agents recruited by Navarre from all over France. She would give them the questionnaires sent by the British and outline their assignments.

In mid-July, Navarre was arrested by Vichy police, and Marie Madeleine had to shoulder the heavy responsibility of commanding the *réseau*. She reported Navarre's arrest to SIS and promised that the network would continue, using the code name POZ/55 so that she could prove herself before the British discovered that she was a woman. This she did, to the extent that even the irascible Claude Dansey, who did not take kindly to enlisting women as agents, much less chiefs of networks, became fond of her, and so protective that he later refused her pleas to be sent back to France after she had come to London to consult about the *réseau*.

Carrying out the task bequeathed to her by Navarre, Marie Madeleine organized intelligence sectors throughout France. In all the important cities and ports, including those along the Biscay coast, agents collected vital information about German submarines and ships. This information was transmitted to England from 12 locations stretching from Normandy to Nice. In 1942 she selected as her chief of staff in charge of military affairs Maj. Leon Faye, who had been released from a Vichy prison at the end of 1941. Although he was also acting as subchief of the headquarters staff of the North African Air Forces, he planned to serve Alliance until he could resume fighting fulltime.[70]

Alliance continued to grow rapidly, and Marie Madeleine was able to send quantities of information to England before disaster struck. SIS had unknowingly sent to France an English radio operator, known as Bla, who turned out to be a fascist sympathizer. He betrayed a number of Alliance members, necessitating several immediate steps on the part of Marie Madeleine. She moved at once to decentralize the *réseau*: each sector would have its own radio service and air operations, and would communicate directly with England. She also promptly changed the pseudonyms of her agents, giving them the names of animals. She became Hedgehog; Faye was Eagle; and her personal courier, Ermine.[71]

The ability of a woman to head a network successfully was acknowledged in November 1942, when Marie Madeleine was asked by SIS to arrange with her key agents for the transfer of General Henri Giraud from the Riviera to Gibraltar for a meeting with General Eisenhower. Giraud, who had escaped from a German prison, had been suggested as a man who could rally the French army and navy in North Africa, and persuade them not to resist the American forces already landing on their shores. Although he reached Gibraltar safely by submarine, he proved not to be the man for the job. Alliance was seriously endangered by this fruitless mission, for the increased radio traffic had attracted attention. In following up this clue the Vichy police arrested Marie Madeleine, her chief of staff, and others at her headquarters on November 7, 1942.

Shortly thereafter Hitler violated the 1940 armistice agreement and German troops began moving into southern France, an event that could have meant death to the Alliance members under arrest if the Vichy police had not permitted them to escape. The presence of Germans everywhere in France greatly increased the risks. More Alliance agents were arrested, and although Marie Madeleine frequently moved her headquarters, she was well aware that she might be caught at any time.

She was especially concerned about her two children, because under the Family Hostage Law of 1942 they could be arrested in her stead. She therefore arranged for them to go to Switzerland.[72] By July 1943 Marie Madeleine had been chief of Alliance for almost two years. The Gestapo was eager to capture her, and Claude Dansey insisted that she come to London for consultation. Very reluctantly she agreed and selected Paul Bernard, known as Swift, to be her successor until her return. She met with her top agents before taking off for England and many discussions with SIS. At their conclusion she hoped to return to France, but Dansey was convinced that she would be arrested immediately.

Unhappy but forced to resign herself to his decision, Marie Madeleine led the network as best as she could from London. She had trained Bernard, and although he was inexperienced, he had the advantage of not being known to the police. She helped him and the other subchiefs by reading all of the Alliance messages and by sending detailed instructions to the subchiefs of the *réseau*, such as the following:

> For Pétrel [Georges Lamarque] and Grand Hotel. Give priority to the parachute and Lysander landing fields of Pétrel and Caïman [Gilbert Beaujolin] in guaranteeing that Gibet [Gestapo] does not know about pending secret operations. Send intelligence mail to Guingamp, Brittany, I repeat Guingamp, for sea operations organized by Donjon. . . . Give Caïman one of your codes. Thank you. Warmest regards, Hedgehog.[73]

For almost a year Marie Madeleine remained in London, saddened by the news of arrests of her associates in France. Faye had been in London but was arrested when he returned to France. Her successor, Swift, had been arrested after only six months on the job; and his replacement, after six weeks. Dansey thought these arrests proved his point and was patronizing: "You see, my dear child," he said, "there's absolutely no point in your returning now."[74]

In the spring of 1944, however, an organizational change occurred that enabled Marie Madeleine to go back to France. She and other leaders of Alliance had been criticized earlier because they reported directly to the British rather than BCRA. This was changed by de Gaulle, who coordinated the French resistance organizations, making them part of BCRA. Marie Madeleine disliked the bickering among the French groups, but she supported de Gaulle wholeheartedly and welcomed this decision. In July 1944 she boarded a Hudson plane that would land her in France.

Dansey's fears proved well founded, however. In Aix-en-Provence, where she had handled 60 pounds of intelligence mail, the Gestapo found Marie Madeleine working alone in the apartment of the chief of the sector, Captain le Comte des Inards, known as Grand Duke. Taken to a detention cell at a nearby military barracks, she was told that she would be interrogated the next day. She knew that she must escape before being transferred to a prison and that she must warn Grand Duke. Marie Madeleine found that she could just squeeze through the bars of her cell by taking off her clothing, holding her dress between her teeth until she was safely outside. Then she ran as fast as her hip would permit and reached Grand Duke at his farm in time to warn him.[75]

Marie Madeleine became one of the most famous leaders in the resistance, rising from the ranks to head the intelligence section of Alliance and finally to be chief of the entire *réseau*. Her achievements were recognized by the French government, which awarded her the Legion of Honor, the Medal of the Resistance with rosette, and the Croix de Guerre. It was a great satisfaction to her to see how well women had proved their ability to handle dangerous and difficult work during the occupation.[76]

In escaping from the Germans their leader was more fortunate than many Alliance members, who paid a heavy price for its successful record. Approximately one-sixth of the entire membership were women, and about 9 percent of them died for the cause. Marie Madeleine gave them full credit for their heroism. "When women in Alliance were arrested and tortured they never revealed the names of their associates," she said.[77]

One of the network's most important contributions was a 55-foot detailed map of German defenses around the Cotentin peninsula in Normandy, the site of the American landings.[78] The network was also instrumental in forwarding to the Allies some of the most remarkable intelligence findings concerning the Germans' secret weapons known as V-1 and V-2.

They were contributed by Jeannie Rousseau, who was only 20 years old when France surrendered. Daughter of a high government official and brought up in a strongly republican tradition, she was a graduate of the greatly respected Ecole des Sciences Politiques and spoke four languages.[79]

Jeannie's first move into espionage came when the mayor of Dinard, where she was living at the time of the surrender, asked her to be his interpreter in his dealings with the Germans. She soon realized that what she heard and observed might be of use to the Allies.[80] In the following year, however, she came under suspicion and was warned to stay away from the coastal area. Still resolved to work for the resistance, she went to Paris, where Georges Lamarque, a friend from the university, asked her to join his intelligence group, the Druides, which he had organized at the beginning of 1943. At that time he was serving as an agent for Alliance under the name Pétrel, and his group was still closely associated with Alliance.

Looking for a cover for her clandestine activities, Jeannie joined an organization designed to help French industrialists work out their problems with the Germans. This job brought her into contact with a German group working on a top-secret program, and she became the interpreter for the purchasing commissions negotiating contracts for the project. Among them she found sources of valuable information about the highly secret program and its head, Colonel Wachtel.

In August 1943, under the pseudonym Amniarix, Jeannie wrote a remarkable intelligence report detailing what she had learned about the secret weapons that Hitler was boastfully touting as the means of changing the course of the war. Her report revealed that the administrative services for the new weapons were at Peenemünde, on an island off the Baltic coast, and that research was concentrated on two bombs. The first was a flying bomb (which became the V-1) that would be launched from 400 catapults in northern France and Belgium. German experts believed that 50–100 of these bombs would suffice to destroy London. The catapults would be sited so that most of Britain's large cities would be destroyed during the coming winter. The second was an entirely new stratospheric bomb that would be launched vertically from a concrete platform. (This became the V-2 rocket.) Although it had encountered some difficulties, it had been successfully tested. Jeannie thus gave ten months' warning of the V-bombardment of London.[81]

Her report, forwarded via the Alliance *réseau* to Kenneth Cohen of MI 6, was turned over to a small team of scientists, headed by Professor Reginald Victor Jones, who were watching for new developments in offensive weapons, such as pilotless aircraft and long-range rockets. At about the same time Jones had received a report that a small flying bomb had crashed on the Danish island of Bornholm. The information, accompanied by photographs and sketches, had come from a Danish naval officer on the island. Putting these facts together with other reports, Jones was convinced that the Germans were working both on a pilotless plane and on a long-range rocket, although one scientific adviser to Churchill doubted that such rockets existed or could be developed.[82]

Jeannie continued to send information to London about Colonel Wachtel. She reported that Operation Crossbow, the large-scale bombing of the launching sites being prepared for the new weapons, carried out by the American Eighth Air Force, had apparently forced Wachtel to move his headquarters south to a chateau at Creil, only 33 miles from Paris. She also noted that Wachtel would not be in continual residence at the chateau, having to make frequent trips "to supervise the finishing touches to the stratospheric rocket."[83]

The British now wanted Jeannie to come to London. She was to cross the Channel by gunboat on April 23, 1944, since no Lysander was available. Her companions would be two other agents, and they were to bring packets of intelligence reports. It was a dangerous time for such a crossing. The British were experienced in carrying out these operations; but D Day was only six weeks away, and the Germans had become even more watchful. In fact, at Bonaparte Beach, only 20 miles southeast of Tréguier, where Jeannie and her party were to be picked up, the Shelburne escape line had suspended its cross-Channel ferry until after the invasion.

The watchfulness of the German defenders proved fatal to the enterprise. Jeannie was arrested and deported before she could know how much good her work had done. Thirty-three years after the war, when she had survived the hardships of three concentration camps, including Ravensbrück, to become the Vicomtesse de Clarens and the mother of two children, she wrote: "It is not easy to depict the lonesomeness, the chilling fear, the unending waiting, the frustration of not knowing whether the dangerously obtained information would be . . . passed on in time or recognized as vital in the maze of intelligence mail."[84] Others were in less doubt about the value of her reports. According to Professor Jones, her achievement stood out "brilliantly in the history of intelligence."[85]

Jeannine Picabia led a smaller group than Alliance, but one that was noteworthy because many of its members were artists and writers. She was the daughter of the surrealist painter Francis Picabia and of Gabrielle Buffet Picabia, who worked in the Brandy escape line.[86] Unlike his daughter and former wife, Francis refused to be involved in World War II, declaring that it was not his affair.[87]

In 1939, just before the outbreak of the war, Jeannine had received her diploma as a nurse, and during the French retreat she served in the Ambulance Corps on the Western Front, caring for the injured and sick. When the armistice was announced, she was in the unoccupied zone but continued to travel with a medical group, visiting prisoner of war camps and distributing food and medical supplies to the men.[88]

While she was moving about, Jeannine found it simple to pick up military intelligence about the Germans that would be useful to the Allies, but she had discovered no means of passing it on until a German general in Toulouse permitted her to drive his car to Cannes, where she hoped to see her father for the first time since the war began.[89] At Marseille she stopped at a gasoline station across the street from the U.S. consulate, and on impulse walked inside and reported what she had learned about German troops in the north. Acting cautiously, the official told her to continue her journey and he would look into the matter. A few days later a French colonel came to her father's house and asked her to return to Paris to gather more intelligence.[90]

Back in Paris in October 1940, Jeannine organized an intelligence *réseau* to which she gave her own code name, Gloria. Among her recruits were prominent intellectuals, professors, artists, and writers, as well as civil servants and a marine officer. One of the writers was Samuel Beckett, a friend of her mother's, who was living quietly in Paris as an Irish neutral. He agreed to translate into concise English the intelligence reports that F2 would transmit to England. Couriers climbed the seven flights to his apartment to pick up the messages that he had typed and put on microfilm. They were then concealed in the bottom of a matchbox.[91]

The *réseau* grew rapidly, developing sectors not only in Paris but also in Normandy and Brittany, eventually acquiring some 300 members. In January 1941 Picabia was summoned to the American consulate in Marseille and told to communicate in Paris with Jacques Legrand, the pseudonym of Jacques Moreau, who would become co-director of Gloria.[92] The name of the *réseau* was now to be SMH Gloria, the initials made by the reversal of the HMS denoting His Majesty's Service.

Many of the intellectuals in the resistance had been pacifists in the 1920s and early 1930s, but when the Germans invaded their country, their attitudes had changed. One of these was Simone Lahaye, a member of Jeannine Picabia's network. Her home, 25 miles from Sedan, had been destroyed in World War I and her family uprooted. She had grown to hate war and to pin her hopes on the League of Nations. When France was conquered, however, although she was working on a thesis in philosophy at the University of Paris, she volunteered to obtain intelligence in Paris and in Lille, in the north of France, where she had many acquaintances.[93]

Germaine Tillion, the anthropologist who was associated with several resistance organizations, also had contact with SMH Gloria.[94] As part of a dangerous assignment that she had been asked to undertake with its co-director, Jacques Legrand, she talked to Father Robert Alesch, the vicar of the parish of La Varenne. She found that he was a genuine priest, but she did not discover that he was also a Gestapo agent. Although she was too wary to tell him about the resistance groups with which she worked, he was nevertheless able to betray her.[95]

On August 13, 1942, Germaine and a colleague were arrested at the Gare de Lyon, at a rendezvous arranged by Alesch. Germaine's mother was also arrested, betrayed by someone else; both were deported to Ravensbrück, where Mme Tillion died.[96] Simone Lahaye was caught in the police net with many others, and she also was deported to Ravensbrück.

Although her *réseau* ceased to function at the end of August 1942, Jeannine Picabia remained in Paris and escaped arrest. The Gestapo had come to Mme Picabia in search of her daughter, however, and it was clearly time to leave Paris. While Mme Picabia resumed her work of providing shelter for escapers and set about organizing a new escape route, Jeannine hid in Lyon.[97] Both mother and daughter received awards for their contributions to the resistance. In February 1943 Jeannine became one of the earliest recipients of the Medal of the Resistance, an award established that month by the Free French.[98]

In contrast with Marie Madeleine Fourcade and Jeannine Picabia, whose organizations sent their intelligence to the British in SIS, Suzanne Bertillon organized and led the *réseau* HI HI for the American OSS. Born in Paris in 1891, she was a member of a prominent French medical family. Her Jewish mother, Caroline Schultze, had come from Warsaw to study medicine in Paris, as her friend Marie Curie had done.[99]

Suzanne was interested in the arts and attended the Ecole Nationale des Beaux Arts and the Schola Cantorum. In 1931 she became a journalist, traveling to the Soviet Union, Central Europe, Germany, and Spain. She also lectured widely in France, Britain, and Switzerland. After the French defeat she held a key post in the censorship service at Vichy. Since all types of correspondence crossed her desk, she was approached in April 1943 by an OSS agent sent on the recommendation of Virginia Hall, the remarkable American SOE agent. Virginia had known Bertillon in Vichy when she was on her first mission to France in 1941–42.[100] Virginia, who was about to leave London for an assignment in Madrid, provided the password for the OSS agent: "I come on behalf of the woman journalist [Virginia Hall] you were working with and to whom you came and recently read a large part of your novel [November 1, 1942] . . . ."[101]

Suzanne eagerly agreed to the request that she form a trans-Pyrenees clandestine network to aid the Allies, the first American intelligence chain to operate in southern France. She made up for her initial lack of training by following directives from Henry Hyde's SI headquarters in Algiers.[102] She was soon able to recruit and train friends and associates who consistently gathered valuable material, such as carbon copies of reports by regional prefects, information on the German order of battle, and details about rail traffic and maritime activity in Toulon.[103]

At the outset Suzanne, who had the temporary rank of commandant, was her own courier. She picked up and carried all the intelligence reports, delivering them to couriers who would cross the Pyrenees into Spain. The job meant traveling long hours by bicycle or train, and passing pouches filled with incriminating material through the stringent German controls. The *réseau* soon numbered 100 members as new agents were recruited, and in turn found and trained others. It extended from Vichy south along the Rhone valley, west to the Spanish frontier, and east to Cannes and the Italian border.[104]

HI HI became one of 14 OSS trans-Pyrenees chains functioning in southern France. It had a place in what was called the Medusa plan, whose aim was to furnish intelligence to London and Algiers for the invasion of Normandy and the assault on the southern coast of France. With remarkable daring Suzanne kept her office in Vichy, so that she could remain in touch with the various ministries of the regime and monitor its relations with the Germans. In this way she provided the Americans with valuable military and political information. Other HI HI agents also did outstanding work, and

Medusa headquarters in Barcelona was "simply delighted with the bulky pouches" of intelligence reports they received. In May 1944 agent no. 41 was commended by Medusa for providing "very complete particulars of fortifications, evacuations, morale and the situation all along the [Mediterranean] coast from St. Raphaël to Menton." The agent was urgently requested to obtain similar data eastward for 50 kilometers.[105]

Suzanne's responsibilities included paying her full-time agents and reimbursing the others for their expenses; she herself refused any pay. She had a problem, however, because she did not receive the entire sums of money sent to her by Medusa in Barcelona. One courier, although paid 75,000 francs per month to cover travel and liaison costs, opened the pouches before forwarding them to her. When she received them, she found that some of the money was missing. Her courier was not the only greedy one. Two chiefs of chains were always asking for more money, and one even sold some pouches filled with intelligence to French, British, and Belgian agents. For this he was dismissed.[106]

Bertillon ran grave risks maintaining her office in Vichy. On July 10, 1944, she was arrested in Moulins, 35 miles north of Vichy, and imprisoned. Six weeks later her friends obtained her release by telephoning a fake order to officials at her prison that all female prisoners were to be freed. Although she then had to go into hiding, she remained in contact with several of her groups, and they continued to provide tactical intelligence to American units advancing from the south.[107]

The intelligence network known as Cohors, which operated in Paris and eight other regions, including the industrial north and the coast of Brittany, established an impressive record from its inception in April 1942 until the liberation of France. It was headed by Jean Cavaillès, a member of the executive committee of Libération Nord. He had been a lecturer in philosophy at the University of Strasbourg and was temporarily at the Sorbonne. He chose as a key assistant in the new organization Mme Suzanne Tony Robert, a soft-spoken but singularly forceful woman who had been working at his side in Libération Nord since the previous September. She was born in Lorraine in 1900 and, like Cavaillès, was deeply aware of the destruction caused in eastern France by three invasions from Germany in 70 years.[108]

Married to the president of Raffineries Say, Suzanne lived in the Chateau de Forcilles, near Brie Comte Robert, 20 miles south of Paris. When the Germans occupied the region, they attempted to conduct military exercises in the park of the chateau. She was not only outraged by their intrusion but concerned because among the 17 people living in the chateau were several refugees from Belgium. Appeals to the local commandant and to authorities in Paris proved fruitless, but she temporarily solved the difficulty by posting large signs reading "Eingang Verboten" at each entrance to the park.[109]

Not long after this incident Suzanne made contact with the organized resistance and avoided personal confrontations with the enemy. At the end of 1940 she was gathering intelligence about German troops in Seine et Marne, including the complete plans of the German airfield at Villaroche and information about the hangars where gasoline and munitions were hidden. She sent her reports to the Libération Sud organization through a British friend. Her work with Cavaillès began in September 1941, about seven months before they set about establishing Cohors.

In three months they made the *réseau* a reality. Jean, with the help of Suzanne and several others, had started by recruiting many patriots from Libération Nord, who then held membership in both groups. In addition to recruiting friends, Cavaillès, a Protestant, worked through a minister to reach a large university group. Thanks to the various factories owned by Tony Robert, Suzanne's husband, contacts were found in the ports of Bordeaux, Nantes, Dunkerque, and Calais.[110]

Suzanne played a key role as Cohors developed, first as Jean's assistant and then as secretary-general of the organization. Initially she arranged with Rémy's CND to send the bulk of the intelligence to London by radio or Lysander plane. Later Cohors had its own radio operators, including three women, but they were betrayed.

In August 1943 Cavaillès was arrested. Suzanne continued as adjunct to his young friend and successor, Jean Gosset, the name of the *réseau* now being changed to Asturies.[111] When Gosset was arrested, she asked Albert Guerville to become chief. He worked for the SNCF in southwest France and had been a member of the *réseau* since its beginning. She continued as his adjunct until the liberation.

During all this time Suzanne was also chief of a subnetwork comprising 66 members that she had created in the vicinity of Brie Comte Robert. Ten of her agents were full-time volunteers; 32 were part-time; 11 served as liaison agents; 4 made false documents; and several more were occupied with clandestine social service. Organizing such a group in the area was noteworthy because many residents were wealthy and complacent — in contrast with those in Lorraine, the Ardennes, and Brittany, for example, who responded eagerly to opportunities to help the Allies.[112]

Despite many difficulties Suzanne's sub*réseau* established an impressive record during almost three years of clandestine activity. It furnished the Allies with complete data about several German airfields and detailed architectural plans of the broadcast facilities of German-controlled stations in the department of Seine et Marne and in Bordeaux. It also obtained the plan of the new headquarters of the German navy set up by Adm. Karl Doenitz in Angers. In the spring of 1943 Suzanne received part of the code used by the German navy to communicate with its submarines. This she carried to headquarters in Paris, hiding it under cabbages in her shopping basket.[113]

Like all networks, Cohors was usually short of funds. Full-time agents had to be paid, and members had to be reimbursed for expenses. When money from BCRA failed to arrive, Suzanne and her husband, along with her sister, Mme Marcelle Ogliastro, contributed 700,000 francs to the cause without expectation of being repaid. The money was sent to them after the war.

Like Suzanne Robert, Mme Yvonne Le Roux was an early resister who organized an intelligence subnetwork. The widow of a French naval attaché in Washington, D.C., she was living in the United States in 1940. She had chosen to remain there because her two daughters had married Americans. When France surrendered, however, although she was 58 years old, she was determined to return to Brittany and discover some way of serving her country. At Morgat, south of Brest, she found a vacant villa, but soon the Germans requisitioned it and forced her to move to more modest quarters in the rear.[114]

In December 1940, with her son Yann in London preparing to join General de Gaulle, Yvonne looked for an assignment in the resistance. Three months later Robert Alaterre, the newly arrived chief of the BCRA intelligence *réseau* Johnny, asked her to serve as an agent. Her primary assignment was to obtain detailed information about the German battle cruisers *Scharnhorst* and *Gneisenau*, which had sunk 22 Allied ships in the Battle of the Atlantic and were in Brest for repairs.

Now known as Tante Yvonne, Mme Le Roux recruited a subgroup of liaison and intelligence agents. She herself went frequently to Brest, where she collected information about the naval base from friends of her late husband, one of them a marine engineer who was director of the arsenal and an enthusiastic supporter of Pétain. At tea in the home of friends he gave her, perhaps unwittingly, information of the highest importance: as a member of a German commission charged with inspecting the damage to German ships, he had learned the estimated time it would take to repair the two warships. The *Scharnhorst*, which had serious engine trouble when it arrived at the base, would not be ready for action for several months. The *Gneisenau* had been hit by a torpedo and four bombs. The *Prinz Eugen*, a new cruiser that had accompanied the ill-fated battleship *Bismarck* into the Atlantic, had also slipped into Brest, damaged by British attacks.[115]

The bombing of these German battle cruisers not only prevented them from carrying out their patrols but also disrupted the repair and maintenance of the U-boats operating along the coast. Adm. Karl Doenitz complained to Naval Headquarters that 800 dock workers had to be taken from other bases to carry out repairs at Brest, and consequently the effectiveness of his submarines was seriously impaired by delays in maintenance.[116]

Throughout 1941 Tante Yvonne and her associates watched the progress being made in refitting the warships. Information from her *réseau* was a valuable supplement to intelligence from other sources. Intercepts of German radio messages deciphered by Enigma gave important clues to German intentions, and other BCRA agents as well as SIS were also at work in the area. Photographs were taken from RAF Spitfires, although it was difficult to judge from them the extent of damage to the ships, and impossible to know how long the repairs would take.[117]

Eventually the engines of the *Scharnhorst* were overhauled, and Tante Yvonne notified London that the cruiser would soon be sailing to the base at La Pallice, near La Rochelle. It made the trip safely, but was bombed soon after its arrival and had to be towed back to Brest for repairs. The captain of one of the two tugboats bringing it to Brest was one of Tante Yvonne's agents.[118]

The Johnny *réseau* suffered a series of arrests late in 1941, and Alaterre returned to England, leaving Tante Yvonne with responsibility for the whole network as well as for her own group. She kept London informed about the activities at the base and warned, at the end of January 1942, that the battle cruisers were preparing to break out of Brest. Finally she reported that they would leave one hour after the next Allied night bombardment.[119]

Despite her report and those from other sources confirming the intelligence, the *Scharnhorst* and *Gneisenau* executed a brilliantly planned sortie from Brest, though it proved to be a Pyrrhic victory. Both ships were damaged by mines in the Channel. The *Gneisenau* was bombed in dock at Kiel and never sailed again. In December 1943 the *Scharnhorst* was sunk off the northern coast of Norway while pursuing an Allied convoy to Russia.[120]

Not long after the disappointing escape of the warships, another wave of arrests of members of *réseau* Johnny was caused by the infiltration of a traitor. By Easter 1942 Tante Yvonne reluctantly agreed to her colleagues' urging that she go to London for discussions with BCRA about problems facing the network. Her insistence on delaying her departure until she could put her papers in order at Morgat and pick up $500 she had left with a friend cost her dearly. She was arrested on April 8, imprisoned for a while in France, and then deported to Ravensbrück. She lived to see the camp liberated but died in a Paris hospital before she could return to Brittany. Her achievements were officially recognized in the series of French postage stamps honoring heroes of the resistance.

Another BCRA intelligence group, the Mithridates *réseau*, with headquarters in Lyon, had a woman as chief of its Paris sector. At the time of the armistice, Simone St. Clair, an established journalist and novelist in Paris, was recruited into an intelligence group by her literary agent and friend Denise Clairouin.[121] A knowledge of English and facility in writing helped Simone handle messages and deal with agents, and the Lyon chief taught her to code and decode messages. Under her leadership in Paris, she and her friends recruited some 40 members, including her student son, who helped her make false papers and decode messages. Another young volunteer, 18-year-old Paule Mayet, recruited women students as couriers. Energetic and intelligent, she became one of Simone's most effective agents and a lifelong friend.[122]

Until the middle of 1943 all went well with the network, but in June the Lyon sector was infiltrated through the work of Hugo Bleicher, the highly successful Abwehr counterintelligence specialist. He had already turned several imprisoned resisters, including La Chatte, into his double agents. In Lyon his task was easy because a disloyal radio operator in the French navy volunteered to offer his services to the *réseau* and report back to Bleicher. Since radio operators were scarce, he was welcomed with open arms, given a transmitter and code, and assigned to operate in Clermont-Ferrand and Lille.

By October 1943 he had enough incriminating evidence to enable Bleicher to strike. Denise Clairouin and five other agents in Lyon were arrested. In Paris, Simone learned of their arrest and was told that the police had taken her code as well as documents she had sent from Paris. Her informants said that the police would surely seek out Mithridates agents in Paris, and that she would be wise to leave the city.

Simone warned her Paris confederates, and went briefly to Lyon to alert all the agents there and pick up some important documents relating to the German defenses of the Mediterranean coast. She refused to abandon her family; if the police were unable to find her, they would take her husband and perhaps her son as hostages. Carefully she disposed of all evidence of her underground work in her apartment, in preparation for the visit she knew the police would soon make. They arrived on December 2, 1943, and although their search for incriminating papers was fruitless, they took her to the rue des Saussaies. From there she went to Fresnes and eventually to Ravensbrück. Like so many others at the camp, she refused to let the terrible hardships break her spirit. She wrote brief accounts of the horrors on bits of paper, guarding them until the liberation and eventually using them as the basis for her book *Ravensbrück, l'enfer des femmes.*[123]

Most chiefs of intelligence networks and subsectors were recommended for awards and honors after the war. All too many did not live to receive them. One of these was Marcelle Pardé, the director of the Lycée de Jeunes Filles in Dijon, who gallantly remained at her post with the school until she was arrested for leading the local sector of the intelligence *réseau* Brutus. The honor she received was exceptional. After her death at Ravensbrück, the lycée she directed was renamed for her, and at the entrance a plaque was placed, quoting a sentence from a letter she had written while in prison: "La patrie vit tant que ses enfants sont prêts à mourir pour elle" (Our country will live as long as its children are ready to die for it).[124]

At the age of 49 Marcelle was pursuing an academic career when war broke out. A graduate of the Ecole Normale de Sèvres, she had taught French for ten years at Bryn Mawr College before returning to France in 1929. Although she was offered a chance to return to the United States and teach at a college near Bryn Mawr after the invasion, she refused the invitation. Instead, throughout 1941 and 1942 Marcelle tried to join General de Gaulle's exiles in London, believing that her knowledge of the British and the Americans would make her useful in their dealings with the French. When reaching England proved too difficult, friends in Toulouse asked her to organize a sector of Brutus, an early Gaullist group with ties to the Socialist Party, and in 1943 she agreed to begin the work in Dijon.[125]

By May, Marcelle had set up her headquarters in the lycée, a large, rambling building in a strategic location less than two blocks from the railroad station and about the same distance from the imposing Hôtel de la Cloche, which the Germans had taken over as the regional headquarters of the Gestapo. The school was also convenient because of the cover provided by constant traffic in and out of the building.

Marcelle recruited women in her school, including her secretary, Simone Plessis, and a few faculty members. Because Dijon is an important rail center on the main line from Paris to Lyon to Marseille, and a junction for trains running to industrial centers in France as well as to Germany and Switzerland, the little group specialized in gathering information about German troop and munitions trains. Assisted by contacts in the SNCF, they also obtained detailed plans of the principal stations on the Paris-Marseille line.[126]

Marcelle's companions found her to be an intelligent, understanding, and courageous leader. To confuse the Gestapo, they adopted "Bryn Mawr" as one of their passwords. Since she did not have a radio operator, Marcelle prepared her messages for Toulouse or Paris to send on to London. Sometimes her secretary wrote them in invisible ink on small pieces of thin paper and carried them on the train. At other times they hid them in packages of vegetables mailed to friends in Paris.[127]

They continued in this way until December 1943, when the Gestapo in Paris seized André Boyer, the chief of Brutus, and ransacked the command post where membership lists were kept. From that point on, Marcelle and her group knew that they could be under surveillance, but she was unwilling to leave her work and go into hiding. On August 3, 1944, she and Simone Plessis were arrested; both died at Ravensbrück. They received the Medal of the Resistance posthumously, and Marcelle the Legion of Honor as well.

Details about the number of people, particularly women, who were engaged in intelligence and what happened to them are, by the very nature of their work, hard to obtain. Marie Madeleine Fourcade has estimated that 17 percent of the members of Alliance were women.[128] About one-fifth of the members of F2 were women. In Cohors-Asturies, which had 992 registered agents, more than 200 were women; and in Mithridates, which had 1,987 agents listed in its records, 340 were women. Without doubt these figures understate the case, since many women who assisted in networks were never registered.

Numbers do not tell the whole story, of course. One woman like Jeannie Rousseau could turn up, by herself, details about secret weapons that were acknowledged in London as being of inestimable value. Such intelligence successes, however, were based on the daily routine of collecting bits and pieces of information. Most intelligence agents, including those who are little known and were in unheralded *réseaux*, contributed information to the intricate mosaic of strategic and tactical intelligence that helped bring down the enemy.

Notes

1. Paul Paillole, *Services spéciaux*, p. 207.

2. See chapter 1. SIS's liaison was actually with the French Cinquième Bureau, a new organization for gathering intelligence, which had been split from the Deuxième Bureau at the beginning of the war.

3. Francis H. Hinsley, *British Intelligence in the Second World War*, 1:162; Gustave Bertrand, *Enigma*, p. 103.

4. Charles de Gaulle, *The Complete War Memoirs*, p. 284.

5. André Manuel, interview, Paris, June 1974.

6. Hinsley, *British Intelligence,* 1:276, 2:18.

7. Paillole, *Services spéciaux,* pp. 205, 207, 218. Frenay took armistice leave in February 1941, but he was told by the French army commander that his departure was final.

8. Arthur L. Funk, *Charles de Gaulle*, p. 22.

9. U.S. War Department, Strategic Services Unit, History Project, *War Report of the OSS*, 2:231–32; Bradley Smith, *The Shadow Warriors*, pp. 187–88, 218–22.

10. The OSS agents were French. *War Report of the OSS*, 2:207–09.

11. Belgian, Dutch, and other agents also sent intelligence to their governments in exile in London.

12. M. R. D. Foot, *Six Faces of Courage*, p. 23.

13. Jeanne Berthomier's younger brother Pierre was chief of parachute drops for the network. Both he and Jeanne later received the Medal of the Resistance. Marie Madeleine Fourcade, *Noah's Ark*, pp. 134–35 (the English edition is abridged). For a full account see the original French edition, *L'arche de Noé*.

14. Mme Paule Letty-Mouroux, interview, Paris, June 1974. The entirely French subnetwork was integrated in February 1941 into F2 under the code name P.O.4. *Revue historique de l'armée*, "Le Réseau F2"; Henri Noguères, *Histoire de la résistance en France*, 1:308. Mme Letty-Mouroux later became secretary-general of the important Federation of Intelligence and Evasion Réseaux.

15. Marguerite Claeys, interview, Paris, June 1974; RG 332, ETO, MIS, MIS-X Section, France, Mme Marguerite Claeys, dossier.

16. Arthur Calmette, *L'O.C.M.*, p. 176.

17. Extract from biographical files of "héros de la résistance," Archives CHG. The Order of the Liberation was not awarded after January 23, 1946.

18. U.S. War Department, *War Report of the OSS*, 2:210.

19. According to Rémy, Jeannette was arrested and imprisoned for two to three months prior to her escape to London. Gilbert Renault, *Mémoires d'un agent secret de la France libre*, 2:254.

20. Ibid., 2:256.

21. Ibid.; also 2:564-65.

22. Elizabeth MacDonald, *Undercover Girl*, p. 196; Renault, *Mémoires,* 2:47-50. The French called the mail drops, boîtes aux lettres.

23: After the war she married M. Gauthier. She received the Legion of Honor from the French as well as the American Distinguished Service Cross. She was one of only two women to receive the award. Rear Adm. R. H. Hillenkoetter, director of CIA, to Maj. Gen. William J. Donovan, "List of Decorations to OSS Personnel and Foreign Nationals Associated with OSS," with covering letter, March 8, 1948. The names of women recipients of OSS awards were obtained from Geoffrey M. T. Jones, president of Veterans of OSS. Despite the high award to Jeanne Guyot, the CIA refused to release any documents about her under the Freedom of Information Act.

24. U.S. War Department, *War Report of the OSS*, 2:209-10.

25. Maj. Justin O'Brien to Col. John Haskell, "Arrest and Execution of Salaud, Colère and Filan B," August 22, 1944; "Cinq de la France libre," Francis Pickens Miller Collection, George C. Marshall Research Library, Lexington, VA, pp. 14-15, 19; memorandum, "Recommendation for Award of the Silver Star to Evelyne Clopet," October 31, 1944, CIA.

26. "Cinq de la France libre," pp. 14-15, 19; Report, August 1945, CIA.

27. "Cinq de la France libre," pp. 23-32.

28. Unless otherwise stated, the information about Hélène Deschamps Adams was obtained in an interview in West Palm Beach, FL, January 1980.

29. Hélène Deschamps, *The Secret War of Hélène de Champlain*, pp. 187-90; U.S. War Department, *War Report of the OSS*, 2:240-42.

30. U.S. War Department, *War Report of the OSS*, 2:242-43.

31. Henry Hyde, telephone interview, New York City, November 1979.

32. RG 332, ETO, Adjutant General Section, Correspondence Regarding Medal of Freedom Awards, 1945-46, Annie Thinesse, "Recommendation for Award of the Bronze Star Medal," June 18, 1945. All such correspondence regarding Medal of Freedom awards in this chapter has the same citation. H. M. Cole, *The Lorraine Campaign*, pp. 205, 208.

33. Thinesse, "Recommendation for Award of the Bronze Star Medal."

34. Ibid. Annie was recommended for the Bronze Star, a military award; but since she was a civilian, she received instead the Medal of Freedom with bronze palm.

35. Hyde, interview.

36. Hillenkoetter, "List of Decorations to OSS Personnel." The figures on the number of men and women who received awards for service to the OSS are from Brig. Gen. Robert M. Gaynor, national adjutant, Legion of Valor, 1961-80.

37. Ann Willets Boyd, letter to author, May 12, 1980.

38. Boyd, letter, February 26, 1980.

39. The grandson of the founder of the Equitable Life Assurance Society, he was born in Paris, brought up in Franco-American circles, and educated at Cambridge University and Harvard Law School.

40. Hyde, interview.

41. Boyd, interview, Sewickley, PA, May 1982; Joseph Persico, *Piercing the Reich*, pp. 327-30.

42. Unless otherwise noted, the information about Mme de Hautecloque was obtained in an interview in Paris, June 1974.

43. Renault, *Mémoires*, 2:134–35.

44. Ibid., 1:552–53.

45. After the war she was awarded the Legion of Honor, Croix de Guerre, and Medal of the Resistance with rosette.

46. Like many in the resistance, he added his code name to his family name after the war.

47. Henri Gorce Franklin, letter to author, February 8, 1977.

48. Paillole, *Services spéciaux*, p. 256; Roman Czerniawski, *The Big Network*, pp. 119, 194.

49. Mathilde Carré, *I Was the Cat*, pp. 115, 131–36, 144–57; Gordon Young, *The Cat with Two Faces*, pp. 114–15, 128.

50. Gorce Franklin, letter to author, February 8, 1977.

51. Henri Frenay, *The Night Will End*, p. 257.

52. She was awarded the Legion of Honor and Medal of the Resistance. Gorce Franklin, letters to author, February 8 and June 13, 1977; attestation of Gorce Franklin about Dr. Batier, February 22, 1958.

53. OSS Aid to the French Resistance in World War II, "Report of Jedburgh Team Julian II," Report no. 981, Marquat Memorial Library, Ft. Bragg, NC.

54. Christiane de Renty Beaujolin, letter to author, June 30, 1977. She was awarded the Legion of Honor and Medal of the Resistance.

55. Gorce Franklin, letter to author, June 13, 1977; Gallia report, personal archives of Gorce Franklin, pp. 5–8. The number of agents is considerably higher if members of a sub*réseau* called Reims Noël are included.

56. Mme Claire de Forbin, "Recommendation for Award of Medal of Freedom," November 28, 1945.

57. Claire de Forbin received the Medal of Freedom, basic, for services through March 1945. Geoffrey M. T. Jones, interview, New York City, October 1979.

58. Marguerite Petitjean Bassett, interview, Coral Gables, FL, December 1976.

59. Isabel was a first cousin of Sen. Clairborne Pell of Rhode Island. Sketch of Isabel T. Pell, "Pelliana" series 1935–65, pp. 30–31, Ft. Ticonderoga, New York, from John H. G. Pell.

60. Marie Madeleine Fourcade, in *Vie et mort des français*, pp. 335–36.

61. M. R. D. Foot, *SOE in France*, p. 102.

62. Marie Granet, *Cohors-Asturies*, p. 22.

63. De Gaulle, *War Memoirs*, pp. 849–51.

64. Odette Lioret, "Recommendation for Medal of Freedom," March 19, 1946.

65. Foot, *SOE*, p. 103.

66. Ibid., pp. 479–80.

67. Fourcade, *Noah's Ark*, pp. 251–52.

68. Fourcade, interview, Paris, June 1974. Her husband's surname was Méric, but she is better known by the name of her second husband, Hubert Fourcade, whom she married in 1947.

69. Fourcade, *Noah's Ark*, p. 52.

70. Contrary to the views of some writers, Faye was not the head of Alliance. Paillole, *Services spéciaux*, p. 302.

71. This led the Germans to call the group Noah's Ark. Fourcade, *Noah's Ark*, pp. 115–20.

72. Ibid., p. 232.

73. These messages were sent to the author by Christiane Beaujolin, June 30, 1977.

74. Fourcade, *Noah's Ark*, p. 310.

75. Ibid., pp. 328–38.

76. Fourcade, interview.

77. Ibid.

78. Fourcade, *Noah's Ark*, p. 301.

79. Jeannie Rousseau de Clarens, letter to author, August 13, 1980.

80. R. V. Jones, *The Wizard War*, pp. xiii, 355.

81. For the English text of her report, see ibid., pp. 351–52.

82. Ibid., pp. 35–51, 356.

83. Ibid., p. 374.

84. Ibid., p. xiv.

85. Ibid., pp. 353, 375.

86. See chapter 2.

87. William Camfield, *Francis Picabia*, pp. 59, 255, 259.

88. Gabrielle Buffet Picabia, taped interview with my research assistant, Constance Greenbaum, Paris, March 1979.

89. Deirdre Bair, *Samuel Beckett*, p. 310.

90. Ibid.

91. Ibid., p. 311.

92. Legrand was also in contact with Jacques Lecompte-Boinet of CDLR.

93. Simone Lahaye, interview, Paris, October 1976.

94. See chapter 1.

95. Tillion, letters to author, February 5 and 15, 1980.

96. For more about Germaine Tillion, see chapter 6.

97. Gabrielle Buffet Picabia, interview. Jacques Legrand, Jeannine's co-director, escaped the earlier net but was arrested in November 1943 and died in Germany.

98. She died in an automobile accident in 1977.

99. Bertillon family archives.

100. For information about Virginia Hall, see chapter 8.

101. Suzanne Bertillon, form, 1943, CIA.

102. Because of the restrictions placed on the OSS in Spain by U.S. Ambassador Carlton J. H. Hayes in accordance with the Hayes-Donovan agreement of November 1943, "no large scale organization for agent recruiting, briefing and dispatching was established at S1/Spain bases similar to that which the Algiers office was developing." U.S. War Department, *War Report of the OSS*, 2:231.

103. Suzanne Bertillon, "Recommendation for Award of Legion of Merit," January 4, 1946.

104. Ibid.; Bertillon family archives.

105. "Memorandum to Medusa, Barcelona, from Medusa, Madrid," May 4, 1944, CIA.

106. Elton, Lisbon, pouch letter to Philip Horton, chief, S1 branch, Paris,

September 11, 1945; report, "French Chains Operating from Spain, 1943–1944," 1944, pp. 4–10, CIA.

107. Bertillon family archives; Suzanne Bertillon, "Recommendation for Award of Legion of Merit"; Headquarters 2677th Regiment, Office of Strategic Services (Provisional), Suzanne Bertillon, "Recommendation for Award of the Distinguished Service Cross," June 22, 1945; Adjutant General, War Department, AGPD-B, 091.713, Bertillon, Suzanne, letter to director of Strategic Services Unit, approval of Medal of Freedom with bronze palm, June 13, 1946, CIA.

108. Unless otherwise noted, the information about Mme Robert was obtained in an interview in Paris, October 1976.

109. Later, however, the Germans took possession of the chateau and destroyed much of the interior.

110. Granet, *Cohors-Asturies*, pp. 2, 6–11.

111. After the war it was known as Cohors-Asturies.

112. Mme Suzanne Tony Robert, personal archives. Other women also served as chiefs of subnetworks in Normandy and Toulouse.

113. Ibid. Her decorations included the Legion of Honor, Croix de Guerre, and Medal of the Resistance with rosette.

114. Dr. A. Vourc'h, "Une femme debout dans la tempête: Tante Yvonne," *Cahiers de l'Iroise*, 1958, pp. 118–19; Extract from biographical files of "héros de la résistance," Archives CHG.

115. Adm. Karl Doenitz, *Memoirs*, p. 165.

116. Ibid.

117. Hinsley, *British Intelligence*, 1:332; 2:179–80. Nine Spitfires were lost on these photographic missions over Brest.

118. Vourc'h, "Une femme," p. 119.

119. Ibid., p. 121.

120. For details about the escape see Hinsley, *British Intelligence*, 2:179–88; Jones, *The Wizard War*, pp. 233–35. For details about the *Scharnhorst*, see Doenitz, *Memoirs*, pp. 371–84.

121. Her married name was Simone Leduc, but she is better known by her pseudonym St. Clair.

122. Paule Mayet letter to Mme Mireille Best, November 14, 1977.

123. *Bulletin de l'Association des écrivains combattants*, March 1975.

124. Prof. Pauline Jones, "Notes on Marcelle Pardé," July 1, 1975, pp. 19–20.

125. *A la mémoire des sèvriennes, mortes pour la France*, pp. 42–43; P. Jones, "Notes," pp. 1–4.

126. P. Jones, "Notes," pp. 6–10; Mme M. Jorré, letter to author, August 13, 1975.

127. P. Jones, "Notes," pp. 5–6; Jorré, letter.

128. Fourcade, letters to author, July 8 and September 21, 1974.

6 THE PEN BEFORE THE SWORD

When the Germans occupied three-fifths of France, they sounded the death knell for the free press. As part of their military regime they censored the press, including newspapers, pamphlets, and books. German officials directly managed some 45 percent of the Paris papers and subsidized many others. In Vichy France the General Secretariat of Information issued restrictive guidelines for editors and imposed penalties on those who ignored the injunctions.[1]

Patriots responded to censorship by reproducing news items from BBC broadcasts and Swiss newspapers. The underground press began with typed sheets, then advanced to mimeographed pages and finally to printed newspapers. Despite the problems of obtaining paper, ink, printing facilities, and funds, the clandestine press grew from a few papers in 1940 to 100 national and 500 regional and local papers in 1944 with a circulation of 2 million copies. This expansion took place in defiance of a German ordinance of December 18, 1942, which warned that anyone producing or distributing unauthorized papers would be punished with forced labor, or in serious cases with death.[2]

The underground press had several functions. The first was to provide accurate military and political information to counter the so-called news provided by the Germans through French publications they controlled.[3] For example, on January 1, 1942, *Défense de la France*, a large and influential underground newspaper, presented a brief general statement about the war and then discussed the German-Russian front in detail. It compared Napoleon's campaign in Russia with that of Hitler's and noted that history was repeating itself.[4]

A second function of the clandestine press was propaganda. The papers were anti-German, but some had been pro-Vichy before de Gaulle won their support. Early in the war the underground press denied that the "perfidious" British would fall before the German onslaught and, hence, the only alternative for France was to join the New Order of Europe as a partner of Germany. For instance, the newspaper *Résistance* of the Musée de l'Homme group urged Parisians on December 15, 1940, to organize resistance groups and transmit information to the executive committee of the paper, whose only wish was to revive a pure and free France.[5] Other papers questioned the legality of the Vichy regime, stating that it was neither free nor legal, and that it came to power under the pressure of enemy armies.[6]

Clandestine journalists denounced the pillage of France by the Germans, which led to rationing and shortages of food, clothing, and coal. They blamed German requisitions, not the British blockade, for the shortages. One journal printed detailed figures about the huge shipments of French food and other products to Germany.[7]

The underground press also encouraged people to take part in demonstrations. General de Gaulle's BBC broadcast urging his compatriots to observe an hour of hope on January 1, 1941, was printed in France, and many people, particularly in the occupied zone, stayed off the streets from 3:00 to 4:00 in the afternoon. The demonstration succeeded despite a German announcement that scarce items like coal would be available during the hour of hope.[8]

The Communist Party and its press also spurred demonstrations. Wives and mothers were urged to demonstrate for increased food rations. In July 1944 *Femmes françaises*, an organ of the Union des Femmes Françaises (UFF) under the Front National (FN), instructed women to place red, white, and blue flowers, the colors of the French flag, on war monuments on July 14, Bastille Day, and then to march to the prefectures demanding bread.[9]

The clandestine press was also a recruiting vehicle for resistance organizations. The papers reported on the organizations' activities in undermining the German grip on France and encouraged people to join in the resistance. The mere existence of the papers showed dissenters that they were not alone.

The underground press also presented and discussed new ideas about the postwar structure of France. Resistance groups were not fighting to restore the discredited Third French Republic. All wanted a change to what was often described as "a pure and strong Republic." In January 1944 the Défense de la France movement printed in its *Cahiers* a proposed constitution similar to others appearing at the time. It outlined a strong presidential system of government with one legislative assembly. One section provided for proportional representation and the enfranchisement of women — not surprisingly, because the group included many women, particularly among the students, of whom about one-third were female.[10]

Producing clandestine newspapers and documents was a major operation in which scores of resisters took part, including women working as editors, writers, printers, distributors, general secretaries, liaison agents, and couriers.

Although not many women had been editors or writers of newspapers and journals before the war, they were well represented in the clandestine press. Many were Communist or left-wing. One such woman was Edith Thomas, who edited pamphlets of the UFF and helped plan demonstrations by women against Vichy and the Nazis.[11] After the Germans imprisoned and shot a number of writers, Edith became a leader in re-forming the Comité National des Écrivains, an organization of writers under the Front National that included Gaullists, Communists, democrats, Catholics, and Protestants.[12] She also wrote for *Les lettres françaises*, the organ of the Comité, which had a circulation of about 15,000. In the October 1942 issue she wrote a moving appeal to writers to leave their ivory towers and dare to speak the truth. The truth, she noted, was yellow stars on chests, children being torn away from their mothers, men being shot, and the systematic degradation of an entire people. Not to speak the truth was to be an accomplice.[13]

Another radical editor was Madeleine Braun, a reserved young woman of the upper middle class who "went through a conversion when exposed to social issues through communism." After joining the Communist Party in 1942, she helped organize the FN in the south of France and became the co-ordinator of its executive committee. Simultaneously she served as editor of *Le patriote* in Lyon, and under her direction a compilation of news bulletins taken from Allied broadcasts was mimeographed and distributed to 52 papers of the FN in the south.[14]

Louise Weiss presented a Gaullist point of view in *La nouvelle république*, which she edited. Born in 1883, she held degrees from the universities of Paris and Oxford, and was a well-known editor and feminist. She had been president of Femme Nouvelle, an organization with a six-word program for women: equality of civic and political rights. Tired of waiting to be enfranchised, she ran as a write-in candidate in the Paris municipal elections of 1935 and received 25,000 votes in the 18th arrondissement. She had many supporters, including those in the press, radio, and cinema who aided her campaign.[15]

Jacqueline Bernard, a coeditor and linchpin of the newspaper *Combat*, had a law degree and experience working on an economics journal.[16] She was a member of a well-to-do Jewish family that had left Paris and moved to unoccupied Lyon. Her father, a retired colonel in the colonial army, made substantial contributions to the Combat movement.[17]

Jacqueline had been recruited by Bertie Albrecht, Henri Frenay's "chief of staff," a heroine of the resistance.[18] Bertie asked her help with the paper, and Jacqueline began by typing copies of the two-page bulletin that became

Combat in December 1941. It was published roughly once every three weeks. Fifty-eight regular issues plus special numbers appeared, and the circulation expanded from a handful of copies to 200,000 in 1944. Combat also printed some 100,000 copies of other resistance journals, such as *Défense de la France* and *Témoignage chrétien.*[19]

Jacqueline assembled information about what the Combat movement was doing, and added news from the BBC, the Swiss papers, and the Deuxième Bureau. She and René Cerf, an editor and professional journalist, wrote news items and sought out other people to write special articles. When Frenay was in France, he usually wrote the editorial. In preparing copy for the printers Jacqueline spent many hours counting and shifting words and spaces so that the text would fit the format exactly. In fact, she later recalled:

> Everything in the resistance took an awful lot of time. We were continually fixing small things which were not working. We were also trying to overcome little difficulties such as getting a suitcase, proper identity cards, or climbing onto a train through a window because it was so crowded. We had to spend time finding an inconspicuous place to live and work where we would not be observed.

Jacqueline was aware of the risks she was taking. On one occasion she was saved from arrest by a concierge. Most concierges were women, and many aided the resistance by providing food and shelter for evaders, serving as letter drops, and warning people when the police were in their buildings.[20] For instance, an associate of Jacqueline's phoned her and, between sobs, asked her help. Jacqueline went to her apartment, but cautiously checked with the concierge. Learning that two men, probably from the Gestapo, were upstairs, she beat a hasty retreat.

By January 1943 Combat had fused with the two other large Gaullist movements in the south of France, Libération and Franc Tireur, to form the Mouvements Unis de Résistance (MUR). Only their respective newspapers remained independent. Jacqueline moved the editorial offices of *Combat* to Paris in September 1943, after the executive committee of MUR began meeting there. Later she worked with some new editors, among them Albert Camus, who edited the paper professionally after the war.

In January 1944 the Gestapo arrested Jacqueline's brother Jean Guy, a key assistant to Frenay, and Jean's wife, Yvette, who had been chief of the social service of MUR. Jacqueline remained at her post and tried to arrange for their escape, but without success. Six months later she, too, was arrested, having been betrayed by a new contact. Despite the bathtub torture she did not break under interrogation, and she survived deportation to Ravensbrück. She was awarded the Medal of the Resistance with rosette for her service to Combat.

Just as difficult as writing and editing issues of the clandestine newspapers was the task of duplicating them. Paper, typewriters, stencils, mimeograph machines, printing ink, and presses were scarce. Resisters had to be resourceful to meet the various needs, and women were particularly helpful because of their office skills. One who stood out was Hélène Mordkovitch, born in 1917 to parents of Russian origin. As librarian of the physical geography laboratory at the Sorbonne, she worked under Professor Lutaud, who was outspokenly anti-Nazi.[21]

Hélène, along with friends and students, decided that since they could not fight the Germans with weapons, they would resort to propaganda and produce a clandestine paper. Philippe Viannay, a co-worker who was from a Catholic, conservative family that admired Pétain, became a key editor; funds for the paper were provided by Marcel Lebon, an industrialist.

Lebon purchased a German Rotaprint machine for the group, and Philippe and an accomplice stole an essential but scarce special typewriter from the Ministry of Agriculture. With this machine several women typed the text of the paper directly on aluminum sheets that served as plates.[22] The newsprint was purchased on the black market, and later from friendly dealers at a fair price. A total of 15,000 copies of the first issue of *Défense de la France* appeared in August 1941. As was usually the case, the name of the journal became the name of the resistance organization that developed around it.

Keeping the Rotaprint in a secure yet accessible place was a problem, but Hélène, who married Viannay in 1942, provided a solution. She found an obscure corner in the basement corridors of the Sorbonne where the machine was kept for more than a year—until the spring of 1943. She had the keys to the physical geography laboratory, which gave access to those corridors; and the journal was printed two nights a week in the deserted building.

In 1943 Défense de la France purchased regular presses, and two patriotic printers instructed Philippe, Hélène, and Charlotte Nadel, a colleague of Hélène's, on printing techniques. Soon Charlotte took charge of printing, which expanded into several workshops, some for typesetting and others for presses—they were kept separate. Women generally specialized in typesetting while the men ran the machines.[23] With the use of presses the number of copies grew to 100,000, and in January 1944 a special issue reached a peak of 450,000.[24] A total of 47 clandestine issues of the paper appeared from August 1941 to August 1944, making it one of the most important underground papers in northern France.

Like Charlotte Nadel, Mme Marie Catherine Servillat, who is better known by her pseudonym Lucienne and her postwar name Guézennec, was involved with printing a clandestine newspaper.[25] At the beginning of 1941, when she was 23, Lucienne started to distribute the underground paper *Le coq enchaîné*. A year later she began working for André Bollier, a 22-year-old former student at the Ecole Polytechnique who was in charge of the printing and distribution of *Combat*. Based in Lyon, Lucienne served as a courier running errands that included carrying 30–40 pound suitcases of lead type to a printer.[26]

Lucienne's responsibilities increased early in 1943, when André decided to buy a printing press with funds from BCRA and publish the bulk of the newspapers with his own team. He set the press up in the cellar of an isolated house in Crémieu, some 20 miles east of Lyon. He solved the problem of obtaining paper by boldly ordering seven tons from Germany in a complicated game of false papers.[27] He also continued to use a few printers in the region, and Lucienne carried the heavy cases of type to two printers twice a month. In this way the printed copies of the paper reached 50,000.[28]

Except for a brief period in 1943, when she was assigned to help Jacqueline Bernard in the editorial office, Lucienne spent much of her time in the printing shops. Her involvement with printing increased after André decided in the spring that Crémieu was no longer a safe location for the press. He leased a factory in Villeurbanne, a suburb of Lyon, and set up a fictitious company as a cover for the operation. He named the company the Bureau de Recherches Géodésique et Géophysique (Bureau of Geodetic and Geophysical Research), and by duping the authorities he obtained a telephone and a priority in the use of electricity.[29]

Lucienne worked long hours as part of the team in the new factory printing *Combat*, for it was now a major operation. She took turns running two printing presses: the one from Crémieu and a huge one, called Minerva, that André had purchased in Grenoble. It had been taken apart, carried in sections, and reassembled in the factory. In 1944 she also operated a third printing press, an American automatic one, provided by Philippe Viannay in an exchange agreement with Combat. André and his team would print and distribute copies of *Défense de la France* from photographic plates and type cast from cardboard molds. The plates and molds would be brought by courier from Paris. In return Philippe's group would print and distribute *Combat* in the northern zone.[30] Couriers like Suzanne Guyotat, a librarian and childhood friend of Philippe's, found it easier and less dangerous to carry lightweight molds than lead characters from one zone to another.[31] Things went smoothly, and soon 100,000 copies of *Défense de la France* were being run off in Lyon.

One morning in mid-December 1943, Lucienne was in charge of running the big Minerva when she noticed that a blob of ink was spotting an illustration. Without thinking and without stopping the machine, she wiped the type. In a fraction of a second her arm was crushed between the rollers. She was in excruciating pain as she was rushed to the nearby hospital of Grange Blanche. She told the surgeon that her injury was caused by a printing accident, but that she was not free to furnish any details. She refused to have her arm amputated, and after some six weeks left the hospital and returned to duty with the presses.[32]

On June 17, soon after D Day, Lucienne was working in the factory with André. He had escaped following a second arrest by the police, but during his absence someone had burglarized the factory. Suddenly the police and Gestapo arrived, and shots rang out. André and Lucienne ran into the courtyard; as they fled across the street, Lucienne was shot in the chest and legs, and André was gravely wounded. He refused to be taken alive, he told Lucienne, and calmly shot himself in the heart. It was a tragic end to a brilliant resistance career.[33]

The Germans took Lucienne to the hospital of Grange Blanche, where she had been only six months previously. The sister in charge recognized her, but said nothing. In July, when she was strong enough, Lucienne's friends brought her a set of clothes. During visiting hours she walked out of the hospital unnoticed. She was free, and she knew how lucky she was to be alive.[34]

Distributing copies of clandestine newspapers was still another operation that taxed the ingenuity of resisters. When Bertie Albrecht took charge of circulating the early information bulletins that she and Henri Frenay prepared in Lyon, she put some directly in mailboxes, inserted others inside magazines, and sent still others through the mail. In Paris about eight people, including the Countess Elisabeth de la Bourdonnaye, distributed copies of *Résistance* of the Musée de l'Homme group.

The countess, the mother of six children and separated from her husband, had come in contact with Boris Vildé of the Musée de l'Homme while searching for an escape line for her eldest son, Geoffroy, a tank officer who wanted to join General de Gaulle. In November 1940, when Vildé had set up a line via Spain, she offered her family Chateau de Chantérac in the Dordogne as a refuge en route.[35]

After the departure of her son, the countess typed articles for pamphlets and for the newspaper *Résistance*, including some written by Dr. Robert Debré, a close friend who had been her children's doctor. The son of a rabbi and a noted physician and professor in Paris, Debré ignored the anti-Jewish laws and refused to wear the yellow star prescribed by the Nazis.[36] He was one of 108 Jewish doctors, comprising only 2 percent of the medical profession in Paris, permitted to practice.[37]

The Countess de la Bourdonnaye was arrested in March 1941 along with many others in the Musée group, primarily because she sheltered Leon Nordmann, a Jewish lawyer who distributed *Résistance*. He was betrayed while attempting to escape to England.[38] The countess was released in August after being imprisoned for six months in the filthy, cold Cherche Midi. She was in poor health and had given her word that she would return to prison to stand trial with her unfortunate colleagues.[39] Her precarious situation, however, did not deter her from resuming her resistance activities. She assisted Dr. Debré, who was chief of the medical clinic at the Hôpital des Enfants Malades, and hid Jewish children in her apartment, furnished them with false papers, and sent them to live in a safe refuge in the country. She obtained blank identity cards and official municipal stamps from a naval officer in Nantes, and her son Guy helped her prepare new cards and falsify old ones for the children.[40]

Both the Countess de la Bourdonnaye and Dr. Debré went underground in the Vallée aux Loups in the fall of 1943 after she was arrested briefly, and he evaded the Gestapo agents who had come to arrest him in his examining room. Both emerged from hiding before the insurrection in Paris; and the countess, who had worked earlier with the UFF, continued to organize first aid stations and to supply emergency medical kits containing compresses, bandages, needles, syringes, medicines, and ampules of morphine and heroin. She also aided Dr. Debré, who was serving as chief of the Service de Santé (Health Service) of the Front National, and they set up the headquarters of the service in her apartment. This was an exciting time, and she was overjoyed when she embraced her son Geoffroy, who had arrived with General Leclerc's division.[41]

Distribution continued to be a challenge to the underground press. As more newspapers were printed, chains or large committees were required for their circulation. Hélène Viannay took charge of the distribution of the early issues of *Défense de la France*. She divided the 15,000 copies among a dozen of her friends, each of whom divided her papers among three friends, and so on.[42] Renée Cossin, the mother of two small daughters and a Communist Party member, organized 60 women to deliver pamphlets and newspapers in Amiens. She was arrested in 1942 and deported to Auschwitz, where she died.[43]

Other large-scale distribution systems were developed. In the cities distribution was organized by lycées, sections, and streets. Couriers carried suitcases filled with newspapers to regional centers, where they were circulated by chains. Adrienne Cazajus, for example, was in charge of distributing *Défense de la France* in the department of Nord and neighboring departments. She was a professor in the lycée of Lille; and with the help of her colleague Lucienne Idoine, she organized chains among the students, former students, and parents that reached various groups of the population.[44]

To reduce their risk, couriers often registered suitcases containing papers as accompanying baggage on a train. The couriers did not travel on the train, but forwarded the receipts to others, who picked up the suitcases at their destination. Because it was dangerous to call for the luggage, distributors tried to have a baggage employee as a member of the resistance group. This was not always possible, but some employees were sympathetic. On one occasion a courier escaped arrest when she went to retrieve three suitcases filled with copies of *Combat*. She was tipped off by a note from a baggage clerk asking that in the future the shipper put straw around the papers in the suitcase so that they wouldn't move around and attract attention.[45]

In addition to mass distribution, some organizations mailed copies of their papers to special groups. The editors of *Défense de la France* in 1943 decided to reach intellectuals—professors, doctors, priests, and lawyers—who were influential in the community. They instructed a group of students to compile lists of names and addresses from professional directories and to mail copies of the paper to each individual. This service was first headed by Genevieve de Gaulle, niece of the general, who, like so many members of the organization, was a student at the Sorbonne.

Genevieve had come to Paris in the fall of 1941 and had lived with her aunt Mme Madeleine de Gaulle, who took part in several resistance activities, including escape lines. In April 1943 Genevieve met Philippe Viannay in Paris. He asked her to serve on the executive committee of the movement and, as one of her responsibilities, to take charge of the special mailing of the paper. She agreed to help and set up her office in the apartment of an old friend, Madame Lepage. It was here that the envelopes were addressed and some 10,000 newspapers were prepared for mailing. As a precaution, Genevieve did not live there, but in the vacant apartment of another friend.

Genevieve did not confine her work to the office. By summer the Allies were on the offensive and hope was widespread that they would win the war. The leaders of Défense de la France therefore decided to make a dramatic gesture that would demonstrate the strength of the resistance and its press. Genevieve, Philippe, and 19 colleagues working in teams boldly passed out papers to parishioners leaving a church after mass, to passengers on subway trains, and to others walking along the street.[46]

Some 200,000 copies of *Défense de la France* were being circulated when disaster struck in Paris on July 20, 1943. A large number of the papers to be distributed were stored in a busy bookstore on the rue Bonaparte that served as a letter drop. Here the subchiefs of circulation, posing as customers, came to pick up their packages of papers. One was Marongin, a pharmacy student at the university who proved to be working for the Gestapo. With his cooperation the police set up a trap and arrested some 50 distributors, one after another, as they came to pick up their papers.

One of them was Genevieve de Gaulle. Seeing the Gestapo agents, she had put down her briefcase filled with incriminating documents and asked innocently for the Bible she had ordered. When she was told that the proprietor, Madame Wagner, was busy, Genevieve said she would return, and started toward the door. She was stopped by the police, who demanded to see her identity papers (which were false) and opened her briefcase. She was arrested and interrogated by Pierre Bony of the notorious Bony-Lafont gang, whose members were auxiliaries of the Gestapo. Realizing that she could not deny the evidence in her briefcase, she told Bony her real name. Genevieve was imprisoned in Fresnes for six months and deported to Ravensbrück, where she arrived on February 3, 1944. Eight months later SS officers moved her from a squalid blockhouse to a special cell, and on February 28, 1945, she left Ravensbrück with the American Virginia Roush d'Albert Lake (whose story appears in chapter 8).

Coordinating the various branches of the clandestine press was another essential task. Couriers and liaison agents carried messages and materials to editorial offices, printing shops, and distribution centers, which were separated for security reasons. Agents also maintained contacts with various newspapers.

Denise Jacob was one of the valiant liaison agents of Franc Tireur.[47] She had been living with her parents, two sisters, and a brother in Nice, which had been occupied by the Italians since November 1942. Because the Italians were less anti-Semitic than the Germans, many other Jews had sought refuge in the area. Denise, although aware of the dangers, wanted to take part in the struggle against the Nazis; and in June 1943, at age 19, went to Lyon to make contact with the resistance.

Two months later the director of a Girl Scout camp gave her an introduction to a member of Franc Tireur and she became a full-time liaison agent posing as Miarka, a university student. Denise found that the life of an agent was very hard. She received 3,000 francs a month for expense money, which she used to rent an unheated room for 500 francs (heat was extra) and to buy a little food to eat in her room. Denise was always hungry when she left the table, and black market food was out of the question because it was so expensive. She was lonely because she had no friends in the city, and for security reasons she could not socialize with other agents. She was also very busy making about 12 resistance contacts a day while transporting messages, journals, and other material.

After carrying out her assignments for almost a year, Denise was caught at a German roadblock, imprisoned in Montluc, and deported to Ravensbrück, where she arrived at the end of July 1944. She survived the ordeal, and for her courageous service to Franc Tireur she was awarded the Medal of the Resistance with rosette.

Meanwhile, by July 1943, soon after Denise left Nice to work for the resistance, the situation had become very dangerous for all Jews because Mussolini had fallen from power and the Germans had replaced the Italians in southeastern France. Denise's younger sister, Simone, who later became a high cabinet minister as Madame Veil, was forced to leave the lycée at the end of 1943. She went into hiding with her family at the home of some friends who shared their meager food with the Jacobs. With the cooperation of some classmates, Simone was able to take the exam for the baccalaureate in March 1944, the day before she and the others in her family were arrested.[48] The Jacobs were deported to Auschwitz, where the parents and brother died.

Jacqueline Bordelet, another courier, was in her twenties when she began working for the Musée de l'Homme group.[49] A tall, slim brunette, she had been a part-time typist at the museum for several years before the war. When war broke out, she took an accelerated one-year course in nursing but continued to work at the museum as a volunteer. She knew the staff members, including Yvonne Oddon, the librarian and a founder of the group; soon after the armistice she asked Yvonne if she could join in the surreptitious activities. Yvonne, realizing the risks, told her she was too young.

Jacqueline did not give up, however, and later proved to be both determined and courageous. Following the arrest of Yvonne and Anatole Lewitsky, a staff anthropologist, in February 1941, Jacqueline came regularly to the museum to help in the library. She also accepted the invitation of Pierre Walter, whom she knew only as Didier, to be his courier and to work with him under the guise of being his fiancée. As part of her duties she went to Muller's bookstore several times to deliver and pick up Pierre's mail, and she met him twice a week to provide him with cover as they moved around the city making contacts. All went well until April 18, when she and Pierre were to have lunch with Albert Gaveau. At the door of the restaurant Gaveau said he was not feeling well and excused himself. The Gestapo then appeared and arrested Pierre and Jacqueline. Gaveau was an unsuspected traitor who had infiltrated the group and had betrayed many of those arrested in the Musée de l'Homme affair.[50]

Jacqueline was imprisoned in Cherche Midi with 18 of her colleagues, released briefly under surveillance, then transferred to Fresnes for the trial, which began in January 1942. Thanks to the generosity of Pierre Walter, she was acquitted for lack of proof and released along with four men on February 18. Except for the six-month sentence given to the Countess de la Bourdonnaye, which she had already served, most of the other sentences were extremely harsh. Seven men, including Vildé, Lewitsky, and Nordmann, were condemned to death, as were three women, Yvonne Oddon, Sylvette Leleu, the leader of an escape line,[51] and Alice Simmonet, a student.

The situation was desperate for the seven condemned to death, and Germaine Tillion, an associate of the museum staff, promptly sought the aid of the Catholic hierarchy to obtain clemency for her friends. She had an introduction to Cardinal Baudrillard, rector of the Catholic Institute in Paris. Germaine believed that since he was a collaborator, he might have some influence with the Germans, and she asked him to write a letter to Hitler requesting clemency for those condemned to death. At first he ridiculed her suggestion but grudgingly agreed to write the letter. The appeal was not dispatched to the Führer, however; the seven condemned men were executed on February 23, 1942, and the three women were deported to Germany.[52]

Jacqueline Bordelet had accompanied her friend Germaine Tillion on some of her visits to ecclesiastical offices, and she was shocked and saddened by the execution of her colleagues. She would have had good reason to withdraw from the resistance, for she knew what the consequences could be, and her parents were not sympathetic. Her father, a World War I veteran, believed that the war had been lost and that people must accept the fact. Jacqueline did not agree with her parents, and after a brief respite she rejoined the resistance. She worked with the *réseau* Manipule, and in May 1944 she became the secretary to Jacques Lecompte-Boinet, chief of the Ceux de la Résistance (CDLR) movement. On Saturday, August 19, when shots were fired to signal the insurrection in Paris, she and her chief climbed over the wall of the Ministry of Public Works and occupied some vacant offices. Lecompte-Boinet had been nominated by the De Gaulle government in Algiers to be the head of the ministry, and this was the first one to be liberated. It was an exciting climax to Jacqueline's long resistance career.[53]

Génia Deschamps was another liaison agent, as well as a member of the executive committee of Défense de la France. A childhood friend of Hélène Mordkovitch Viannay, she was also a part of the Russian community and most of her friends were politically "socialist revolutionaries." Her mother had come to Paris in 1910 to study medicine and had remained. Although born in France, Génia felt more Russian than French because she had been treated as an unwelcome foreigner. Her father and husband had been mobilized, and although she did not feel very patriotic, she gave civilian clothing to French soldiers who escaped from the Germans and responded to Hélène's request that she assist Défense de la France. She believed that helping one's friends was a tenet of the Russian community and good training for the resistance.[54]

Génia was the only married member of the embryonic executive committee and the only one with an official job: she was a nurse in the Beaujon Clichy hospital before transferring to a maternity hospital. This gave her the necessary credentials to rent apartments for Défense de la France editorial and printing groups, and to obtain a card permitting her to move about the city freely. She therefore became a liaison agent between the executive committee and the other groups of the organization.

After July 1943, when Défense de la France was shaken by the arrest of many of its distributors at the rue Bonaparte, Génia gave up her job at the hospital and worked full-time for the movement. She became Philippe Viannay's principal liaison agent and the general secretary of Défense de la France.[55] Her jobs were varied. She coordinated activities, transmitted orders, and established a central liaison service consisting mainly of young women. She also arranged meetings of the executive committee, and took charge of closing offices and printing shops and moving equipment to new locations — frequent changes of address were essential to keep the Gestapo in ignorance.

Génia's job became more complex in February 1944, when Philippe decided that Défense de la France should play a military role in addition to publishing the journal. At his request he was appointed chief of the maquis or guerrilla groups of the Forces Françaises de l'Intérieur (FFI) being formed in the northern part of Seine et Oise, some 20 miles northwest of Paris.[56] Génia was responsible for maintaining the liaison between Philippe's headquarters and the sections of the movement in Paris, and for providing some food supplies for those in the maquis.

Génia was arrested in May 1944 when a member of the Paris organization revealed names of colleagues and the address of the main printing plant in Paris to the police while being routinely questioned. Most of the members of the team, including Charlotte Nadel, were rounded up. Fortunately they were in the hands of the French police and were put in French prisons, from which they were released on August 17, shortly before the Paris uprising.[57]

After her release Génia returned to the maquis and resumed her liaison work. She was glad to see her good friend Hélène Viannay, who had given birth to a son on July 14, 1943, just before the rue Bonaparte disaster, and had fled with her baby to escape arrest. After D Day Hélène left the baby with his grandparents and joined Philippe in the maquis, where she too became a liaison agent. It was a very dangerous period, she later reported, because they constantly had to dodge the Germans, and "it was only because of good luck that our son did not become an orphan."[58] The tension finally eased for those in the maquis when the Germans retreated in early September.[59]

By 1942, when a number of people working for *Combat* and other services of the movement were arrested and imprisoned, Bertie Albrecht decided that something must be done to assist these unfortunate colleagues. As Frenay's "chief of staff" she knew that resisters in prison were poorly fed and harshly treated, and that they worried about what was happening to their families.[60] Bertie felt strongly that these confederates must not feel abandoned, and she proposed to Henri that she set up a social service, an entirely new venture, to aid them and their families. Henri agreed, and BCRA promptly sent the necessary funds to launch the program.[61]

Bertie had been a social worker and had demonstrated her abilities in many ways. Born in 1893 into an upper-middle-class Protestant family in Marseille, she had married a Dutch banker in 1918 and had a son and a daughter, Frédéric and Mireille. A petite woman with a zest for life and a talent for music, languages, and gourmet cooking, Bertie enjoyed life and had an outgoing personality; she was also strong-willed.[62]

After living in the Netherlands and England, Bertie returned in 1934 to France, where she had ties with intellectuals of the Left. She enjoyed helping people, and the following year she decided to become a specialized social worker in labor relations. She entered the Ecole des Surintendantes d'Usines, which Jeanne Sivadon directed,[63] and was well established in her profession by March 1941, when she went to Lyon to join Frenay in organizing some kind of resistance. She obtained a job as a regional women's unemployment officer in the Vichy-financed Commissariat du Chômage Féminin, and found an apartment for herself and 16-year-old Mireille. By early the next year, however, she was devoting all her time to Combat and had set up the social service that became the model for other clandestine organizations.[64]

Under Bertie's leadership the social service grew into a specialized operation staffed almost entirely by women, for such work was considered to be uniquely feminine. Many staff members were social workers whom Bertie and her friends had recruited into the movement in Lyon, Paris, and several cities in the south of France. They prepared hundreds of food parcels and distributed them to prisoners, and they provided subsistence funds to families whose breadwinner was in prison or a concentration camp.

One of the social workers who assisted Bertie was 22-year-old Yvette Baumann, who later married Jean Guy Bernard, the brother of Jacqueline. Yvette had also been trained at the Ecole des Surintendantes d'Usines, and Jeanne Sivadon suggested that she join Bertie at the Commissariat du Chômage Féminin. Yvette soon learned that her chief was in the resistance and offered to help.[65]

Yvette took charge of the social service after Bertie was arrested by the Vichy police in May 1942. Bertie was imprisoned for seven months before escaping on Christmas Eve from a psychiatric hospital in Lyon, where she was incarcerated after feigning mental illness. She rested briefly before assuming the position of chief of the social service of the Mouvements Unis de Résistance (MUR) when Combat became part of the new organization. The service was organized, as before, in six regions with departmental and local units. The chiefs were women. Marcelle Bidault, a nurse and the sister of resistance leader Georges Bidault, was in charge of the Marseille region.[66]

On May 26, 1943, Bertie was captured in a trap set for Frenay and imprisoned in Fresnes, where she died two days later. It was said that she was decapitated by the enemy; but at the end of the war, when Frenay investigated her death and had her body exhumed, he believed that she had hanged herself rather than reveal information under torture.[67] Bertie was one of the six women awarded the Cross of the Liberation (four of them posthumously).

Following Bertie's arrest, Yvette took her place as chief of the social service of MUR. Several months later she went to Paris, where the headquarters of MUR had been transferred. Her work came to an abrupt halt on January 28, 1944, when she and her husband were seized by the Gestapo and deported to Auschwitz, where Jean Guy died.[68]

Not long after Yvette had gone to Paris, 39-year-old Bernadette Ratier took over as chief of MUR's social service. The work of the agency had greatly expanded as more and more resisters were imprisoned and deported. What had begun in 1942 as a small operation costing 10,000 francs a month grew in 17 months into a large enterprise with a monthly budget of 400,000 francs.[69]

Early in 1944 the social service expanded even more when MUR joined with some Gaullist organizations in the north, including Défense de la France, to form the Mouvement de Libération Nationale (MLN). At this time the Algiers government decided to unify the social services of the various resistance organizations in the Comité d'Oeuvres Sociales de la Résistance

(COSOR), with headquarters in Paris. It was headed by Father Chaillet, editor of the clandestine newspaper *Témoignage chrétien*, whose chief assistants were Marcelle Bidault, secretary-general, who had come to Paris to escape from the Gestapo in Marseille, and Mme Hélène Lefaucheux of the Organisation Civile et Militaire (OCM). The structure of the service in the south remained unchanged when it became part of MLN.

By early August so many resisters and their families needed assistance that Bernadette requested a monthly budget of 25 million francs for her regions in the south. The largest sums were for financial assistance to the families and for food parcels. A typical parcel contained 250 grams of sugar and of butter, 300 grams of cheese, 500 grams of roasted meat, 1 kilo of vegetable salad, 1 kilo of cooked stew, and 2 kilos of bread. Parcels going to the same prison had to be different, lest the Gestapo suspect that the prisoners were from the same resistance organization.[70]

The social services were so effective in bolstering the morale of imprisoned resisters with their food parcels and notes hidden in laundry, that the German security forces arrested many of their leaders, including Bertie Albrecht, Marcelle Bidault, and Bernadette Ratier.

In an effort to make her talk, Bernadette was handcuffed and forced to crouch in a bathtub of icy water with a wooden pole placed under her knees and arms in such a way that her tormentors could turn her repeatedly in the water. She refused to reveal information and survived the torture. At least 17 other women in responsible positions in the south were arrested; they too were badly treated, and some were deported.[71]

During the war women made a significant contribution to the clandestine press. Along with men they fought with pens and printing presses to publish and disseminate their papers. They provided news, propaganda, calls to action, and plans for future French policy. The struggle, however, was not without many casualties, and the social services of the underground developed their own system of aid to its victims and their families.

Notes

1. Claude Bellanger et al., *Histoire générale de la presse française*, 4:13–24; Robert Paxton, *Vichy France*, p. 394.
2. Henri Michel, *Histoire de la résistance en France*, pp. 69–70.
3. Claude Bellanger, *Presse clandestine, 1940–1944*, p. 7.
4. Marie Granet, *Le journal "Défense de la France,"* pp. 33–34.
5. Bellanger, *Presse clandestine*, pp. 51–52.
6. Dominique Veillon, *Le Franc Tireur*, p. 277.
7. Granet, *Le journal*, p. 29.
8. Manifestations Ordonnées en France, "Manifestations du 1ᵉʳ janvier 1941,"

France Libre Service, document 27E.3, French Press and Information Service, New York.

9. *Femmes françaises*, July 14, 1944, Bibliothèque Nationale, BN [Rés. G 1470 (130)], pp. 1–2.

10. Texts of the *Cahiers* are in Marie Granet, *Défense de la France*, pp. 205–99.

11. Edith Thomas, *The Women Incendiaries*, p. xiii.

12. Bellanger, *Histoire générale*, p. 130.

13. *Lettres françaises*, October 1942, Bibliothèque Nationale, BN [Rés. G 1470 (209)].

14. Madeleine Braun, interview, Paris, October 1976; *Cahiers d'histoire de l'Institut Maurice Thorez* no. 10 (November–December 1974): 84–85.

15. French Press and Information Service, Research Division, New York City, "French Women in the War," 2:61.

16. Unless otherwise noted, the information about Jacqueline Bernard was obtained in an interview in Paris, October 1976.

17. Henri Frenay, *The Night Will End*, pp. 53–54, 111.

18. See below.

19. Marie Granet and Henri Michel, *Combat*, p. 141.

20. The husbands of concierges usually had other jobs during the day.

21. Unless otherwise noted, the information about Hélène Mordkovitch Viannay was obtained in an interview in Paris, October 1976; in her *témoignage* of May 6, 1957; and in her letter to the author, January 23, 1977. All *témoignages* referred to in this chapter are in the archives of the Comité d'Histoire de la Deuxième Guerre Mondiale.

22. Granet, *Défense de la France*, p. 21.

23. Charlotte Nadel, *témoignage*, October 21, 1957.

24. Granet, *Défense de la France*, pp. 26–27.

25. Mme Servillat, née Morat, was divorced after the war and married Hughes Guézennec.

26. Marie Catherine Guézennec, *témoignage*, June 10, 1955.

27. Jacqueline Bernard, interview.

28. Guézennec, *témoignage*; Bernard, *témoignage*.

29. Guézennec, *témoignage*.

30. The molds were called *flans*. Bollier, an engineer, developed photographic plates to replace letterpress type.

31. Guyotat also helped to distribute the paper. She was arrested in 1944 and deported to Ravensbrück. Guyotat, *témoignage*, November 12, 1955.

32. Guézennec, *témoignage*; Henri Frenay, *Volontaires de la nuit*, pp. 288–89, 305–08.

33. Guézennec, *témoignage*.

34. Ibid. She was awarded the Medal of the Resistance.

35. "Souvenirs de Madame de la Panouse de la Bourdonnaye," 1946, pp. 2–4, in family archives of her daughter, Dr. Bertranne Auvert.

36. Robert Debré, *L'honneur de vivre*, chapters 21–27.

37. Robert Paxton, *Vichy France*, pp. 178–79.

38. "Souvenirs de Madame de la Bourdonnaye," pp. 3, 5.

39. See below.

40. Guy was later caught by a German patrol while trying to cross the Pyrenees to join de Gaulle in England. He died at age 20 in Mauthausen concentration camp. "Souvenirs de Madame de la Bourdonnaye," p. 11.

41. Ibid., pp. 12–13; Dr. Bertranne Auvert, "Mémoires," p. 9. Geoffroy was 25 when he died fighting in Alsace in 1945.

42. Hélène Viannay, interview.

43. Union des Femmes Françaises, *Livre d'or dédié aux femmes héroiques mortes pour que vive la France*, pt. 5, pp. 30–31.

44. Mme Adrienne Cazajus Grandclément, *témoignage*, July 2, 1958.

45. Bernard, *témoignage*.

46. Genevieve de Gaulle also wrote two editorials for the paper about her uncle. She included detailed information about his family, education, military career, and ideas. She stressed that he left France only because he wanted to continue the battle for a strong and independent France. Granet, *Le journal*, pp. 175–76, 181–83.

47. Unless otherwise noted, the information about Denise Jacob Vernay was obtained in an interview in Paris in October 1976 and from letters.

48. The exam was given in March instead of in June because of the anticipated Allied invasion of the south of France. After the war Simone learned that she had passed. Ménie Grégoire, "Interview du ministre Simone Veil," *Marie Claire*, September 1974.

49. The information about Jacqueline Bordelet is from a telephone interview, New York City, February 1980, and her "Rapport sur mon activité dans la résistance," Musée de l'Homme Collection, Bucknell University.

50. Germaine Tillion, letter to author, October 19, 1979. For an account of the arrest and trial of those involved in the Musée de l'Homme affair, see Martin Blumenson, *The Vildé Affair*.

51. See chapter 2.

52. Germaine Tillion, "Statement About Cardinal Baudrillard," August 30, 1945, Musée de l'Homme Collection, Bucknell University.

53. Marie Granet, *Ceux de la résistance*, pp. 228–29.

54. Unless otherwise noted, the information about Génia Deschamps is from her letter to the author, October 5, 1978, and her *témoignage*, April 23, 1947.

55. She replaced Jacqueline Pardon, a student at the Sorbonne who was an early member of Défense de la France. Pardon was arrested in the rue Bonaparte disaster, but later was released and served as an aide to Claude Monod, who became regional chief of the FFI in Burgundy and Franche Comté. Pardon, interview, Paris, October 1976.

56. For information about the FFI and the maquis, see chapter 7.

57. Marie Granet, "Défense de la France," *Revue d'histoire de la deuxième guerre mondiale*, April 1958, p. 53.

58. Hélène Viannay, letter to author, January 23, 1977. She and her husband were awarded the Medal of the Resistance with rosette.

59. After the war Génia married Jean Gemahling, who had been chief of intelligence for Combat.

60. Mireille Albrecht, letter to author, April 12, 1977. "It is often said that my

mother was Henri Frenay's secretary. I who lived with her at the time would say that she was his right arm and the one who inspired him."

61. Frenay, *The Night Will End*, p. 153. This book has many references to Bertie Albrecht.

62. Mireille Albrecht, letter.

63. See chapter 5.

64. Association Nationale des Anciennes Déportées et Internées de la Résistance, *Voix et visages*, January–February 1974; Frenay, *The Night Will End*, p. 153.

65. Yvette Bernard Farnoux, interview, Paris, October 1976.

66. Marcelle Bidault, *témoignage*, February 25, 1947.

67. Frenay, *The Night Will End*, pp. 271–79, 359.

68. Yvette Bernard Farnoux, interview. Both Jean Guy and Yvette were awarded the Medal of the Resistance with rosette.

69. Granet and Michel, *Combat*, p. 191.

70. Bernadette Ratier, "Un rapport de Bernadette Ratier, alias Dorothée, assistante nationale du service social pour la zone sud," August 15, 1944, Archives Départementales de Marseille. The document was sent to the author by Madeleine Baudoin.

71. Ratier, "Rapport de Bernadette Ratier, alias Dorothée, sur la vie à Montluc et la fusillade du 14 juin 1944," August 16, 1944, pp. 376–79, 386. She was awarded the Medal of the Resistance.

7 WOMEN AT ARMS

Some of the most dramatic actions in the French resistance were carried out by saboteurs who derailed trains, blew up bridges, cut telephone wires, and slowed factory production, and by small, armed groups who ambushed and attacked German troops. Although fewer in number than in other resistance organizations, women played a significant part in these paramilitary groups. By serving as couriers, liaison agents, nurses, doctors, and radio operators, they gave needed support to the guerrillas, most of whom were men. Nor were women's roles always secondary: some became organizers and chiefs of the armed groups, instructing recruits in the use of weapons and explosives, organizing the reception of parachute drops and the distribution of funds and supplies, and at times taking part in sabotage and combat.

They started with the small armed units known as Groupes Francs, whose purpose was to take direct action that could weaken the Germans' hold on France. Some units were free-lance and undertook only special missions, such as arranging escapes from prison. Others had a definite structure, with departmental and regional chiefs and a national head. In fulfilling their purpose of hindering enemy operations and harassing collaborators, they depended on resistance networks already established by BCRA, the operations and intelligence unit organized in London by the Free French, and SOE to supply them with explosives, weapons, and money; but for security reasons each group acted autonomously.[1]

The organizational structure of paramilitary units in the south of France was established by Combat, led by Henri Frenay. In each of its six administrative regions it had small Groupes Francs as well as paramilitary reserves called the Armée Secrète (AS). In 1943, when Combat joined with the other two important movements in the south, Libération and Franc

Tireur, to form the Mouvements Unis de Résistance (MUR), the military units were coordinated.[2]

The best-known groups who fought against the Germans were collectively called the maquis, a name derived from the scrubby underbrush of Corsica, the traditional hiding place for outlaws. They had their beginning late in 1942, when small groups of men fled to the mountains and forests of France to avoid being sent to Germany as forced laborers. Although some only wanted to escape from the Germans, most volunteered to train and fight for the liberation of their country. By 1944 hundreds of maquis were harassing the Germans, about one-third of them being under the Francs Tireurs et Partisans (FTP), the military arm of the Front National.[3]

The Germans unwittingly became the best recruiters for the maquis when they began to demand foreign workers for Germany to replace their own factory workers, whom they had drafted for the army after the heavy losses on the Russian front. Succumbing to the pressure to supply the needed labor, Pierre Laval, chief minister of the Vichy government, launched an elaborate propaganda campaign to entice French volunteers to work in Germany. Posters depicted a smiling mother and daughter, and in the distance a father happily waving from a factory: "The bad days are ended! Papa earns money in Germany!" To cloak the campaign in patriotic tinsel, the Germans agreed to the relève: For every three skilled laborers who consented to work in Germany, they promised to release one prisoner of war. Despite these inducements, however, the program failed to produce the increasing number of workers demanded by Gauleiter Fritz Sauckel. On September 4, 1942, Laval introduced the hated Service du Travail Obligatoire (STO), under which able-bodied males between 17 and 50 years of age and single women between 21 and 35 would be subject to compulsory work.[4]

However, it was not until February 1943, in response to Sauckel's demand for a contingent of 250,000 male and female workers, that Vichy began to draft entire male age groups, beginning with those born in 1920–22. Three months later Sauckel, still insatiable, demanded 220,000 additional workers. Young Frenchmen bitterly resented the substitution of work in Germany for the former military service, and although 120,000 left for Germany, 50,000 refused to report. Undeterred, Sauckel in August presented a new demand to Laval for half a million workers: 300,000 men and 200,000 women. Few of the workers demanded in August were in fact sent to Germany. One reason was that Albert Speer, Hitler's minister of armaments, had succeeded in having many French enterprises classified as S (for Speerbetriebe), which meant that they were considered essential to the German war machine and their employees were exempt from transfer to Germany.[5]

Before drafting French women for work in the Reich, German officials in 1942–43 attempted to induce them to volunteer, either accompanying their husbands or going on their own. Notices were placed in newspapers stating, for example, that 500 women were needed immediately. Those without jobs were urged by employment bureaus to sign labor contracts for work in Germany.[6]

Unlike the men, women were not conscripted by entire age groups and, rather than being sent to Germany, most were forced to serve the enemy in France, working in factories, filling clerical posts, and doing household chores for German officers quartered in the towns. Some young women joined the resistance rather than work for the Germans.[7]

At first only young, single women had been subject to the call for forced labor. Beginning on February 1, 1944, however, when the Germans desperately needed workers, Sauckel resumed his demands. This time the demand was for 1 million; and women from 18 to 45 years, both single and married women without children, were included in the labor draft. At the same time the age groups for men were extended to include those from 16 to 60 years of age.[8]

Some Catholic groups immediately protested, insisting that mobilization of women would endanger their health and virtue. Protestants also opposed the drafting of women for work in Germany. By spring, however, everyone was aware that the Allied landings would soon take place, and both men and women refused to report to the authorities. In fact, only 38,000 French workers went to Germany in 1944.[9]

Women may also have been persuaded to refuse the call by the joint appeal of three resistance groups issued in 1944.[10] They urged that women neither register for the labor service nor get the medical clearance that included a rough, degrading gynecological examination similar to the one given to prostitutes. They also asked women not to replace men in munitions factories, reminding them that the men would then be sent to Germany. Instead, women should join the resistance. "Not one French woman for the Reich" was the slogan.[11]

Although the threat of forced labor in Germany and the prospect of the Allied assault gave impetus to armed resistance, the seeds were sown much earlier, particularly among couples like Lucie Samuel and her Jewish husband Raymond, an escaped prisoner of war who had been captured while serving as an engineering officer in the French army. After his escape, carried out with Lucie's help, Raymond had joined the Armée Secrète in Lyon, where the two had settled and where Lucie was able to obtain a post teaching history at the lycée.[12]

Lucie, like many educators, was disturbed by the Vichy attitude toward women. The regime glorified motherhood and accorded women no public role. The elementary schooling of girls was changed to reflect this emphasis in August 1941. After studying the girls' curriculum an American historian observed, "One is forced to conclude that Vichy preferred women barefoot and pregnant in the kitchen."[13]

Lucie's parents were vine growers in Burgundy, and although they were poor, she had managed to take a degree at the University of Paris and pass the stiff examinations required for a lycée professor. She and Raymond had married in 1940, when she was 28. Using her position at the school as a cover for her work in the resistance, she helped to found Libération Sud, a movement whose members were primarily intellectuals of the Left, as she was, and trade unionists. Under her resistance name of Aubrac she also wrote articles for the clandestine newspaper *Libération*. Although she now had a small son, Lucie continued to be a leader of Libération Sud and became a talented organizer of Groupes Francs in Lyon. Unlike those in the maquis, who lived in camps, the men in these groups usually carried on their normal occupations until action was needed. Then Lucie rounded up the requisite number, outlined the mission, and at times led it herself.[14]

In one mission that she arranged, five resisters escaped from police custody in Lyon. Since it was easier to organize the escape of prisoners from a hospital than from a prison, Lucie first visited the men in St. Paul Prison, where she gave them a drug that would induce a high fever and make them seem seriously ill. Once the men were transferred to the hospital annex, young recruits of Lucie's Groupe Franc, posing as German officers, tricked the authorities into releasing the five men.[15]

Meanwhile, Lucie's husband had become a leader in the Armée Secrète and in June 1943 had been among the resistance chiefs betrayed and arrested in Caluire at the ill-fated meeting with Jean Moulin. Learning that Raymond was in Mountluc Prison in Lyon, but was being taken to Gestapo headquarters for questioning, Lucie devised a scheme for waylaying the van carrying him back to Montluc. The situation was desperate not only because Raymond had been sentenced to death but also because he was being interrogated by Klaus Barbie, chief of the Lyon Gestapo and notorious for his cruelty, who beat Raymond with riding crops and truncheons in a vain effort to make him inform on his comrades.

For the escape plan to succeed, Raymond would have to be alerted, and Lucie undertook this task. She was pregnant, and using this as a pretext, she showed a Gestapo agent a set of false identity papers and asserted that Raymond had seduced her. She pleaded for a chance to speak to him and persuade him to marry her for the sake of her reputation and their child's welfare. Surprisingly, she was permitted to talk to her husband privately when he was brought to headquarters for interrogation, and she told him of the scheme. That evening Lucie and a dozen men of her Groupe Franc attacked the van, freeing Raymond and 13 other patriots.[16]

After this episode it was, of course, more dangerous for Lucie and Raymond to remain in France. On February 9, 1944, a Hudson plane, arranged for by BCRA, flew them and their young son to England. Three days later Lucie gave birth to a daughter they named Catherine, the name Lucie had adopted in the underground. Her work for the resistance did not stop, for she was the first woman appointed to the Consultative Assembly of the French Committee of National Liberation in Algiers.

In recognition of her accomplishments, Lucie was awarded the Croix de Guerre and the French Medal of the Resistance. To some it might have seemed surprising that a young pregnant woman could carry a 12-hour teaching schedule, manage a household that included a small child, and fulfill her resistance tasks. To Maurice Schumann, the spokesman for the Free French on the BBC, it seemed necessary to reassure listeners that she was more like the mother of a family than a lycée professor or a courageous and determined leader of Groupes Francs.[17]

In addition to the Groupes Francs, a large number of other resistance organizations took part in sabotage and combat operations. Many of the big resistance movements that developed spontaneously in France and were later supported by the Free French organization BCRA had paramilitary sections as well as underground journals and intelligence services. Others, like those financed and supplied by the British SOE, specialized chiefly in sabotage and guerrilla operations. The Communist-led Front National encouraged patriots of all political persuasions to fight for the liberation of France. Its FTP consisted of small fighting units operating chiefly in their own localities.

In Paris one of the first small groups that attacked Germans was organized by Communists, including Danielle Casanova. Born in Corsica, she studied dentistry in Paris and set up her office there in 1933, at the age of 24. Three years later she organized and led the Jeunes Filles de France. Believing, with the editor of L'humanité, that "the best way to emancipate women was to make them lead themselves," she trained young women to run their own organizations and was soon recognized as a national leader of Communist women.[18]

When war came, many of these women served as members and leaders of the National Front's Comités des Femmes Françaises, which later became the Union des Femmes Françaises. In the summer of 1941, after Hitler's armies invaded the Soviet Union in violation of his pact with Stalin, Danielle and other Marxist leaders decided that demonstrations against the Germans and strikes were not enough. Communists not only should sabotage German operations, according to the party, but also must shoot German soldiers. With this aim Danielle and her colleagues organized small armed groups of partisan fighters. Two young men from one such group shot the first German in the military services to be killed in France after the armistice. He was a naval cadet, and the shooting took place in August, in the Barbès-Rochechouart metro station.[19]

Furious over such an overt act of rebellion, the German authorities took French hostages, warning that they would be executed if any more assassinations occurred. The Germans also demanded that six imprisoned Communists die in reprisal for the cadet's murder. Danielle was arrested in February 1942 and a year later was deported to Auschwitz, where she died of typhus in May 1943.[20]

Long before D Day, General de Gaulle had become fearful that the resistance by armed groups was being weakened by duplication of efforts, lack of coordination, and inadequate leadership. From the time that thousands of patriots defied the forced labor laws and fled to the maquis, the various units had gradually become more organized; but now it was imperative to bring them under one command.

In March 1944 de Gaulle ordered the formation of the Forces Françaises de l'Intérieur (FFI), which in theory would include all underground fighters who would accept his authority, such as the Armée Secrète, the Groupes Francs, and the maquis.[21] He then appointed Lt. Gen. Pierre Koenig to command the FFI under the Supreme Headquarters Allied Expeditionary Force (SHAEF) of General Eisenhower. After D Day, Koenig directed the tripartite headquarters of the FFI (EMFFI), in which staff members of BCRA, SOE, and OSS worked, sometimes ineffectively, to coordinate their activities in support of the Allied forces. Finally, in July, in preparation for launching Operation Dragoon, the command of the FFI in the south of France was assigned to Maj. Gen. Gabriel Cochet, who, like General de Gaulle, had his headquarters in Algiers.[22]

In Britain, SOE, flying in the face of tradition, had decided that women should be sent to France as agents. It recruited women not only because of a shortage of qualified men in England but also because they believed that women would make good radio operators and would be less conspicuous couriers than men. Soon SOE was training women in the skills necessary to assist organizers in the field. When the need arose, several women served as instructors in the use of explosives and weapons, and a few advanced to positions of organizers and leaders of maquis groups.

As a cover, most of the women in F section of SOE were enrolled in the First Aid Nursing Yeomanry, known as FANY, a distinguished civil organization dating from 1907.[23] Fourteen women trained by SOE were given honorary commissions in the Women's Auxiliary Air Force (WAAF). This was partly to help them command respect from Frenchmen they would be dealing with, and partly in the hope that if captured, even though they wore civilian clothes, they could claim officers' status and thus escape the firing squad.

Most of the 39 women dispatched between May 1941 and July 1944 by SOE to support paramilitary operations in France were trained in the United Kingdom. The schedules were tough and demanding. Women trained along with the men, and the courses took them to three or four specialized schools. They were first assigned to country estates like Wanborough Manor in southern England, where they were put through rigorous basic military and physical training. They learned to handle weapons and explosives, read maps, and code messages. Until June 1943 the program at Wanborough was relied on to screen out those not considered fit to serve in the field. Later the screening was done by an assessment board of psychologists and psychiatrists.[24]

By the end of 1943, several women agents were being sent, along with men, to the west coast of Scotland near Arisaig for a stiff course in commando training. Among other skills they learned to use British and enemy light weapons, to kill silently, and to handle the new plastic explosives in demolition exercises. Their next course was at Ringway Airfield in Manchester, where they received parachute training, since most agents were flown to France and dropped by parachute. At first some doubted that women ought to land by parachute. The harness was tight and binding across the chest and through the legs, but women performed as well as the men in the required four practice jumps, one of which had to be done at night.[25]

The last school that prospective agents attended was at Beaulieu, near Southampton, where they had to master the clandestine techniques and security procedures that would help them avoid capture by the Gestapo. They were given new identities and cover stories to match. To help them withstand Nazi interrogations, they were grilled by officers in SS uniforms, who employed every trick to shake their cover stories.

Women who were to be radio operators did not go to Scotland for the commando training. Instead they were assigned to special radio schools, such as the one at Thame Park. In addition to becoming skilled transmitters in Morse, they learned special codes, safety checks, and methods of concealing the sets that would betray them at once if discovered. Trainees were sent on practice missions that required them to send messages to headquarters from a given city without being detected by an officer who might be following them.

All agents sent into France were given four different kinds of pills to help them in emergencies. Some were to keep them awake during long hours of working alone; others would knock out an adversary for about six hours if slipped into a drink; still others would cause intestinal symptoms if the agent needed to feign illness. The most controversial was the so-called L tablet, a cyanide pill that would cause almost instant death, a grim reminder that capture could mean torture so brutal that one might choose death rather than risk betraying comrades if the pain became unbearable.

Women agents who completed their training in SOE's F section were briefed before leaving for France by Vera Atkins, a key figure in the section. Initially she was personal assistant to Maurice Buckmaster, head of the section and formerly manager of the Ford plant at Asnières, outside of Paris; she had worked her way up to the post of intelligence officer with the rank of captain, and by the end of the war she had been promoted to major.

Clever, thorough, and unruffled, Vera gave the agents leaving for France the latest information about rationing and about work and travel regulations. She checked their clothes, made in the French style by refugee Polish tailors in London, taking care that no British coins, tickets, cigarettes, or matches remained in their pockets, and making sure that their money belts fit well under their outer clothing. Although brisk in manner, she made them feel that she was concerned about them and would do whatever she could to help them at headquarters. Those who returned from missions kept her informed about current conditions and special problems they had encountered.[26]

Jacqueline Nearne was one of the early couriers trained by SOE. She was born in London and her family moved to France in 1923, when she was seven. In 1942 Jacqueline and her younger sister Eileen were determined to take some active part in helping the Allies and in April they managed to reach England by way of Gibraltar.

Both were invited to join SOE. Eileen trained as a radio operator. Jacqueline underwent only the standard early training, which did not include the rugged regime in Scotland. She did not understand some of the military lectures and was bored with theory, but she was a good shot and liked the practical side. Her early familiarity with both French and English had developed in her the curious tendency to think in French but to dream in English. She told her superiors about this habit, since it could be dangerous if she were awakened suddenly.[27]

Overruling the recommendations from the training center at Beaulieu that opposed sending her to France, Maurice Buckmaster arranged for Jacqueline to be parachuted into France on January 25, 1943. Since she was slim and chic, her cover was that of a cosmetic saleswoman. Her companion on the flight was the chief of the Stationer *réseau*, Maurice Southgate, who had come to SOE from the RAF. His parents were English but he had been born and brought up in Paris, where he had become a furniture designer.[28]

For the next 15 months Jacqueline traveled over a large area, maintaining contact between her chief and the various sectors of the maquis, and with another SOE network. Some of her journeys were by bicycle, some by train. Because the trains were crowded and she often traveled at night, sitting on her suitcase, the job was tiring, with the added strain of knowing that every new contact might betray her.

Eventually the Gestapo did pick up her trail, and Buckmaster ordered her return to England. The farm near Châteauroux where she waited for a Lysander pickup was run by a couple who permitted the Allied planes to land and take off in their fields. Although during Jacqueline's stay the wife was pregnant, she cheerfully cooked for the incoming and outgoing agents, and took the same risks as her husband of being caught by the Germans. Jacqueline was flown out on April 9, 1944.[29]

BCRA also sent women agents to France, but not until 1944. Generally the French women were trained in British schools, and 11 of them reached France mostly by parachute. Among the first was Marguerite Petitjean, who arrived in late January. Born in Strasbourg, she had no liking for the Germans and had worked for Gaullist organizations ever since the armistice. By the spring of 1943 she was a coding clerk at the Free French headquarters in Algiers, but she was restless to take more direct action against the enemy. After much effort she persuaded BCRA to send her to England for training, and from August to November she attended three schools.[30]

French agents being trained in sabotage at that time took the names of garden tools. Marguerite chose the code name Binette, the French word for hoe. It took three attempts for her to reach France by parachute. The first two flights were aborted because of bad winter weather. On her third try, at the end of January 1944, she landed without mishap, but the impact set off the little alarm clock attached to her side. In the dark she could not find the right lever, and the ringing continued. Despite her fear and frustration, she could not help laughing; fortunately no Germans were nearby. Her good luck would continue through her mission.

Although she had been trained for sabotage, her chief, Louis Burdet, selected Marguerite to be his courier. Under the name Circonférence he was de Gaulle's regional military delegate in the area of France designated Region 2, whose chief city was Marseille. His job was to assure the liaison between the headquarters of the FFI in London (EMFFI) and the regional FFI. Marguerite's job was to travel throughout the region, taking instructions to leaders of the FFI and maquis, and bringing information back to her chief. She walked a good deal but sometimes rode first class on the train, where her blonde good looks and her fur coat gave the impression that she was the mistress of an important official. Her expensive clothes had other uses; on one occasion the padding in the fashionably exaggerated shoulders of her jacket concealed plastic explosives. To hide the characteristic almond odor, she splashed herself with perfume. Molded against a railroad track and fitted with a detonator and time fuse, the plastic could derail a train on impact. Marguerite derailed one train with 21 cars in this fashion.

The arrest of Burdet at the end of June 1944 put a stop to Binette's missions. Knowing that she was in serious danger, she did what she could to wrap up the loose ends that might betray those she was leaving behind. One of her last tasks was to distribute the sizable remaining funds to various agents and groups. She took the balance to BCRA in Algiers after crossing the Pyrenees and reaching Spain on August 10, 1944.

Unlike the women agents trained abroad at special installations, most of the several hundred women couriers for the maquis simply volunteered to carry messages and set off on their assignments with hardly any instructions. Annie Kriegel, who would become an important Communist intellectual and writer, began her work as a courier in this way. In 1942 one of the professors at the lycée she attended in Grenoble put her in touch with the Jewish Young Communist movement, which included many foreign Jews. At the direction of this organization, although she was only 16 and looked even younger, she served as a courier between the FTP in the city and those in the hills. Although she was small, she could travel 60 miles a day by bicycle, thanks to a strong constitution and the gymnastics she had excelled in at school.

Life was very dangerous in the maquis; and when she was in the hills, Annie carried arms like the others. Her chief was only 20 years old, but she felt that his guardianship was necessary. Solidarity at that time, she noted, "meant that women would help the men and the men would protect the women." But she also relied on her own intelligence and managed to outwit the Germans until the area was liberated. She later became head of the department of social sciences at the University of Paris-Nanterre.[31]

Nurses and doctors also served the maquis, and in many parts of France they gave medical aid to guerrilla groups. Often under fire and exposed to the risk of deportation, they provided skills that were indispensable to men in isolated outposts who could not risk seeking medical help from strangers or travel long distances for treatment. In fact, the need for nurses was so great that some maquis battalions would accept women only in this capacity, though they had to be prepared, like the others, to defend themselves.

Micheline Blum-Picard signed on as a nurse because she wanted to take part in the liberation of Montluçon in central France. This city had been the refuge of her family since 1940, when they had fled from Paris. Her father had been chief engineer of mines in the Saar region before its people voted to return to Germany in 1935. His loyalty to France and the fact that, although a practicing Catholic, he was classified as a Jew under the Nazi racial laws put him on the Nazi black list. Through Micheline's resistance contacts he escaped from France and joined de Gaulle's government in London.[32]

Micheline had begun her underground career as a courier for the Libération Sud movement in 1942, when she was only 18. She carried messages for her chief, Pierre Kaan, a former lycée professor who had been dismissed because he was a Jew. Kaan became a leader of Libération Sud and a close associate of Jean Moulin.

With her accreditation in Red Cross first aid, Micheline was attached as a nurse to the Pierre Thimbault company, Battalion 203 of the FTP. Though technically a noncombatant, she carried a rifle and grenades, since the Germans did not grant the same recognition to the FTP that they did to the FFI. She served in the maquis with another nurse and 300 men, many of whom were Spanish refugees who had fought in the civil war in Spain. When Montluçon was liberated along with much of the department of Allier, Micheline asked to be demobilized, but her service to her country did not end. In Paris, where she was reunited with her parents, she joined the newly organized Corps Auxiliaire Volontaire Féminin (CAVF), a special administrative unit whose some 300 women members had taken part in the resistance. Although the women wore a distinctive uniform, they were not a military corps. They served as administrative assistants, social workers, secretaries, drivers, interpreters, and radio operators for the de Gaulle government. Micheline was attached to the interpreters' section and was a liaison officer with various British and Canadian headquarters.

Before the Allied landings in the south of France, the chief doctor of the Armée Secrète of MUR in the Basses Alpes had needed a colleague who could organize the medical service for the maquisards, including those in the FTP units in the southern sector of the region. He chose Dr. Marie Elise Seror, a young physician who became known to the Germans as "the woman doctor of the maquis." She had started to care for the sick and wounded in the local maquis a year after she had arrived in the department of the Basses Alpes with her Jewish parents.[33]

The new assignment was a challenging one for the 30-year-old Dr. Seror. She had to create the entire service, and proved to be an excellent organizer with a special gift for persuading local doctors to aid the wounded in their districts. At her request the military chiefs of the maquis selected isolated farms and houses in which she set up medical stations. This done, she recruited the wives of farmers and workers to serve as auxiliary nurses. At first they had to make field dressings out of old linen cloths, sterilized in wash boilers. By August, however, Dr. Seror could obtain proper dressings and other medical supplies at the district center of the Service d'Atterrissages et Parachutages (SAP), though it required a 20-mile trip by motorcycle to pick up the items dropped by BCRA. Medical instruments came from a double agent who stole them from the Germans.[34]

In addition to medical services, radio communications were an essential lifeline for large maquis groups. Only through radio contact with Free French and British organizations could they obtain the funds, weapons, and supplies needed for their military operations. Messages had constantly to be exchanged about sites for parachute drops and the timing of operations.

Radio operators were in short supply because of the long training period required and the large number arrested after a few months' service. Few women supporting the sabotage and combat operations of the maquis were more valued than the radio operators, or more deserving of praise for their courage. The efficient German detection vans could track down illegal transmissions; and if an operator was caught with a set, they needed no further evidence of guilt.

The first female radio operator sent to France by SOE was a descendant of the last Moslem ruler in south India on her father's side, and a grandniece of Mary Baker Eddy on her mother's. Her father, the Indian leader of the Sufis, a mystical branch of Islam, had been invited to Russia by Tsar Nicholas and was establishing a Sufi order there when Noor Inayat Khan was born in the Kremlin on New Year's Day, 1914.[35]

Later the family moved to France and settled in Suresnes, outside of

Paris. By the time Noor was 24, she had acquired a degree from the Sorbonne and had begun writing children's stories for Radio Paris. As with other French families, their peaceful life was shattered by the German invasion. They fled to Britain from Bordeaux, and when Noor's elder brother signed up with the RAF, she enlisted in the WAAF in November 1940.

Her fluency in French made Noor a prime candidate for the first group of 40 young women to be trained as clandestine radio operators. After seven months of tedious training and many more as a radio operator at an advanced school for bomber crews, she was more than ready to accept Selwyn Jepson's invitation to serve in SOE.[36] Jepson, an author in civilian life, fully understood the role women could play in the resistance. He believed that when it came to personal danger, women were singularly endowed with what he called "lonely courage." They did not need companionship in arms, he said, to support their bravery as men did.[37] Such courage was precisely the kind required of radio operators because they had to work long hours in solitude and anxiety.

During her training Noor had the reputation of being gentle but aloof, a Sufi mystic. She remained apart from the others and seemed to prefer a solitary life.[38] One of her instructors believed she was too emotional and nervous to do field work; but Buckmaster and Atkins thought otherwise, and on the night of June 16, 1943, she took off for France with two couriers, Cecily Lefort and Diane Rowden. She had been given the cover of a children's nurse and a headquarters code name of Madeleine.[39]

All agents could expect betrayal, but theirs happened with unusual swiftness. The SOE agent who met them at the landing site southwest of Le Mans had contacts with the Gestapo.[40] Only a week after Noor reached Paris and met her chief, Henri Garry of Cinema-Phono, a subréseau of the Prosper organization, the Germans arrested several SOE agents. They included the chief of Prosper, the radio operator, and a woman courier, Andrée Borrel, who had trained in Britain under SOE.

Noor transmitted the alarming news to SOE, and Buckmaster ordered her to return. But since she was now the only radio operator in Paris until a replacement arrived, she was determined to try to restore part of the organization. Buckmaster approved her decision but warned her not to use her radio.[41] Although Noor took the precaution of changing her lodging and bleaching her dark hair, she also took unnecessary risks. Disregarding Buckmaster's warning, she sent messages on behalf of her chief, requesting parachute drops of arms and explosives for maquis groups around Le Mans. In an effort to rebuild the Paris sector, she visited friends in Suresnes, where she had grown up and might easily be recognized by collaborators.

The end came after three and a half months in the field. Men of the SD burst into Noor's apartment, placed her under arrest, and seized her radio codes and security checks.[42] The Germans transmitted messages purporting to be from Noor in a radio game to lead SOE to continue sending her information and money. At first SOE suspected that she had been arrested but later decided the calls were genuine. The mistake put other agents at risk.

Noor's behavior as a prisoner demonstrated the steel beneath her sweet and gentle manner. She was taken to the SD headquarters at 84, avenue Foch and put in a cell on the top floor. Despite harsh interrogations she revealed nothing useful to her captors. She made two attempts to escape, both ending in failure. On the second she managed to crawl across the roof with two male prisoners, Maj. Leon Faye, a leader of the Alliance *réseau*, and John Starr, an SOE agent. They were recaptured before they could leave the area, and a furious Josef Kieffer of the SD counterintelligence service in Paris demanded that they sign declarations promising not to attempt any more escapes.

Both Noor and Leon were to die for their refusal to give their word. The slightly built Noor — she normally weighed only 108 pounds — was classified as a desperate case and sent on November 26, 1943, to a prison in Pforzheim, where she was put in chains and kept in a solitary cell. Even under this inhuman treatment she did not break. On September 13, 1944, she was shot at Dachau. Three other SOE women died with her: Yolande Beekman, one of the two women who had trained with her in Britain as a radio operator, and two couriers, Eliane Plewman and Madeleine Damerment. Andrée Borrel, the courier arrested with the leaders of the Prosper network, had already been executed at Natzweiler, along with two other couriers from SOE, Vera Leigh and Diane Rowden. Diane had been one of the three passengers on the plane that took Noor to France. The third passenger, Cecily Lefort, was also captured, and died at Ravensbrück.[43]

In recognition of Noor's work and courage, she was awarded the George cross and the Croix de Guerre posthumously.[44] The Sufi order designated her as its first woman saint.

Yvonne Cormeau, the radio operator who had trained with Noor and Yolande Beekman, was the only one of the three to survive. The daughter of a British consular official, Yvonne was born in Shanghai in 1909 and educated in France, Belgium, and Switzerland. In 1937 she was married in London and the next year gave birth to a daughter. When the Germans began to bomb London, the child was sent to a nursery school in the country. Yvonne's husband, on active service with the British army, was killed by a German bomb that destroyed their London apartment at the end of 1940.[45]

Yvonne responded to her loss by volunteering in 1941 for the WAAF and was assigned to a bomber station. Soon she was summoned to London to talk to Selwyn Jepson, who asked whether she would be willing to serve in France. She was concerned about her daughter, who had already lost one parent, but she assumed that she would be living in the unoccupied zone of Vichy France. By the time her release from the WAAF was arranged, however, the Axis powers had occupied all of the country.

Nevertheless, Yvonne undertook the standard training for radio operators and on August 22, 1943, under the code name Annette, she parachuted
into the department of Gironde. She was to set up her radio in a village 75
miles northeast of Bordeaux and to work with George Starr, chief of the
Wheelwright *réseau*, who was known as Hilaire. This network, covering ten
departments, was chiefly concerned with organizing, arming, and training
men to fight in the maquis.

Annette owed her survival in part to the caution she exercised in carrying
out her assignments. Until Easter 1944 she took pains never to spend more
than three days in one place. She usually made a point of not carrying her
radio with her when she moved, relying on local people, who would attract
less attention, to perform this dangerous service. When she was transmitting
from a relatively secure location, Annette put the long aerial up in a garden;
otherwise she set it up inside an attic. To avoid attracting the attention of
the Germans, she never transmitted for more than 15 to 20 minutes at a time.
Thanks to the flexible schedules of the SOE, she could change the hours and
wavelengths of her transmissions.

In the spring of 1944, in anticipation of D Day, Annette moved her radio
apparatus to Hilaire's headquarters in a farmhouse in the village of Castelnau-
sur-Auvignon, some 60 miles northwest of Toulouse. Radio traffic became
heavy, and she was assisted by another radio operator from England, Dennis
Parsons, a young man she had met during training.

On June 1 Annette, Parsons, Hilaire, and his young SOE courier, Ann
Marie Walters, discussed the message on the BBC about the approach of D
Day. Hilaire undertook to set up a maquis group around the village with the
many Frenchmen who volunteered, and with a dozen Spanish Republicans.
When one of the Spaniards revealed their location to the Germans, the enemy
attacked the village and Hilaire and his assistants, including Annette, joined
another maquis group. This group, together with men under French Colonel
Parisot, made up a group of some 1,200 fighters called the Armagnac Battalion. Although Annette was constantly on the move with the men, she continued to send and receive messages for Hilaire, who had become one of the
important chiefs in southwestern France. In early September, when Toulouse
was liberated, she and her chief headed a maquis column that entered the city
to celebrate its restored freedom.[46]

By the time Annette returned to England with Hilaire on September 25,
she had spent 13 months in the field and transmitted 400 messages. Her contribution to the success of the Wheelwright *réseau* was recognized with the
British award of the MBE. She insisted, with the reserve characteristic of so
many women in the resistance, that she had merely done her bit.

BCRA also trained women as radio operators in France, recruiting 31
women for this work, most of them already in the country. In 1943 operators
for BCRA were instructed at a station near Lyon that had the clandestine

name Service National Radio. By then French operators either transmitted or received; no one did both. Despite this security measure, the risks were still great, particularly for those sending messages that could be picked up by the German vans cruising in the vicinity.[47]

Compared with the male operators, very little is known about the women carrying on this hazardous work, and nothing about the fate of 12 of them. But four women trained under the wing of BCRA in England and dropped by parachute into France survived: Josianne Somers Gros, Germaine Gruner, Germaine Heim, and Danielle Reddé. One of the few bits of information reported about them is that when 19-year-old Josianne Gros landed by parachute in France on July 6, 1944, the reception committee was led by her mother.[48]

Although radio operators sometimes coded messages, specialists were needed when traffic was heavy. The inter-Allied mission Union was fortunate to have Marie Thérèse Arcelin as its chief cipher clerk. This team, headed by Col. André Fourcaud, was one of the first dispatched to the maquis, arriving in January 1944. Its two officers and one radio operator quickly established contact with the regional maquis headquarters in Lyon and with the FFI chiefs of the departments of Savoie, Drôme, and Isère, which included Vercors. Their network of radio operators and couriers provided communication among the three departments as well as with London; there were many messages to be encoded, and Marie Thérèse worked full-time, using her home as a base of operations. The arrest of her elder sister inspired her to work even harder.

On May 20, 1944, she was arrested and subjected to torture. Refusing to reveal information about the Union team, she fought the German prison guards and was "a magnificent example to her fellow prisoners." At length she was deported to a German concentration camp, as were five of her children who had been active in the resistance. After her liberation Marie Thérèse, also known as Madeleine, received the Medal of Freedom with bronze palm for her work with the OSS.[49]

Another need that some women helped to fill for the paramilitary groups was training saboteurs and volunteer fighters in the use of weapons and explosives supplied by the Allies. Thousands of containers packed with arms, ammunition, and explosive devices were dropped to the maquis in 1944. Sometimes military men were available to instruct volunteers in their use, but women were also trained for such assignments. Two of these were Jeanne Bohec of BCRA and Lise de Baissac of SOE.

In 1939 Jeanne took a job as a chemist in a gunpowder factory in Brest to help with the war effort. On the eve of the armistice she escaped to England by boat and joined the ranks of the Corps Féminin, established in 1940 by the Free French on the model of the British ATS.[50] To her dismay, her first assignment was a secretarial job, but soon she was making use of her training in a laboratory devoted to discovering how to manufacture explosives out of products that could be purchased in a store. For a while she also showed several young men how to teach maquisards to make explosives, but her request to be sent on a similar mission was refused by what she called "a misogynistic BCRA." Unlike the French group, she said, "the British had understood for a long time that a woman was as capable as a man of carrying out certain missions."[51]

Not quite five feet tall and weighing only slightly more than 100 pounds, Jeanne did not look like a potential instructor of saboteurs, but she was persistent and persuasive. Luck came when Henri Frenay, chief of Combat, visited her laboratory. He was in London serving as a leader of the permanent resistance delegation to the Free French and Allied services.[52] He knew what women like Bertie Albrecht had contributed to the cause. On his recommendation Jeanne was accepted by BCRA in September 1943, and in February 1944 she parachuted into Brittany after completing her training in the British schools.

The reception team knew only that an instructor code-named Râteau, the French word for rake, was arriving. After getting over the surprise of finding that a woman would be instructing the recruits, the local FFI was glad to avail itself of her expert knowledge.

From then until D Day, Jeanne traveled hundreds of miles by bicycle to meet and train sabotage teams. On one occasion she taught a course in sabotage to lycée professors in Quimper. After the Normandy landings, however, the maquis in the coastal regions were too occupied with hindering the Germans from bringing in more troops and supplies to spend time in training. Jeanne was eager to fight because she knew better than some of the men how to handle weapons, but she was told that a woman should not fight when men were available.[53]

Instead she joined a team of the Bureau d'Opérations Aériennes (BOA), an organization of BCRA responsible for supplying Gaullist groups in northern France. Her team was stationed close to a maquis group of 2,000 in southern Brittany, and Jeanne took charge of the reception of several arms drops. Her service was recognized by the French, who awarded her the Croix de Guerre, the Medal of the Resistance, and the Legion of Honor. In May 1974 she was named deputy mayor of the 18th arrondissement of Paris.[54]

Lise de Baissac, originally assigned by SOE to serve as a courier, also instructed young men in the use of arms in the course of her second mission to France. Both she and her brother were born in Mauritius, a British colony in the Indian Ocean, and were bilingual in French and English. When the war broke out, they were working in France but escaped to England and were accepted for training by SOE.[55]

On her first mission, which began in September 1942, Lise had organized a network called Artist in the Poitiers area. After 11 months the numerous arrests in the region caused her to be recalled to London on August 15,

1943. The danger was very real. Only a few weeks after her departure, the Germans came to her Poitiers address and later seized her principal helpers.[56]

On April 9, 1944, Lise arrived once more in France, this time serving as her brother Claude's chief assistant. D Day was less than two months away, and he was now in south Normandy, organizing maquis units to harass German reinforcements. Lise went from one maquis camp to another, helping to arrange and receive shipments of arms and supplies by parachute. Some drops included as many as 60 containers, all needing to be moved quickly and without attracting notice. Since the young men in the maquis were unfamiliar with the weapons and explosives, she taught them how to use the Sten submachine guns, hand grenades, Bren light machine guns, and plastic explosives.[57]

The assaults on the beachheads of Normandy increased the pressure for Lise and her companions. During the day she rode her bicycle to the maquis camps, carrying orders from London. At night she decoded and coded radio messages or waited in the fields for parachute drops. As long as the Germans were in the area, the dangers and difficulties were great, and she had to be constantly on guard. But it was exciting when the beachheads were secured and the Americans arrived in her area, making it safe for her to put on her FANY uniform to welcome them.[58]

With few exceptions the chiefs of maquis groups were men, but one was a British woman, Pearl Witherington, who was born in France in 1914. At the outbreak of the war she was working in Paris for the British air attaché and living with her widowed mother and three younger sisters. As the Germans advanced, the family moved to Marseille and finally, in July 1941, to England.[59]

Pearl had no trouble being accepted for training with SOE, where they could make good use of anyone who was fluent in French and English. She completed the courses at Wanborough, Ringway, and Beaulieu; and although she did not go to Scotland, she was trained in the use of explosives and weapons. On September 22, 1943, she parachuted into France with an assignment to serve as courier, along with Jacqueline Nearne, in the Stationer network led by Maurice Southgate, a former school friend.[60]

Like other couriers, Pearl had to travel constantly, since messages among resistance groups could not be trusted to the mails or the telephone. She described her experiences thus:

> The trains were unheated and it was hell travelling in an unheated train. For example, once a week I left Toulouse at 7:00 P.M. and arrived at Lyon at 11:30 the next morning. I delivered the messages and then went to a safehouse with no heat and very little food. It was difficult, not only because of the cold but also because of the fear of being caught. We were almost always tense. Of course, life did go on even if we were tense and sometimes we would have a good laugh when an incident which might have been tragic turned out to be funny. We knew an agent who had

his radio set in his suitcase on a train. As a precaution he covered it with bits of string tied in so many knots that a gendarme did not make him open it.

Some seven months later, Pearl's role changed abruptly. In April 1944 Jacqueline Nearne had been ordered back to England by Buckmaster, who feared that her arrest was imminent. On May 1 their chief, Maurice Southgate, was arrested by the SD and taken to their Paris headquarters on the avenue Foch. Someone had to assume charge of the organization, and Pearl stepped in. Although she was a woman and English, the French knew her as a straightforward, tough, and able agent with excellent training.[61] Known to the French as Lieutenant Pauline, she organized a new *réseau* called Wrestler in the northern part of the Indre department. It became the nucleus for four maquis groups that expanded dramatically after D Day. The maquisards looked to her for help and she did not disappoint them, supplying them with funds and matériel from the parachute drops that she arranged.

Pearl's maquis groups were carefully organized. Each had its own territory and a subchief directly responsible to her, and all had teams of specialists in sabotage and reception of parachute drops. In one such team her fiancé took charge of 40 receptions of arms.[62] During this time the Gestapo posted Pearl's picture with offers of a substantial reward for her capture. Although her height and English looks made it easy to recognize her, no one betrayed her.[63]

On the night of June 5 Pearl received one of the hundreds of SHAEF action messages relayed by the BBC, and although she was far from the invasion beaches, she began to issue orders to sever railroad tracks and cut down trees to block a main road. The primary task of her maquis groups was to slow the German troops advancing toward the Normandy beachheads. They did this effectively by cutting the main railroad line from Toulouse to Paris about 400 times in the month of June.[64]

Shortly after D Day, Pearl learned that some maquis groups north of her had not carried out sabotage orders and that the enemy was likely to discover the operations of her own men. Her apprehension was justified, for on June 10 several truckloads of German soldiers arrived in her sector. Pearl and about 150 maquisards were hiding in the wood of Taille de Ruine, near the village of Dun le Pöelier, when the Germans surrounded them and attacked.[65] The fighting began at 8:00 A.M. and lasted 14 hours. Though outnumbered, the maquis had the advantage of concealed positions, and the Germans finally withdrew. As a matter of principle Pearl had not joined the fighting. Later she said, "I don't think it's a woman's role to kill."

Pearl Witherington's great contribution was the leadership she exercised. Like soldiers everywhere, the maquisards chafed under inaction; a cool head and strong will were needed to maintain unity and effectiveness among them, especially when, several weeks after D Day, they numbered 2,000, including new recruits. Pearl had asked for a military man to lead her maquisards in combat operations, and in July, Colonel Perdiset, the commandant of other FFI forces in north Indre, arrived and took command.[66]

Pearl continued to shoulder heavy responsibilities, providing weapons, supplies, and money for the men. Their new task in the summer of 1944 was to harass the German troops withdrawing eastward across central France, who would soon be trapped between the Allied armies in the north and the French and American forces advancing from the Riviera in Operation Dragoon. On two occasions her maquis tangled with units of German panzer divisions: first on the road at Valençay in mid-August, and two weeks later on the railroad at Reuilly, some 25 miles northeast of Châteauroux. In the latter engagement Pearl learned that about 20 tank cars loaded with gasoline were coming along the line, and sent word to headquarters. The message was relayed to bombers, and they destroyed the shipment of fuel. Her men also joined many other maquis groups on September 11, 1944, at Issoudun, ten miles south of Reuilly. Here German Gen. Botho Elster, whose harassed troops were trying to retreat to Germany, surrendered with 18,000 soldiers.[67]

Although Pearl was promoted to the honorary rank of captain, she felt more like a civilian in uniform and did not think it was her job to blow up railroad tracks. Instead, she regarded herself as a liaison officer between Allied headquarters in London and the FFI in the field, and as an administrator of military groups. She was a good administrator, and her men liked and respected her. Michel Mockers, one of the officers in maquis 4, reported:

> Pauline [Pearl] was the great creator of the North Indre Sector. Without any respite and with sang-froid and contempt for danger she and Jean [her fiancé] traveled around the various maquis . . . with extraordinary audacity.[68]

Later the French honored her with the Medal of the Resistance, the Croix de Guerre, and the Legion of Honor. Her British superior officers recommended her for the Military Cross; but women were considered ineligible for this honor, and the government presented her instead with an MBE, Civil Division. This she refused, observing that she had done nothing civil. The Air Ministry then came forward with the MBE, Military, which she accepted.

Georgette Gérard, another woman leader in the maquis, was the only one to become a regional chief of the maquis service.[69] Born in Lorraine in 1914, she grew up in a region newly liberated from Germany after World War I. Concerned with the threat that Germany would not submit to the loss of Alsace-Lorraine, she prepared to take part in any future war by studying engineering and keeping herself in good physical condition by hiking and cycling.[70]

When the feared invasion became a reality, Georgette, better known by the pseudonym Claude, went to Lyon, where she helped refugees from Alsace and Lorraine, gathered intelligence for a British network, and wrote leaflets against the Germans. At the end of 1941 she joined Combat and became the adjunct of André Bollier, who was in charge of printing and distributing the clandestine newspaper *Combat*.

In August 1942 Claude narrowly escaped imprisonment. The French police arrested her on suspicion, but she was able to satisfy them of her innocence and they released her. Two months later the Germans occupied Lyon, a move that gave them access to local police records. Fearing that these might reveal her activities, Claude went underground, organizing Secret Army sectors for Combat in the Dordogne. Cycling from town to town, she set up groups of 30 men. They would live at home but be prepared to undertake sabotage missions and to join in the fighting after D Day. To impress the young reserve officers she hoped to recruit, Claude told them she represented a male military chief in the department. Once she knew them, she confessed that she was the only organizer in the area.

In April 1943 the national chief of the maquis, Michel Brault, made Claude the head of the maquis service of the Mouvements Unis de Résistance (MUR) in R5, the Limoges area. She traveled through the nine departments comprising her sector, making note of existing maquis groups and planning where to organize new ones. The camps, some of them manned by FTP volunteers, had a maximum of 120 men. They were located mostly in forests, the maquisards living in huts or abandoned farmhouses nearby. By November some 5,000 non-Communist fighters were in her region. Arms were provided by the British, and money was supplied by the national chief of the maquis.

In August, Claude became coleader of the region with Gontran Royer. Her job, like Pearl Witherington's, was organizing groups and operations, and administering the distribution of funds and supplies, with Gontran acting as the military commandant. In December 1943 he was arrested, and she was also in jeopardy. Claude therefore left the maquis service and transferred to the BCRA intelligence *réseau* Andalousie, but unwisely did not leave the region. The Germans caught up with her after she had served Andalousie as section chief for several months. Imprisoned in Limoges, she was harshly treated by her captors until she was liberated on August 22, 1944. After the war she was integrated into the regular French army with the rank of major, and placed in charge of female personnel.

Women working with the fighting units were very effective after D Day. At that time thousands of new recruits joined the ranks of saboteurs and guerrillas, swelling their numbers to some 200,000 and giving them a chance to help in liberating their country.[71] Along with the Allied air forces they delayed the arrival of German divisions at the Normandy front by disrupting rail and road traffic, severing telephone lines, and fighting skirmishes like the ones engaged in by Pearl Witherington's men. At a time when additional enemy forces might have driven the Allies back to the Channel, three German infantry divisions stationed in Brittany took an average of ten days, instead of two, to reach the front. In Montauban in southern France, Das Reich, the Second SS Panzer division, first assigned to suppress "terrorists," took 17, instead of 5, days to make the journey to the front. In south-central France two German divisions were prevented from supporting the armies in Normandy.[72]

In all these successes the women who had acted as couriers, doctors and nurses, radio operators, sabotage and weapons instructors, and leaders and organizers of fighting groups rightfully took pride. Men like Maurice Buckmaster and Colin Gubbins of SOE, and Michel Pichard of BOA—all in a position to know—had high praise for the women supporting and working with the fighters and saboteurs. According to Pichard,

> Women proved to be quite as brave as men in their long venture, and in a way better agents as they generally proved stronger than the men when they were arrested and interrogated.[73]

Many of these women were honored by the Allied governments after the war—some posthumously. Others simply resumed their peacetime occupations, satisfied with what they had done. Those still alive in concentration camps when France was at last free had to wait many months for Allied troops to rescue them. For others deported to these camps, there was no rescue.

Notes

1. Madeleine Baudoin, *Histoire des Groupes francs*, pp. 27–41.

2. Henri Frenay, *The Night Will End*, pp. 92, 242.

3. Henri Michel, *The Shadow War*, p. 290; Charles de Gaulle, *The Complete War Memoirs*, p. 590.

4. Jacques Evrard, *La déportation des travailleurs français dans le Troisième Reich*, pp. 41–55; *Journal officiel de l'état français*, September 13, 1942, p. 3122.

5. Evrard, *Déportation*, pp. 143–44, 148.

6. RG 226, Records of OSS, no. 31330, "The Situation in France," April 1, 1943; Evrard, *Déportation*, p. 105.

7. RG 226, Records of OSS, no. L38360, Comité Français de Libération Nationale, "La main d'oeuvre au service de l'Allemagne," pp. 11, 15–16; Evrard, *Déportation*, pp. 61–62; French Press and Information Service, "French Women in the War," 1:22–34.

8. RG 226, Records of OSS, no. 83144, Etat Français, Ministère du Travail et de la Solidarité Nationale, no. 1007/CD, April 20, 1944; Records of OSS, no. L38360.

9. Evrard, *Déportation*, pp. 62, 152; Mgr. Guéry, *L'église catholique en France sous l'occupation*, pp. 86–92. In the spring of 1943, Pastor Marc Boegner, president of the French Federation of Protestant Churches, met with Pétain, who assured him that he would never accept a German demand to conscript young women for work in Germany.

10. Comité d'Action Féminine du MLN, Union des Femmes Françaises (UFF), and Comités Locaux d'Aide aux Réfractaires (local committees to aid those disobeying STO).

11. Elisabeth Terrenoire, *Combattantes sans uniforme*, p. 50.

12. Lucie Aubrac, letter to author, September 27, 1974.

13. Robert O. Paxton, *Vichy France*, pp. 167–68.

14. Aubrac, letter.

15. Ibid.; Marianne Monestier, *Elles étaient cent et mille*, p. 45; Eric Piquet-Wicks, *Four in the Shadows*, p. 75.

16. Les Voix de la Liberté, *Ici Londres*, pp. 219–20; Maurice Schumann, BBC radio address, March 24, 1944; French Press and Information Service, "French Women in the War," 1:78–80. Ironically, Barbie has been a prisoner at Montluc, having been brought back in February 1983 for trial after escaping to Bolivia with the help of U.S. Army counterintelligence agents and living there for many years.

17. Schumann, BBC radio address.

18. Simone Téry, *Du soleil plein le cour*, pp. 22–29.

19. Ibid., pp. 42–44; Michael Marrus and Robert Paxton, *Vichy France and the Jews*, p. 224.

20. *Danielle Casanova*, Héroines d'hier et d'aujourd'hui, pp. 3–4. She was awarded the Legion of Honor posthumously.

21. De Gaulle, *Complete War Memoirs*, pp. 592–93.

22. Cochet was under the supreme commander of the Mediterranean Theater, Gen. Sir Henry Maitland Wilson. U.S. War Department, Strategic Services Unit, History Project, *War Report of the OSS*, 2:191–92; Marcel Vigneras, *Rearming the French*, pp. 300–01.

23. They served under the Women's Transport Service rather than in the Auxiliary Territorial Service (ATS), the British counterpart of the American Women's Army Corps (WAC), since ATS did not allow its members to engage in active military operations.

24. Jacqueline Nearne, interview, New York City, September 1976; M. R. D. Foot, *SOE in France*, pp. 46–48, 54–59. SOE women agents were also sent to other countries.

25. James L. Langley, interview, Woodbridge, England, October 1976.

26. Vera Atkins, interview, London, October 1976; Maurice Buckmaster, *Specially Employed*, p. 77.

27. Unless otherwise noted, the information about Jacqueline Nearne was obtained in two interviews in New York City, September 1976 and March 1977.

28. Maurice Southgate, interview, La Celle St. Cloud, October 1976.

29. Ibid.; Nearne, interview.

30. Unless otherwise noted, the information about Marguerite Petitjean Bassett, married after the war to an American, was obtained in an interview in Coral Gables, FL, December 1976.

31. All the information about Annie Kriegel is based on an interview in Ann Arbor, MI, October 1974.

32. Unless otherwise noted, the information about Micheline Blum-Picard Glover is from her letters to the author, August 28 and September 22, 1974, June 27, 1976, and March 28, 1983. After the war she married an American.

33. Dr. Marie Elise Seror, *témoignage*, October 18, 1946, Archives CHG.

34. Ibid. SAP dropped supplies for Gaullist forces in southern France.

35. Foot, *SOE*, p. 336; Jean Overton Fuller, *Noor-un-nisa Inayat Khan*, pp. 30–35.

36. Fuller, *Noor-un-nisa*, pp. 46–50, 110.

37. Madeleine Masson, *Christine: A Search for Christine Granville*, p. 145.

38. Yvonne Cormeau, interview, London, October 1976.

39. Fuller, *Noor-un-nisa*, pp. 130–31.

40. At a trial in 1948, Henri Dericourt admitted to having such contacts but was found not guilty of charges of intelligence with the enemy. Foot, *SOE*, pp. 304–05.

41. Fuller, *Noor-un-nisa*, p. 150.

42. According to one German official, she was betrayed by Renée, the sister of her chief, Henri Garry. After the war, however, Renée was acquitted of the charge, and a German counterintelligence officer testified that he had found Noor through detection vans. Fuller, *Noor-un-nisa*, pp. 206, 216; Foot, *SOE*, pp. 340–42.

43. Elizabeth Nicholas, *Death be not Proud*, p. 223; Fuller, *Noor-un-nisa*, pp. 222, 238–39; Foot, *SOE*, p. 429.

44. Fuller, *Noor-un-nisa*, p. 250.

45. Unless otherwise noted, the information about Yvonne Cormeau was obtained in an interview in London, October 1976, and from letters to the author.

46. Cormeau, letter to author, April 22, 1983; Henri Noguères, *Histoire de la résistance en France*, 5:116–117; Anne Marie Walters, *Moondrop to Gascony*, pp. 161–71.

47. Michel Pichard, letter to author, June 19, 1980.

48. Ibid.; Foot, *SOE*, p. 202.

49. RG 332, ETO, Adjutant General Section, correspondence regarding Medal of Freedom awards, 1945–46, Madeleine Arcelin, "Recommendation for Award of Bronze Star Medal," June 18, 1945.

50. In November 1942, the Corps Féminin became the Corps des Volontaires Françaises, and in 1944 the Auxiliaires Féminines de l'Armée de Terre (AFAT).

51. Jeanne Bohec, *La plastiqueuse à bicyclette*, pp. 6–9, 14, 29, 40, 68–70.

52. Frenay, *The Night Will End*, pp. 295–97.

53. Bohec, *Plastiqueuse*, pp. 107, 111, 117, 121, 137.

54. Ibid., p. 237. Since the city of Paris now has a mayor, her title was changed to municipal officer.

55. Lise de Baissac Villameur, letter to author, May 30, 1977.

56. Ibid.; Irene Ward, *FANY Invicta*, pp. 215–16.

57. Villameur, letter.

58. Ibid. Like Jacqueline Nearne and Yvonne Cormeau, she was awarded the MBE.

59. Unless otherwise noted, the information about Pearl Witherington Cornioley was obtained in an interview in Paris, October 1976.

60. Southgate, interview.

61. Ibid.

62. Henri Cornioley, interview, Paris, October 1976.

63. Michel Mockers, *Maquis SS4*, p. 16.

64. Foot, *SOE*, pp. 381, 389.

65. Information from Pearl Cornioley.

66. Noguères, *Histoire*, 5:718.

67. He technically surrendered to American officers of a Jedburgh team, "his conscience horrified at the notion of surrendering to the French" maquis. De Gaulle, *Complete War Memoirs*, p. 696.

68. Mockers, *Maquis*, pp. 11, 15.

69. Noguères, *Histoire*, 4:670-71.

70. Unless otherwise noted, the information about Georgette Gérard is from an interview in Paris, October 1976, and from her *témoignage*, January 31, 1950, Archives CHG.

71. 200,000 Frenchmen served in the French First Army, which landed on the Riveria on August 15, 1944. This number expanded to 290,000 as the campaign continued. Vigneras, *Rearming the French*, p. 186.

72. Max Hastings, *Das Reich*, pp. 1, 169-75; John Keegan, *Six Armies in Normandy*, pp. 156, 336-37. Das Reich was responsible for the massacre of 642 people at Oradour sur Glane.

73. Pichard, letter to author, July 28, 1983.

IV AMERICAN WOMEN IN THE RESISTANCE

8 SIX WHO LOVED FRANCE

Like the women of other nationalities, American women who volunteered to help the Allied cause in France engaged in various tasks: gathering intelligence, serving as couriers, organizing sabotage and guerrilla actions, and aiding the escape of downed Allied airmen. They also faced the same hazards. Even before the U.S. entry into the war, they were targets of German suspicion, since few refrained from sympathizing with the Allies.

After Pearl Harbor they became enemy aliens. At first they had only to register once a week at the *mairie*, but in September 1942 the Germans began to intern all American women who still qualified as American citizens at Vittel, a spa in eastern France where British citizens were already being held. Only women over 65 and mothers of young children were exempt, though some internees were later released because of real or feigned illness.[1]

Among the American women who evaded the German net by hiding or fleeing to Britain, many joined the resistance. Of the six whose stories follow, all but one was interned, imprisoned, or deported to a concentration camp, and all received medals for their services.

Virginia Hall was born in Baltimore in 1906, the daughter of a prominent family who gave her the traditional start in life: enrollment at the Roland Park Country School and summer vacations at the family's farm in Parkton, Maryland, where her energetic nature and eagerness for new experiences led her to milk the cows and care for other farm animals, not dreaming how useful the work would be when she became a secret agent in France.[2]

By the time Virginia went to college in 1924, she showed signs of jumping over the traces and not following the traditional patterns of well-bred young ladies from Baltimore. She was strong-willed and, although a bright student, she was not happy with the rigid academic requirements as a freshman at Radcliffe or in her sophomore year at Barnard. She rebelled at the curriculum and persuaded her father to let her continue her studies in Europe. She took off for Paris and spent 1927–28 at the Ecole des Sciences Politiques before moving on to Vienna and graduating from the Konsular Akademie and the Schule der Orientalischer Sprachen. In 1929 she returned to the United States for one year of graduate study at George Washington University. Her goal was to be a foreign service officer, and while in Washington she took the written foreign service examinations. She passed with flying colors, but the diplomatic corps at that time rarely accepted a woman; despite her excellent qualifications and high test scores, Virginia was excluded. She was disappointed but undaunted, for she was determined to serve in American embassies abroad in some capacity. In 1931 she accepted assignment as a clerk in the American embassy in Warsaw, explaining to a friend, Elbridge Durbrow, who was a vice-consul there and later a U.S. ambassador, that since top officials of the State Department did not welcome women into the service, she would enter by the back door.[3] She was in Poland for two years before transferring to Izmir (formerly Smyrna), Turkey.

There a tragedy occurred. As she recounted the episode, she and some friends were snipe shooting outside the city. She had been carrying her gun pointed toward the ground, but it slipped from her grasp, and in grabbing for it she hit the trigger, discharging shot into her left foot. The wound became septic, and in order to save her life her leg had to be amputated below the knee. Undaunted, Virginia learned to walk with an artificial leg and continued to fulfull her duties in the consular service in Venice and Tallinn, Estonia. She enjoyed the excitement of serving abroad, but her work was not challenging; she was still a clerk.

In October 1939, after the war started, Virginia decided not to remain in Estonia, but to play an active role in defeating the Nazis. She felt that after 12 years in Europe, it was her battle as well as that of her friends. She resigned her post and went to England, where she tried to enlist in the British Auxiliary Territorial Service (ATS). The British, however, refused to accept American women, and she may have been rejected because of her physical handicap as well.

Undeterred, Virginia went to Paris, where in early 1940 she enlisted in the French army as an ambulance driver and served with an artillery regiment near Metz on the Western Front. When the French surrendered, she resolved not to give up the fight. Since the United States was not yet in the war, she went to London and resumed working for the Department of State, this time in the office of the military attaché at the embassy. She soon met officers of the British SOE who were looking for suitable recruits. They found Virginia impressive. Slim and handsome, with aristocratic features, she did not look as if she would suffer fools gladly or seek the limelight, but she was friendly and soft-spoken. By all accounts she also possessed the courage, energy, self-confidence, and cool judgment that the officers were looking for. In March 1941 they asked her to join F section and return to France as an agent.[4]

Known for its unorthodox policies, SOE set a high value on women as agents, and it was quickly evident that Virginia's qualifications far outweighed her physical limitations. She was five feet, seven inches, tall, walked with a long stride that concealed any limp, and was otherwise healthy. Her command of French, German, and Italian was a great asset; summer courses at the universities of Toulouse, Grenoble, and Strasbourg, supplementing her Paris studies, had made her fluent in French and knowledgeable about the country. She was consequently sent to France via Spain, with no further training than a political briefing. She was to pose as a reporter.

Virginia's credentials as a foreign correspondent were obtained with the help of a British official in New York. He had persuaded the owner of the *New York Post* to make her a string correspondent working out of Vichy; and in August 1941, after registering with the Vichy authorities, she began the double life of a foreign agent. No woman had ever been a resident SOE agent in France, but she quickly won the confidence and respect of her associates.

Virginia's first dispatch to the *Post* described the difficulties caused by the strict rationing of food, clothing, and fuel under the Pétain regime. Women could no longer buy cigarettes; men were limited to two packs every ten days. Vichy was crowded with government officials and employees, and even bathrooms were used as offices.[5]

For the sake of her real mission Virginia soon moved to Lyon, registered with the gendarmerie, and set up headquarters for F section in her apartment on the place Olier. Although she was to organize the Heckler network, in practice her activities were broader than that. Using the pseudonym Marie, she briefed SOE agents who came to Lyon, gave them advice about crossing the demarcation line, and distributed radio sets to clandestine operators who transmitted her intelligence reports to London. Virginia helped endangered agents and Allied soldiers make contact with the Pat O'Leary line so that they could escape to Spain. Three men left behind in the Dieppe raid owed their freedom to her and to a friendly policeman who had brought them to her apartment. She also traveled extensively as a liaison agent and kept in close touch with George Whittinghill, American vice-consul in Lyon.[6]

Virginia still found time to write for the *Post*, not only to protect her cover but also to awaken Americans to the plight of the French. Because of the food shortages, she wrote on October 16, 1941, countless people resorted to the black market or forged ration cards at the risk of imprisonment or even death. On November 24 she summarized the anti-Semitic laws that cruelly restricted the rights of Jews in business and the professions. Her last article, appearing on January 22, 1942, was filed from "Somewhere in France." Germany had now declared war on the United States, and even in unoccupied France her situation was precarious. From now on, she was an enemy alien.

By 1942 the Germans realized that resistance groups were forming almost everywhere in France. Now such groups would receive even more support from the Allies, and stronger measures against the movement were called for. As Virginia heard of more and more arrests, she increased her precautions, meeting her contacts only in certain bars and restaurants in Lyon, learning all she could about the Vichy methods of surveillance, and being careful not to trust strangers without credentials. Her discretion paid off, allowing her to continue her assigned work for 14 months despite the increased difficulty of communicating with agents in the field and with London.

Finally time ran out. The Allied invasion of North Africa, posing the threat of attacks across the Mediterranean, brought German troops pouring into unoccupied France in November 1942. With them, inevitably, were Gestapo agents who knew about Virginia's activities and offered her no choice but flight. Characteristically, she did not appeal to the overworked Pat line, but seized the initiative herself. She hired a Spanish guide and took two London-based Frenchmen and a Belgian army captain with her across the Pyrenees.

Difficult as the journey was in the cold November weather, an even more bitter trial lay ahead. None of the fugitives had entry papers for Spain, and they were immediately arrested by border police and thrown into jail at Figueras. Despite the onerous living conditions, Virginia kept her sense of humor and made friends with the women inmates, some of whom were prostitutes. When one of the women was released, she smuggled out a letter from Virginia and mailed it to the U.S. consulate in Barcelona. Thanks to the intervention of the consular officials, Virginia was released after six weeks in prison. She returned to England early in 1943.

Although Virginia was eager to continue her work in France and willing to risk arrest on a second mission, Maurice Buckmaster, head of F section, knew that the Gestapo might be looking for her and feared for her safety there. Her height and appearance attracted attention, and her accent might betray her if she were questioned. To her great disappointment, she was assigned to work for SOE in Madrid.

Whatever her feelings, Virginia accepted the decision, knowing that she could be valuable in the new post. Spain was alive with agents from Axis countries who were bent, among other things, on uncovering resistance leaders. For nearly a year, beginning in May 1943, she worked in Madrid. In January 1944, however, she was back in England, still determined to embark on another mission to France.

Preparations for D Day were going forward with all speed, and Virginia wanted to be part of the action. She knew that radio operators were vital and still scarce, and decided to study Morse code and qualify as an operator. This training, she reasoned, would not only help persuade SOE to send her back to France but would also make her more self-sufficient once she was there, since she could transmit her own reports promptly, and perhaps more accurately and safely. She believed that many radio operators were careless of security.

Meanwhile, Virginia decided to request a transfer to the Special Operations section of OSS, which was working in tandem with SOE as the Special Force Headquarters (SFHQ) under the supreme Allied commander. She talked with her OSS friend Capt. William Grell, former assistant general manager of the St. Regis Hotel in New York, about the possibility, and he arranged for her to be interviewed. Although she enjoyed working with the British, Virginia wanted her salary to go to the bank account of her mother, who was living at the farm in Maryland, and such a transaction was almost impossible under SOE. Another reason she wanted to move to OSS was that as an American, she would have the simulated rank and pay of an army officer and be insured for $10,000, with her mother as beneficiary. Virginia did not ask what her rank would be, but she was no doubt taken aback to discover later that despite her skills, experience, and important assignments, she was given only the rank of a second lieutenant.[7] Ironically, the papers for her government insurance were never processed.

Virginia's plan to return to France worked, and since there was not enough time to transfer to OSS, she was authorized by SOE to prepare to leave. The British would not have permitted her to return, however, if they had known that her real name and her role in her first mission had been communicated to the Germans late in 1943, in the course of a radio "game" supervised by the British Secret Service, SIS. Believing that Virginia would not return to France, SIS, which was controlling the transmitter of an arrested German agent in England, sometimes sent genuine, outdated information to the German intelligence service so that it would have confidence in the validity of the messages. Such communications would later be used to deceive the Germans about the location and timing of the D Day assaults.[8]

Unaware that the Germans knew a great deal about her, Virginia set off for France. Contrary to the oft-repeated story of her parachuting into the countryside with her artificial leg tucked under her arm, she crossed the Channel in a British motor torpedo boat on March 21, 1944, carrying her radio transmitter and accompanied by Peter Harratt of the Var escape line. They landed near Brest and took the train directly to Paris. There Virginia, now known to headquarters by the code name Diane, stayed overnight with an old and trusted friend, Madame Long.[9] Virginia's field name was Mlle Marcelle Montagne, a Parisian who supposedly was serving as a social worker with the Secours National in Vichy.[10]

Virginia's mission, code-named Saint by the British and Heckler by the Americans, was to organize sabotage and guerrilla groups, and supply them with equipment and funds. Her field of action was again central France, initially in the largely rural departments of Cher, Nièvre, and Creuse, where she spent four months. Virginia succeeded in organizing reception committees in Cher and supplied weapons to a maquis group. In Nièvre her second in command, Colonel Vassereau of the gendarmerie, who had been chief of protocol in Daladier's cabinet, had collected about 100 men whom he and Virginia divided into four maquis groups financed by her. In Nièvre she lived in the attic of a farmhouse whose owner, a 58-year-old widow, waited in the fields with her on the nights when they expected parachute drops and had to be constantly on guard against German patrols.[11]

During this time Virginia managed to blend into the scenery by using the cover of a milkmaid and making use of her childhood experience at the family farm. She dressed like a peasant and established herself in cottages, many times without electricity and water. She spent part of her time milking cows, taking them to pasture, and cooking farmers' meals over an open fire. In the remaining waking hours she carried on her real job: sending and receiving radio messages for SOE headquarters, and organizing committees of farmhands to receive parachute drops of weapons and supplies from England. Her cover had the added advantage that she could convey messages to local helpers while she delivered milk and produce from the farms where she worked. She also kept in touch with her assistants and traveled to Paris once a week.[12]

Virginia had arrived in France in March, more than two months before the Normandy invasion. Originally the Allies had planned to carry out simultaneous landings in the south of France. Aptly named Anvil, the southern attack was to set up a front against the Germans retreating from the northern front. Before D Day, however, Allied leaders decided to concentrate all the available assault troops and ships on establishing beachheads in Normandy.

By mid-July the beachheads, though won at great cost, were joined. Cherbourg was in Allied hands, and the assault was going forward despite bitter enemy resistance. The earlier planned landings in the south at last seemed feasible, and the operation — now called Dragoon — was scheduled for August 15. SOE's and OSS's work in the field, organizing and arming guerrilla groups and reporting their strength and successes to London headquarters, took on added value. If maquis groups could provide intelligence about local conditions, destroy enemy installations, and harass retreating German units, they would hasten the time when all of France would be free.

In June, on a preliminary visit to the Haute Loire sector, Virginia had furnished funds for forming a maquis group; when SOE transferred her to the area on July 14, her original contact had left and the others had quarreled over the money. Five Frenchmen controlled the various maquis groups of the department and showed no inclination to cooperate with her. Although they had been told that she was coming, the leader, known as Gévolde, had arranged no place where she could live or operate her radio.[13]

On her own Virginia chose as her headquarters Chambon-sur-Lignon, a Protestant town whose people had undertaken to hide Jewish children from deportation and probable death. Although her first hostess, Mme Leah Lebret, was trying to run the family farm and bring up two small children while her husband was a prisoner of war, she was willing to shelter Virginia until she found more convenient accommodations. These turned out to be a house and barn owned by the Salvation Army but no longer in use. It had three bedrooms where she could lodge incoming agents, and the barn proved ideal for receiving and transmitting radio messages.[14]

Gévolde and his cohorts continued to be antagonistic, although the prior agreement was that she would give them money and arms, and they would take SOE's orders from her. They remained, she reported, "jealous of their prerogatives and prestige," but the men serving under them were soon won over. She appointed one of these paymaster for the groups, supplied them with arms dropped by parachute, and was pleased to see that sabotage operations were continuing.

The Haute Loire in the Massif Central embraces an area of about 2,000 square miles, but the terrain is very broken, making it difficult both for pilots to pinpoint their drops and for reception committees to locate the weighty metal containers that went astray. The supplies included weapons, batteries, chargers, soap, tea, clothes, and money.[15] London also sent medical socks that Virginia needed to cushion her leg against the prosthesis; they were obtained by Vera Atkins from Queen Mary's Hospital in London.[16]

One of Virginia's most valued helpers was Lt. Raoul Le Boulicaud, known as Bob. He had a maquis group of 30 men to help mark the drop areas, handle the containers, and distribute the goods. His men also kept her radio batteries charged and provided her with security. Another Frenchman, a farmer in peacetime, placed his group of 150 saboteurs at her disposal.[17]

During her stay in Chambon, Virginia began to report to OSS, probably in July. Although OSS began paying her on April 1, 1944, and considered her to be one of its agents, she was unaware of the transfer from SOE before July. Her radio messages and reports were shared by the two agencies, and both the British and the Americans claimed her.[18]

As the maquis groups in the area grew and their activity intensified, more and more weapons were needed, and Virginia was constantly appealing for arms and other matériel, as well as for officers who could train volunteers. Near the end of July three planeloads of weapons arrived, which made it possible for her to arm her groups for a series of actions to harass and kill Germans. Virginia had no training in that kind of warfare, partly because of her physical handicap, but she found that with common sense she could plan and organize operations. The results were impressive. Four bridges were destroyed, a key railroad line was cut in several places, freight trains were derailed, and telephone lines were brought down. Nineteen members of the hated militia were taken prisoner. When the assault was launched along the Mediterranean coast, the maquis of the Haute Loire harassed the Germans who were withdrawing from Le Puy, its capital. The enemy convoy was trapped by blown bridges, and in the ensuing skirmish the maquis fighting along with FFI forces killed approximately 150 Germans and took 500 prisoners.[19]

Finally, on August 25, 1944—belatedly, in Virginia's opinion—she received a Jedburgh team code-named Jeremy, sent to her sector from Algiers. It was a standard team with two officers and a radio operator who were dropped in uniform to work with Virginia's maquis.[20] The chief officers were British Capt. G. M. Hallowes and French Capt. H. Fontcroise, accompanied by a British sergeant radio operator. At Virginia's request they organized and trained three battalions, totaling 1,500 men, whom she continued to finance and arm. For this purpose she received three American planeloads of munitions and supplies from Algiers.

During her last weeks in the Haute Loire, although the triumphant Allied advance from the south was heartening, Virginia's difficulties became more acute. Many of the maquis leaders were willing to forget political differences until France was free. Virginia herself, although she was not naive about the Communists, believed that all Frenchmen who were willing and able to fight should be trained and armed. This view accorded with her instructions, and she had therefore financed one FTP maquis group of 800 men, hoping it would unite with the FFI in a common endeavor. This did not happen, however, partly because of the refusal of Fontcroise to work with the FTP group, half of whom had no weapons. According to Captain Hallowes, the FTP also was unwilling to follow Allied orders:

> In the Haute Loire the FTP were in a minority. . . . We informed them that if they remained in the Haute Loire and took orders from SHAEF as transmitted through us we would continue to supply them; otherwise, we would give them nothing. They declined our offer and decided to obey only the FTP commands.[21]

Another difficulty for Virginia arose because Gévolde, now a self-appointed colonel and leader of the three battalions, and Fontcroise wanted to set out for the Belfort Gap without consulting the regional military delegate of de Gaulle's provisional government, whose function was to assure orderly cooperation between the guerrilla forces and regular units. When Virginia insisted that they obtain permission for taking 1,500 half-trained men toward a major battle zone, the French captain's response was "Who the hell are you to give me orders?" Fontcroise further gave Gévolde permission to take nearly 1 million francs, originally furnished by Virginia for expenses in the Haute Loire, to finance the foray. Virginia's frustration at this point is evident in one of her few complaints to headquarters: "You send people out ostensibly to work with me and for me," she wrote, "but you do not give me the necessary authority."[22]

Since the disposition of the three battalions had apparently been taken out of her hands, Virginia asked two officers who had been dropped by an American bomber on September 4 to train a Corps Franc consisting of 16 young men. She hoped to take them into Alsace, where she had many contacts, and direct as well as take part in a group effort to collect intelligence and to ambush scattered German troops. She, Lieutenant Bob, and the new officers traveled with the group as far east as Bourg, but by this time the professional armies had overtaken the guerrillas. Seven of Virginia's Corps Franc went straight into the Ninth Colonial Division of the French First Army, under General Jean de Lattre de Tassigny; the remaining nine joined the regular troops after visits with their families. Virginia asked Lieutenant Bob and another officer to turn over all the arms, munitions, and explosives of the Corps Franc to the Ninth Division as a farewell gift. Always meticulous about the money and equipment entrusted to her, she asked them to obtain a signed receipt to include in her report.[23]

Virginia's mission of six months was complete. With four officers who had been fellow workers she traveled to liberated Paris, and on September 26 she flew to London. The Germans had not yet surrendered, however, and before long she was back in France and at OSS headquarters in Caserta, Italy, preparing to lead a mission into Austria. A few days before she was to leave for her new assignment, the war ended, but for many years she continued to use her skills and experience as an agent, becoming one of the first women to be employed by the CIA, the successor to the OSS.

Like other agents, Virginia had not been able to communicate with her family or tell them what she was doing. Since she had told her mother that Captain Grell in London would be informed about her, Mrs. Hall wrote to him on April 12, 1944, asking about her daughter. Charlotte Norris, representing the commanding officer of the First Experimental Detachment (a cover title) responded to the letter on June 2:

> From a security point of view there is little I am permitted to tell you about your daughter's work. For this I am sorry; it may, however, be of some consolation to you to know that my own husband knows absolutely nothing of my work. . . . But this I can tell you: that your daughter is with the 1st Experimental Detachment of the United States Army; that she is doing an important and time-consuming job which has necessitated a transfer from London, and which will reduce her correspondence to a minimum. We here are in constant touch with your daughter, and are immediately informed of any change in her status. I shall be happy to communicate whatever news of her to you.

On August 23 Mrs. Norris answered another of Mrs. Hall's letters, assuring her that she must not worry: "Virginia is doing a spectacular, man-sized job, and her progress is rapid and sure. You have every reason to be proud of her." Finally, on September 23, the cheerful but premature news was sent that "it is not unreasonable to suppose that Virginia will soon be returning home."[24]

Virginia Hall was the only American woman to receive the Distinguished Service Cross for extraordinary heroism in World War II. William J. Donovan suggested to President Roosevelt that he make the presentation because Virginia was the first civilian woman to receive such an award. However, when Virginia arrived in Paris from Caserta on June 13, 1945, and learned that the War Department wanted to publicize her receipt of the medal, her reaction was predictable. In a cable from Paris, Donovan was informed that Miss Hall

> . . . feels very strongly that she should not receive any publicity or any announcement as to her award. Understand that at her request the British government made no publicity of an award [MBE] she received from them. She states that she is still operational and most anxious to get busy. Any publicity would preclude her from going on any operation.[25]

Instead, Donovan presented the award to Virginia in Washington on September 27. According to her superiors, "Continually at the risk of capture [she] directed warfare against enemy troops, installations and communications." Maj. Gerard Morel, operations officer for F section, wrote: "Her courage and physical endurance were of the highest order; . . . she never on any occasion allowed [her] physical disability to interfere in any way with her work."[26]

Virginia was also the only one of the six American women included in this chapter to serve in organized Allied groups from early 1940 to 1945. In this period she carried out two dangerous but successful missions to France, spending a total of 20 months under the noses of the Germans. Her record was unique but not surprising, since she demonstrated early in life that she would follow her own path regardless of obstacles, though these turned out to be graver than she could have imagined when she broke with tradition and left college for a career abroad.[27]

Another woman agent of SOE was Devereaux Rochester. Born in New York in 1917, she was the youngest of the six American women. A member of a wealthy family, she lived with her mother, stepfather, and older sister in Paris, and spent the summers at their house in Dinard, Brittany. Devereaux's somewhat haphazard education began with an English governess who introduced her to literature, languages, and history; but soon she was sent to the school of dance conducted by Isadora Duncan's sister Elizabeth in Salzburg. Much of her early training was designed chiefly to give Devereaux the accomplishments thought necessary for a girl of her social class, and soon she changed schools, going this time to the Convent of the Sacred Heart outside of Vienna.[28]

She was 11 years old before she settled into school life at Birklands, an exclusive institution at St. Albans, England, where she spent the years from 1928 to 1934. At this school she principally enjoyed golf, riding, and hunting, at which she excelled; she also loved to read. History interested her, but she confessed that she hated Latin and was banished from her algebra class.[29]

At 17, her formal education at an end, Devereaux found nothing she wanted to do. Members of her class generally thought that jobs were only for those who needed money or had outstanding talents. Dissatisfied and frustrated, she traveled a good deal. She accompanied her stepfather on a business trip to Berlin in 1937, a journey that may have influenced her later resolve to help defeat the Germans. She had been to Munich several times in earlier years, but this was her first visit to Nazi Germany. She found the atmosphere oppressive, and she especially disliked all the uniforms and regulations.[30]

When war did break out, Devereaux was 23 years old. A tall woman, just three inches short of six feet, she liked to wear impeccably tailored tweeds. Feeling the need to do her part, she volunteered to drive an ambulance and was accepted by the American Hospital in Paris. When the German armies approached the capital, Devereaux was assigned to work at a makeshift military hospital in Angoulême, 73 miles northeast of Bordeaux. Driving her own car, she took along her mother and a distant cousin who had also volunteered for nursing duty. Although the hospital proved to be a vacant school, they cared for some seriously wounded soldiers there.[31]

Devereaux hated the presence of the Germans in France; but Paris was her home, and after the armistice she returned with her mother to the capital. Their apartment in the 16th arrondissement was almost opposite the Hotel Majestic, which had been taken over by the Germans. In their own building every floor but theirs had been occupied by the enemy. Devereaux continued to work as an ambulance driver, not only transporting seriously ill patients but also using her vehicle to carry medical supplies, foodstuffs, and blankets to a prisoner of war camp near Compiègne, bitterly aware that in that town a jubilant Hitler had reenacted the armistice of 1918, this time with the Germans as victors.[32]

After Pearl Harbor, Devereaux's stepfather left for the United States. She and her mother moved into smaller quarters, glad to leave their German neighbors but fearful of their future as enemy aliens. They had good reason, for in the fall of 1942 Devereaux's mother was awakened at six o'clock in the morning by Germans pounding at the door. Devereaux happened to be in the country and so escaped for the time being, but her mother was taken to Vittel.[33]

Devereaux's first goal was to avoid being interned, and with the help of friends she crossed the demarcation line into southern France. But when the Germans occupied the entire country at the end of 1942, she decided to escape from France and offer her services to the British or the Free French.[34] In the company of a Red Cross worker named Bridget, who was half English, Devereaux reached Annemasse, a French town almost on the outskirts of Geneva that had become an anchor point for escape lines running in and out of Switzerland. The British MI 6 and MI 9 both had agents there, as did the American OSS. Marie Louise Dissard of the Françoise line and many others in the resistance also crossed the frontier there.

At Annemasse, after one day's rest, the two young women set off after dark with a guide who promised to lead them to the border but stopped well short of it and demanded his money, indicating that Switzerland was over the hill just ahead. Left to fend for themselves in the bitter cold, Devereaux and her companion had to make their way painfully over the barbed wire. The lights of Geneva were at last in sight and the Germans behind them; but now the Swiss border guards challenged them and took them in charge, to be questioned by the Swiss Secret Service.[35]

After a brief internment Devereaux was sent to the U.S. consulate in Geneva, but she had no papers proving she was an American citizen, and her stepfather did not respond to cables. Finally Allen W. Dulles, chief of OSS in Bern, sent for her and an official in his organization provided the needed identification. Dulles, impressed with her knowledge of languages and of conditions in France, believed she would make a useful courier for one of the French networks financed by his group. Although she would gladly have taken such a job and was given a new wardrobe that she badly needed, Devereaux was told on her return to Geneva that the work was considered too dangerous for her and someone else had been assigned to do it. Her disappointment was all the greater because her friend Bridget had obtained a job in the British consulate.[36]

Devereaux was determined to reach Britain, and through Bridget's intervention the British officials consented to hear her story. They immediately recognized her possible value to the Allied cause and made arrangements for the Swiss to let them send her back to France. From there she was to work her way west and attempt to reach England by way of Spain.

Devereaux's first destination, after a Swiss officer drove her to a point on the frontier where she could safely crawl through the barrier, was an isolated farm, Les Daines, in the mountains of the Haute Savoie about ten miles southwest of Geneva. The farm, abandoned by the owner, had been taken over by a couple, Clément and Laurence Blanc, devout Catholics and supporters of Pétain, who had become staunch members of the resistance. Clément had been an Alpine guide before the war and Laurence had managed their small hotel. Now they served as guides and occasional hosts for an escape line that extended from Switzerland across southern France to the Pyrenees.[37]

The shelter they offered was primitive. The farmhouse had a leaky roof, no electricity, and no plumbing. Sometimes, Devereaux recalled, she was awakened in the night by snow or rain on her face. Although she cheerfully endured the hardships, she knew it was time to go. Clément accompanied her on the train trip to Perpignan and arranged for a guide to escort her to Spain. For Devereaux, as for so many others, the journey across the mountains was grueling; but besides the bitter cold and blistered feet, she was feverish and in pain from what was later diagnosed as mumps. At last they found refuge in a farmhouse, and the final stage of her journey to Barcelona was by train, thanks to a safe-conduct pass issued by the U.S. consulate.[38]

When American officials refused to help her continue her journey to England and insisted that she return to the United States, Devereaux turned to the British. A major at their consulate greeted her warmly and at once put her to work translating French messages into English. This was only a temporary assignment. Soon she was in London, being interviewed by a colonel for training by SOE's F section. Once accepted, she was sent with six other young women to Wanborough Manor for basic training.[39]

According to her own later appraisal, Devereaux's training record was mixed. She found the psychological tests rather ridiculous. She could memorize Morse code easily but had difficulty transmitting the coded messages. She loved the obstacle course, where her strength and athletic ability were useful, but she did not like some of the field problems.[40]

Nevertheless, she passed muster and, along with two women and four men, was sent to Scotland for six weeks of commando training. Here Devereaux was in her element. The instruction fascinated her, and she later recalled:

> I thoroughly enjoyed weapon training and was a good shot. I enjoyed learning how to blow up trains using plastic explosives. I also enjoyed learning about the use of camouflage. But I did not like silent killing, nor did I like grabbing a rope and climbing up cliffs. I wasn't afraid, but it was terribly hard work.[41]

Tough and lean after the strenuous course, Devereaux faced only one more step in her training, the only one she feared: learning to parachute from a plane. But this too she took in stride. With her credentials complete, she was informed by SOE that she had been selected by Richard Heslop, one of their experienced agents, to be his courier in France.[42] Heslop would serve as chief of SOE's group, code-named Marksman, in the Ain and Haute Savoie departments in the mountains of eastern France. Working with a coleader, he was to coordinate various maquis groups in his assigned area.[43]

The group left England on October 18, 1943. Heslop, known as Xavier, traveled in the first Hudson plane. The second carried Devereaux, to be known as Elisabeth, and an American radio operator, Denis Johnson, known as

Paul, who had lived most of his life in France and whom OSS had reluctantly agreed to release to SOE.

Their arrival in France was more dramatic than Devereaux wished. Heslop's plane landed safely near Lons-le-Saunier, on a field lit only by flashlights, but the pilot of her plane missed the approach and one of the wings hit the church belfry. Fortunately the plane lurched only enough to shake up the passengers before landing.[44]

Devereaux soon discovered that the work of a secret agent was not as exciting as she had expected. As a courier she traveled some distance relaying messages between Heslop and the radio operator Paul. But days went by when she had no assignments and, in her own words, she was bored to death. She had passed the stiff training for commando operations, but Heslop was unwilling to let her engage in sabotage, perhaps because he had nearly 3,000 men in the maquis whom he could call on in mid-November 1943. Nevertheless, Devereaux felt that she could at least train the men, and years later she was still critical of Heslop's decision. "I don't know why he didn't let me help. He might have been old-fashioned and did not think I could really blow things up, but I could. My training records prove that."[45]

Sometimes Devereaux was able to relax at a cafe-restaurant called Ma Baraque in Annecy. Run by a woman whom everybody knew as Pépette, the cafe was one of Heslop's safehouses as well as a letter drop for couriers. There Devereaux was reasonably comfortable, with a room of her own and plenty of black market food and drink. She greatly admired Pépette, a middle-aged woman who had once been in business in Lyon but had been running the cafe since 1939. Although Pépette now suffered from Parkinson's disease, she was still a spirited woman who gave herself entirely to the resistance. She had housed members of a small maquis group, and they knew that they could come to her for food or help.[46]

Devereaux was proving to be an excellent courier. She had the endurance to travel long distances, and her familiarity with the country and her fluent French enabled her to avoid incidents. The good memory that helped her to learn languages and master the Morse code served her now. Heslop recalled that she was able to recite messages verbatim, a useful protection against discovery if she were stopped and searched. When a message was too long, he wrote it on a half-page, and she hid the paper in the sole of her stocking or in a compact. Heslop was very fond of Elisabeth, as he acknowledged later, because she seemed so English and was his only link with home.[47]

Like Virginia Hall's Heckler group, Marksman was not set up to help evaders, but on several occasions Devereaux had to pick up fugitives and check out escape routes for them. One of the most interesting of these was a Scot, 2d Lt. George Millar, who had been a reporter for the *Daily Express* in Paris. Captured by the Germans in the North African campaign, he had first been imprisoned in Italy and then transferred to Stalag VIIA in Moosburg, Bavaria. He had escaped after being a prisoner of war for 20 months. Like S. Sgt. Lee Carl Gordon, evacuated from Bonaparte Beach, Millar had received help from the French Arbeitskommando workers in the railroad yards at Munich. When he arrived at Pépette's cafe, he had already spent some time in Paris and Lyon seeking an escape line.

Here Heslop came to see him, and after checking his name, rank, serial number, and regiment with London, agreed that Millar could travel with five airmen who would soon arrive from Annemasse, prepared to escape through Spain.[48]

Devereaux was sent to Pépette's to help arrange the escape. The rumor had already spread in the village that a British officer was staying there, and the two moved on to the Blanc farm for safety. Devereaux thought it prudent to warn Millar about the family's disdain for some of the British, and she smoothed his way at the farmhouse.[49] He later escaped via Spain and returned to France as an SOE agent.

Toward the end of January 1944 and without the knowledge of Heslop, Devereaux undertook her only sabotage operation. The youthful leader of a small sabotage group was arrested before it could carry out a planned assignment, and the group asked her to lead them in an attempt to wreck three railroad engines in the yards at Annecy. Not without misgivings, she agreed to join the party. Devereaux herself attached the charges to the bearing rods and set the timers. Proving her capability as a saboteur, the explosions went off in quick succession as soon as the group was clear of the scene. She felt at last that her commando training had not been in vain.[50]

In March, Devereaux was stunned to learn that SOE headquarters had ordered her recall to London. Heslop pretended not to know the reason, but 26 years later he explained in his book that he had initiated the request. He hadn't the courage, he said, to sack her because she had worked very gallantly and given him every assistance. He admired what she had done and the dauntless way she had carried out her tasks. The trouble, in his opinion, was that she looked too British; he feared she would be caught by the police, endangering not only herself but many others.[51]

En route back to London, Devereaux stopped in Paris, where she was betrayed by a supposed friend and arrested by the Gestapo. Taken to Fresnes, she told her interrogators that she had gone into the country to escape internment and had been living off the sale of her jewelry. For three months they held her at Fresnes. Then, unable to shake her denial that she had any part in the resistance, they sent her to Vittel, where she was interned until the liberation in the fall of 1944. Although she missed her freedom at Vittel, it seemed like heaven compared with Fresnes.[52]

Despite the disappointing conclusion to her wartime career, the accomplishments of Devereaux Rochester as an agent do her credit. She stayed out of the hands of the Germans for almost four years, crossed the demarcation line repeatedly, and earned recognition from the French government, which awarded her the Croix de Guerre and the Legion of Honor. In her own appraisal it was all worthwhile.

Among the six American women discussed here, only Virginia Hall and Devereaux Rochester were officially appointed British agents in France. The remaining four devoted their efforts principally to helping soldiers and other fugitives evade capture by the Germans. Of these four, Virginia d'Albert Lake was probably the most important because of her service to the Comet line and in the organization of the camp for escaping airmen set up in the forest of Fréteval.

She was born Virginia Roush in 1910 in Dayton, Ohio. Her father was an army surgeon, but illness forced his early retirement; soon after World War I the family moved to St. Petersburg, Florida, where she grew up. After attending St. Petersburg Junior College, Virginia won a scholarship to Rollins College, where she graduated in 1935.

Intending to become a teacher, she enrolled in graduate courses at Columbia University in New York City. On May 1, 1937, in St. Petersburg, she married Philippe d'Albert Lake, a young French aristocrat whom she had met the previous year on a trip to France. With his French father and English mother he had grown up in Paris and at the family's chateau of Cancaval, near Dinard, Brittany, where they spent the summers. When he and Virginia met, he was working for the British P. and O. Steamship Company. After her marriage Virginia retained her American citizenship, little knowing that this decision would later help to save her life.[53]

A noncommissioned officer, Philippe was mobilized when Hitler seized the Sudetenland in Czechoslovakia, a French ally, and threatened to fight if he were opposed. When the British and French governments backed away from war, Philippe returned to Paris. A year later, Hitler invaded Poland, and Philippe was once more in uniform during the stalemate at the Maginot Line and the Germans' victorious sweep across France. When the French surrendered and he was demobilized, Virginia went to meet him and the young couple returned to Cancaval. To their dismay they found Germans occupying the chateau, but they were allowed to stay one night before returning to Paris. Relieved to be together again, they, like many others, thought the worst was over, though Philippe had lost his job with the British firm. But soon, as he recalled, the mood shifted:

> Little by little things changed as we faced the German occupation every day. We knew that England, which was supposed to be beaten in a few weeks, was continuing to fight and the German invasion of that country had been postponed. The British defense inspired us to do something against the Germans.[54]

In addition to their Paris apartment at 1 bis, rue Vaneau, not far from the Invalides, Philippe and Virginia had a secluded house in Nesles-la-Vallée, 24 miles northwest of Paris. There they came face to face with the resistance when the baker, Marcel Renard, asked them to talk to three American aviaators he was hiding in his shop. Virginia was almost as excited as the young men she joined at a festive dinner prepared by Madame Renard, for they were the first Americans she had seen for three years. This happy encounter persuaded Virginia and Philippe to seek a link with an escape line and work together in the resistance.

Their chance came in December 1943, when Philippe's cousin arranged a meeting with Jean de Blommaert, the Belgian who had worked for Comet and had escaped to England when that line suffered a series of arrests in Brussels. Now he was back in France for MI 9. His mission was to renew his contacts with Comet and organize another evacuation system with landing fields for Lysander planes and parachute operations. In this endeavor Philippe and Virginia both helped by sheltering de Blommaert's radio operator for a time in Nesles, seeking contacts with escape lines, and persuading their concierge in Paris to rent de Blommaert a studio apartment at the rear of their building.

De Blommaert was ordered back to London because the traitor Jacques Desoubrie was looking for him; Philippe continued as his second in command with Virginia as his all-round assistant. For security reasons the two moved into the studio apartment where the coming and going of strangers would be less conspicuous. Soon Philippe was asked by Micheline Dumon to take charge of the Paris sector of Comet, recently broken by arrests. With this link repaired, the line was able to resume operations from Brussels to Bayonne.[55]

Virginia's role was safehouse keeper and guide. She encountered the usual obstacles arising from the scarcity of food and fuel, and the caution one had constantly to observe. She ran a special risk, however, because although she spoke fluent French, her accent was unmistakably American. In addition, her identity papers showed she was born in the United States and married to a French citizen.[56]

Most of the aviators Virginia picked up came to the Gare du Nord in Paris, but it was easier to hide them at Nesles for the few days it generally took to arrange train tickets and guides to the Spanish border. It pleased her that the men made their own beds and helped in the kitchen. One taught her how to jitterbug. Attractive, with a friendly, informal manner, she was becoming a memorable hostess to the men she and Philippe sheltered and assisted in other ways. Among the 67 aviators she made to feel at home, Sgt. Thomas L. Yankus was especially delighted to find that she was born in his hometown of Dayton.[57] Lieutenant Jonathan Pearson, from the same crew, wrote that "she was . . . beautiful, brave and kind to us."[58] Second Lieutenant

Julius D. Miller admired her for staying with Philippe in France rather than returning to the United States.[59]

At that time the Paris sector of Comet had 29 members, 21 of whom were women serving not only as guides and hostesses but also as financial officers and liaison agents with other lines. Some kept shops where guides could meet and transfer airmen. Two were White Russians. Like some of the other Russian émigrés in the resistance, Vera Sakounienko had felt unwelcome in France but joined Comet to help her friends.[60] Another recruit was a fellow American and friend of Virginia, Jessie Ann Foley of St. Paul, Minnesota, who was married to a Frenchman, Paul Blanc. Mme Violet d'Albert Lake, Philippe's widowed mother, was also a member of the group.[61]

In April 1944, Philippe and Virginia embarked on a new venture to help Jean de Blommaert organize the camp in the forest of Fréteval, where the evaders could hide until they could be liberated by the Allied troops due to begin their landings in June. The forest, about seven miles south of Châteaudun in the department of Eure et Loir, was owned by the Marquis de Lévy de Mirepoix. In addition to the densely wooded forest, some six miles long and four and a half miles wide, the site included adjacent open spaces suitable for parachute drops.

Philippe now worked with de Blommaert and Lucien Boussa, another Belgian trained by MI 9, to set up the camp. Soon they were helped by the first group of aviators sheltering there. The Comet guides began escorting other evaders in groups from Paris to Châteaudun. There other helpers picked up the airmen and took them to neighboring farms until they could be accommodated at the camp. By D Day 30 men were at the forest, living in tents camouflaged with green leaves.[62]

The camp was largely supported by local women and men directed by Omer Jubault, military head of the Libération Nord movement in the Châteaudun region. Women kept local safehouses as well as being guides, couriers, and nurses for the injured. Some brought supplies to the camp and others permitted messages to be transmitted to England from their homes. Madame Jubault was her husband's courier, and their teenage daughter and son helped to maintain communications among the various helpers. The central storehouse for the camp was at the farm of a couple named Fouchard. Each day their young daughter drove a horse and cart through the woods, bringing fresh bread to the camp from the local bakery. Mme Henri Lefevre delivered charcoal, which would burn without smoke and thus help to conceal the cooking fires. Among those assisting Philippe and others in charge of the camp was Madame Desprès, a woman in her eighties, who converted her chateau on the edge of the forest into a hospital for five aviators.[63]

On D Day, Virginia and Philippe were in their apartment in Paris, unaware that they were about to be separated for nearly a year. With them were six aviators whom they planned to transfer to Fréteval along with five new arrivals from the Countess Bertranne d'Hespel's apartment. They were jubilant over the landings in Normandy but aware that their Paris apartment might now be even more unsafe. Virginia and Philippe decided it would be prudent for them also to hide in the camp. By this time, however, only one train was still running in that direction, and it went no nearer than Dourdan, leaving 54 miles for the party to cover on foot.[64]

The men had been confined indoors for weeks, some for months, and were in no shape to walk that far, especially in the ill-fitting shoes that were all their hosts could offer. Nevertheless, Philippe and Virginia could only hope that ten of them could at least reach Dourdan by train, along with their guides: Anne Marie Piguet, Michelle Fredon, and Anny Melisson. There it was planned that Philippe and Virginia, along with the eleventh aviator, would arrive by bicycle and meet them in a wood outside of town. The two groups met as scheduled. Moving out two or three at a time, the party began the long walk to Châteaudun. By this time it was raining, and soon many of the men were suffering from painful blisters.

With about 18 miles to go, some of the party could not continue; the only solution seemed to be for Virginia to cycle to Châteaudun and try to obtain a cart from members of the resistance there. Philippe gave her a list of helpers' names and addresses, and she carried more than 100,000 francs in her pocketbook. One of the guides, Michelle, would stay with seven of the airmen until she returned. Four others felt able to go on, and they would make their way to Châteaudun on foot in separate groups, guided by Philippe and the other Frenchwomen.

By the morning of June 12 Virginia had succeeded in her quest and had directed the driver of the cart to the rendezvous where Michelle and her charges were anxiously waiting. One was 2d Lt. Ted Krol, who had spent two months at Bertranne's apartment.[65] Six of the men hid in the back of the cart, and Michelle rode beside the driver. The seventh, Alfred Hickman, remembered by Virginia only as Al, would use the bicycle provided by the driver and cycle ahead with Virginia.

Within sight of Châteaudun three German security men riding in a black Citroën stopped Virginia and her companion. One, speaking perfect French, demanded their identity papers and questioned Virginia gruffly about her reason for being in this area when her home was in Paris. Suspicious of her accent when she told him she was in search of eggs and fresh produce, and having noted that her birthplace was in the United States, he soon discovered that Al was also an American. Next he examined Virginia's pocketbook, containing the bundle of francs and the list of names. By this time he was convinced that he had made a big catch indeed.

Nevertheless he returned Virginia's purse and its contents to her before hustling his captives into the car, and Virginia was able to tear up the list surreptitiously and hide the bits in her pocket. This somewhat relieved her fear of betraying the people in Châteaudun, but she was still anxious about Michelle and the 6 aviators, who had been traveling only about 30 yards behind. In fact, their driver had seen the Germans and stopped the cart in time for the airmen to climb out and disappear into the underbrush. The Germans paid no attention to Michelle and the driver. Only much later did Virginia learn that the six evaders were rescued by local resisters, and that Philippe and the remaining guides and airmen had reached safety.[66]

Virginia and Al were taken to the Gestapo headquarters in Châteaudun. For a few moments Virginia was left unguarded, and she quickly managed to retrieve the torn pieces of paper from her pocket and swallow them one by one. That night she and Al were in prison at Chartres, and the next day were taken to the rue des Saussaies in Paris for further interrogation before being driven to Fresnes. This was the last she saw of her companion, who, she learned later, had revealed nothing to the Germans.

She too held out. For seven weeks she was confined to cell number 431. Once a week she received a food parcel from the Red Cross that she shared with her cell mates. There were always two of them, and sometimes as many as five. Fresnes was notorious for its ill treatment of prisoners. For Virginia the terrible thing was the uncertainty about what was going to happen next: "When were you going to be questioned again and when were you going to be tortured?" Unlike many prisoners, however, she was treated civilly by her interrogator, Herr Geinser. The probable reason, she concluded, was that she was an American.

At Fresnes, Virginia might hope that Allied troops would soon drive the Germans out of Paris and she could rejoin Philippe. But on August 1 she was transferred to the prison at Romainville, on the eastern outskirts of Paris, which had become the staging point for deportation to Germany. Her one comfort lay in the assurance given her by the commandant, who had been in the United States before the war, that she and the other prisoners at Romainville would be freed now that the Allies were so near Paris. On August 15, however, when they could hear the Allied artillery west of Paris, Virginia followed the thousands of other women forced into filthy, crowded boxcars en route to an unknown destination. Her nightmare journey lasted 144 hours and ended, temporarily, at Ravensbrück.

Her experiences there and later, in concentration camps at Torgau and Koenigsberg, testify to the sufferings of the women in the resistance who were caught and deported by the Nazis. At all three camps Virginia was systematically starved and overworked by her SS overseers. The workdays were 12 hours long, and most of the jobs assigned to the women were physically exhausting: digging potatoes, filling swamps with sand, laying slabs of sod for airfields, pulling out stumps, and building roads. Like many of the others, Virginia was without warm clothes or work shoes, and suffered from the cold. The women slept in blocks fitted with bunks in tiers of three, with three women in each bunk. French and Russian prisoners were not permitted Red Cross packages. Always hungry, Virginia and the others talked continuously about food.

Two particular worries plagued many of the younger women. They had heard the rumors about the Nazis sterilizing undesirables to ensure the purity of the master race, and they did not want to be the victims of Nazi doctors. They also did not know why they had ceased to menstruate. Mary Lindell, the agent for MI 9 before her capture, was a nurse in the Ravensbrück infirmary and was among those who thought that the SS had put chemicals into their food to stop the menstrual cycle. It is now believed that vigorous exercise or a diet that severely reduces body fat can cause a drop in sex hormones and prevent ovulation.[67]

When she first arrived at Ravensbrück, Virginia had announced that she was a citizen of the United States.[68] Only two other American women were imprisoned at Ravensbrück at that time, one being the Swiss-born wife of the medical chief at the American Hospital in Paris; and to some extent they, as well as some British women, were at first spared the killing labor assigned to women from other countries. At Torgau, at least, Virginia was detailed to help prepare food along with two other Americans and four British women. She still worked 12 hours a day peeling potatoes, but it was vastly preferable to slaving in the munitions factory, as others at Torgau were forced to do.

Sometimes Virginia was able to shame a guard into a semblance of decency. At first she had kept her platinum wedding ring hidden, but by February 1945, when she was once more at Ravensbrück, she began to wear it openly because this slight gesture of independence bolstered her morale. One day the Polish block captain noticed the ring and demanded it. Her knuckles were too swollen from overwork and malnutrition to allow the ring to slip off, however, and when her tormentor persisted, Virginia shouted, "I am an American. Do you steal wedding rings from Americans too?" The response, so startling from a prisoner, apparently impressed the SS woman accompanying the block captain, and she allowed her to keep the ring.[69]

Meanwhile, Virginia's mother, hoping that her daughter's American citizenship might help matters, wrote to Secretary of State Cordell Hull, to see if Virginia might be exchanged for a German prisoner. Philippe, who had gone briefly to London after Virginia's arrest but was now back in liberated Paris, was working through French intelligence to find her exact location. Although Mrs. Roush received no definite word from Washington at first, a cable was sent by the State Department to the U.S. embassy in Bern, giving the date and place of Virginia's birth. A letter dated February 23, 1945, was sent to Mrs. Roush, notifying her that her daughter was at Ravensbrück and "all right."[70]

By early 1945 even the diehard SS officers in the concentration camps knew that defeat was in sight and were reacting in their own fashion. At

Koenigsberg the camp director had driven off, bag and baggage, to escape the approaching Russian troops. At Ravensbrück, in anticipation of the arrival of Allied forces, the SS began to improve the treatment of some women, including Virginia and General de Gaulle's niece Genevieve, who had been arrested with many of her colleagues in the Défense de la France organization in July 1943.[71]

Both women bore the marks of their ordeal. Genevieve de Gaulle was still thin, but her health had improved in the last five months. She had been transferred from a blockhouse to a private cell, where she had been given more food. Virginia had dropped to only 76 pounds from her normal weight of 126 by the time her release was drawing near. Her body was covered with the bites of lice and by open sores caused by the starvation diet.[72]

On February 25 the block captain called for the American woman who had been in Koenigsberg; Virginia was singled out from the others and given anti-vermin powder and a new outfit, including a pretty, warm coat. Four days later an SS woman asked her to confirm that she was Mrs. d'Albert Lake and to give the date and place of her birth. Satisfied of her identity, her captors told her she could soon leave the camp by train, probably to be taken to Liebenau, a Red Cross camp near Lake Constance, where American and British women were interned.[73]

On February 28, after three days of suspense, Virginia and Genevieve de Gaulle left the hated Ravensbrück camp accompanied by three SS guards. Although Liebenau was only about 425 miles from Ravensbrück, the journey took the party six days, probably because of the destruction to railroads by Allied bombing. At Ulm they had to walk ten miles through bombed streets to make train connections. Weak at the beginning, Virginia grew even weaker; but by sheer grit she kept from collapsing. Her release had come none too soon, she felt. "If I had spent one more week in Ravensbrück I would have died like my friends," she reported later. By contrast Liebenau was a paradise. Upon her arrival she was given the care she so desperately needed, and on April 21 she and the others interned there were liberated by French troops. On May 27 she arrived in Paris after an interval at a repatriation camp in Strasbourg. She was one of the lucky ones, for of her original group of 250 women at Koenigsberg, only 25 survived.[74]

Virginia d'Albert Lake is widely regarded as a heroine, especially by the airmen who were in the forest of Fréteval. Soon after her arrest they knew she was being held, and realized that if she broke under questioning, the Germans would send troops to capture them and destroy the camp. When no attack came, it was clear to all those in the camp that she and Al had withstood the questioning.

The men at the camp had not long to wait for the Allied troops to free them. On August 14 Airey Neave of MI 9 arrived at Fréteval from Le Mans, bringing with him a rescue team of British and Belgian SAS. They found 132 cheering evaders and resisters waiting to welcome them, including Americans, British, Canadians, Australians, New Zealanders, and South Africans. Twenty others had left the previous day to be picked up by American tanks or to celebrate in the villages.[75] Ironically, the men at Fréteval were rescued on the eve of Virginia's departure for Ravensbrück.

Medals do not always indicate the recipient's contribution to the struggle against the Germans, and countless courageous resisters received no medals. In Virginia's case her awards do demonstrate the esteem in which she was held by the French, British, Belgian, and American governments. From France she received the Croix de Guerre and the Medal of the Resistance; from Belgium, the Medal of King Leopold. Britain made her a member of the Order of the British Empire, and from her native country she received the Medal of Freedom with bronze palm. Rollins College, her alma mater, acknowledged her achievements by awarding her its Medal of Honor.

Two American women, Dorothy Tartière and Rosemary Maeght, made singularly valuable contributions to the Burgundy escape line. At the end of the war both were awarded the United States Medal of Freedom.

Dorothy Blackman Tartière worked for the Paris section of Burgundy from 1943 until the liberation of Paris. Her chief accomplishment lay in the food she raised for hard-pressed safehouse keepers. She was born in Kenosha, Wisconsin, in 1903 but grew up on a ranch in Mexico. Before the war she played in screen and stage productions under the name of Drue Leyton. In 1938 she married her second husband, Jacques Tartière, and from early 1939 she lived in France.

After the outbreak of the war, Dorothy worked as administrative assistant to Jean Fraysse, president of Paris Mondiale, the government propaganda shortwave radio station, while her husband served as a French liaison officer with the British army. After the French defeat he joined General de Gaulle's forces while Dorothy, who could have returned to the United States and continued her theatrical career, helped Fraysse in the resistance. She felt that "the real excitement and opportunity to help was in France."[76] She believed it was unsafe in Paris, however, and moved to the Villa l'Ecureuil in Barbizon, 32 miles south of the capital. Here she provided a safehouse for Fraysse and, with the help of her Alsatian maid, Nadine, grew vegetables and raised chickens and rabbits to supplement the meager rations of her friends in Paris.[77]

Dorothy wanted to do more for the cause after learning of the death of her husband, killed in June 1941 while fighting with the Free French in Syria. She would be in jeopardy if the Germans discovered that her husband had been fighting with the enemy, but at least she could grow more food without exciting suspicion. Although farming might have seemed an unlikely occupation for this dashing, blue-eyed actress, she knew she could draw on her ranching experience and was convinced that she could successfully cultivate a larger property. Jean Fraysse used his connections in London to obtain an eight-acre parcel of land in a secluded area close to her villa. The lease included a farmhouse that could be used to shelter evaders.[78]

After Pearl Harbor the Germans, ignorant of her underground activities, required only that Dorothy register once a week at the *mairie*, as other American women did. But in September 1942 the Gestapo took her to their headquarters in Melun, and from there she was sent to Vittel. More foresighted than some, she had persuaded Dr. Porcher, a French radiologist in Paris, to certify that she had cancer; and Dr. Jean Lévy, a prisoner of war serving as a doctor to the internees, supported this false diagnosis. After three months at Vittel, Dorothy was released to continue the allegedly necessary X-ray treatments.[79]

Back in Paris, she was disheartened to learn that her friend Jean Fraysse was missing, probably among those lost on a ship bound for North Africa. Her maid, Nadine, was still at the villa, however, and overjoyed to see her. The need to feign illness had sapped Dorothy's strength, but by the spring of 1943 she and Nadine had acquired farm machinery and planted fields of potatoes, sugar beets, corn, and carrots. Some of the harvest would feed the animals they were raising for slaughter; the rest would be made up into food parcels.

Dorothy took these twice a week to Paris, on the pretext of needing to see Dr. Porcher. Fortunately her interviewer at the SD headquarters at avenue Foch, where she had been ordered to report on her arrival from Vittel, was a sympathetic Austrian, and he had given her a pass to visit Paris at any time for treatment.[80]

In the summer of 1943 Dorothy's success in providing food to Paris friends led the leaders of Burgundy to enlist her help for their safehouse keepers. One of those who made her job easier was Sarah Watson, an American woman released from Vittel at the same time as Dorothy. Miss Watson, from Tennessee, was director of the Foyer International, a center for foreign students in Paris, and she owed her freedom to the hospitality she had shown to German and Japanese students before the war.[81] Now she volunteered to have her handyman meet Dorothy at the bus stop and bring the heavy sacks of food to the Foyer. From there they could be distributed to the safehouse keepers.

Many times Dorothy herself delivered food parcels to the homes sheltering evaders. American fliers remembered their visits with this vivacious actress who not only brought food but also eased the burden of living in hiding.[82] She was officially credited with providing food for 32 aviators, finding lodgings for several others, and sheltering at least 10 in her own villa, 5 of them Canadians.[83]

To the south, on the approaches to the Spanish border, Rosemary

Wright Maeght became a leader of the Pau sector of Burgundy. Because of its mild climate and scenic situation at the foot of the Pyrenees, Pau had long attracted Britons and Americans, and Rosemary's family was well established in the large Anglo-American colony there before the war. Now the town was one more stage on the journey Allied airmen were making to regain their bases after being forced down over France.

Rosemary had been born in Massachusetts in 1915 because her American father, a "gentleman writer" and polo player, and English mother had left Pau to spend the duration of World War I in the United States. Rosemary was brought up in a very genteel fashion hardly designed to prepare her for a future career in the resistance. She was tutored by a governess before attending Heathfield School in Ascot, England. Married in 1939, Rosemary and her husband, Pierre, lived in one of the two villas at Pau that her mother had inherited. In the second villa, across the street, Rosemary's mother lived with her other daughter and her Spanish son-in-law, who was vice-consul for the Franco government.[84]

Like countless others, Rosemary joined the resistance in answer to an appeal from a friend, Madame Rich, who in February 1941 was sheltering ten British soldiers in her basement and needed food and clothing for them. Rosemary willingly answered the appeal, but she and her friend wondered about what they should do with the men, since they could not possibly keep them in the basement for the duration of the war. Rosemary sought help in Marseille and eventually found a British intelligence agent who made arrangements for the men to be interned temporarily in Fort St. Hippolyte in Vichy France. She was dubious about this solution, but at that early date few in the resistance knew about an escape line into Spain.

Later Rosemary received 50,000 francs from an unknown diplomatic source in Spain to arrange for guides to take the men across the Pyrenees. In this way she assisted the Polish leader Gotha, chief of the Visigotha-Lorraine line, who was arrested in November 1943. She also agreed to take charge in Pau of affairs relating to the Kümmel line, organized by Lt. Patrick Hovelacque. He had been recruited by the British from BCRA, but he assured Rosemary that he would not discriminate against American aviators by giving priority to the escape of the British. Without commitment to any single organization, she helped 17 airmen, 2 of whom had been in Pau for 3 weeks.[85]

Rosemary's enlistment as an unpaid volunteer member of the Burgundy line occurred through Mme Jacqueline Cintrat, another friend. Madame Cintrat had begun helping fugitives by arranging for Jews to reach Spain, and she continued that work along with assignments from Burgundy. Sometimes her protégés traveled together. One airman, M. S. Thomas, crossed the mountains with a party of 16 Jewish refugees.[86]

With Jacqueline Cintrat and Etienne Lalou, Rosemary helped to organize the Pau sector of Burgundy, and the three became the chief representatives of the line.[87] It was risky work. Most of the men came by way of Toulouse, where the railroad station was so closely guarded that on one occasion six of the eight men arriving from Paris were picked up by the Gestapo.[88]

Later Rosemary ran the organization, now solidly established, with her good friend Jane Moy-Thomas, a British subject. Unlike Dorothy Tartière and other American and British nationals, neither woman was threatened with internment. In Rosemary's case the Germans may have assumed that she had acquired French citizenship when she married Pierre, though she had renewed her U.S. passport after the French surrender (but before Pearl Harbor).

Part of Rosemary's success in evading arrest was due to her caution. Like Virginia Hall, she avoided unnecessary risks and took pains to conceal incriminating papers and suspiciously large sums of money. One hiding place that she considered safe was her mother's villa, since her brother-in-law should have enjoyed diplomatic immunity as a vice-consul of neutral Spain. It was important to safeguard the money for the line, since mountain guides demanded about 10,000 francs for each man they led across the Pyrenees. Rosemary also had to pay the safehouse keepers for their expenses and sometimes for their subsistence as well. She later learned that the money came from Michael Creswell, the attaché in the British embassy at Madrid, who had worked with Andrée de Jongh. Even more important than the money Rosemary's mother hid was a list requested by Burgundy of the serial numbers, but not the names, of the evaders passing through the Pau sector. These numbers were checked with London as a precaution against spies infiltrating the line.

Until the Allied landings in the north and the threats of landings in the south, the Germans left the two villas unmolested. Then, however, they made an inexplicable raid on the villa where the Spanish vice-consul was living with his wife and Rosemary's mother. Germans armed with machine guns surrounded the house and ransacked the interior. Rosemary's mother managed to hide the money and list of numbers, then eluded the searchers by climbing onto the roof, where she was concealed from the intruders. Rosemary's villa was ignored, and she was able to find safety in the hills until Pau was liberated later in 1944. The list that her mother had kept safe contained the serial numbers of 90 men, a remarkable number that was later confirmed by aviators' reports.[89]

The help that Countess Roberta de Mauduit gave to Allied soldiers in her three months with the resistance cost her the terrible penalty of imprisonment and deportation. Her achievements and her sacrifice were recognized after the war by the United States government, which awarded her the Medal of Freedom with bronze palm.

One of seven children, Roberta Laurie was the daughter of a Scottish gardener who had emigrated to the United States. He and his wife were visiting relatives in Polwarth, Scotland, when Roberta was born on September

24, 1891, but she grew up in America and became a naturalized U.S. citizen at the same time as her father.[90] He prospered and became a well-known nurseryman; Roberta, who was called Betty, went to work as a telephone operator soon after graduating from high school in Mansfield, Massachusetts.[91]

She had initially set her sights on New York City, but by 1928 she had gone from New York to Paris. There, at the age of 37, she married Count Henri de Mauduit and went with him to Brittany, where they lived in the Château du Bourblanc, near Paimpol. Twelve years later, after the French surrender, he escaped to England to join de Gaulle's Free French forces.[92]

At first Betty respected her husband's wish and held aloof from the underground movement; but in 1943 a French intelligence agent attempting to reach England appealed to her for shelter, and for five weeks she kept him hidden until he could cross the Channel.

Unaware of the importance to British planners of this section of the Breton coast, Betty was living only about nine miles from Plouha, which later became the staging point for the Shelburne line's successful evacuations from Bonaparte Beach. At this time the situation for evaders was far different. The attempt to set up the Oaktree line had failed, leaving at least 90 airmen waiting in Brittany for an opportunity to regain their British bases.

Betty heard of their plight and was willing to help, but before promising to shelter four Americans, she asked to visit with them to assure herself that they were not Germans trying to entrap her. One of the men was 2d Lt. Robert E. Kylius, whose escape adventures had continued after he had been hidden by the mother superior of the convent in Malestroit. On their train journey to Paimpol they were joined by others, including Canadian and British fliers, bringing the number of her guests to 15. Most of these spent three weeks hidden under her roof. With the Channel crossings still postponed, they finally went on to Pau and took the mountain route into Spain with 32 other fugitives, an unusually large number.[93]

Other evaders soon found their way to the chateau, where the presence of a fellow American sometimes made them feel so secure that she had to warn them against raising their voices. She also drilled the men in picking up their belongings and going promptly to their hiding place on signal. The chateau, with its 40 rooms and many staircases, was ideal for concealing fugitives; but the safest refuge was in the large, hidden space below the attic floor. This space appeared when an ell was added to the main building and the level of the new ceiling was lower than that of the adjoining room. Betty took care that no one but her two maids knew that she was harboring evaders.[94]

By June 1943 she had safely housed 34 stranded aviators and was hiding 5 more from a bomber that had been shot down on a mission to Lorient. Word of her activities, however, had reached the man called Roger Le Légionnaire, betrayer of Louis Nouveau and Pat O'Leary, and early on the morning of June 12 the Germans arrived to search the chateau.[95] On this trip they found nothing, and Betty might have kept her freedom by flight; but she was unwilling to leave because other helpers would be taken hostage in her place. Loyalty to her commitment proved costly, for the Germans returned that evening. Their second search was also fruitless; Betty was taken away but promised that she would be released after questioning. Instead, it proved to be the beginning of her two-year imprisonment. The five Americans crept out of the chateau that evening and eventually reached Spain.[96]

During part of her imprisonment Betty de Mauduit, like Virginia d'Albert Lake, was at Ravensbrück, and she too made it known that she was an American citizen; but the announcement did not save her from hard labor. With a group of Frenchwomen she spent ten months loading artillery shells at a munitions factory near Leipzig. Their work day was 12 hours long. The nights as well as the days were made fearful by the knowledge that arms factories were prime targets for Allied bombers. Several months after France was free, Betty was finally liberated by the 69th Division of the United States First Army.[97]

The achievements of these six American women prove their courage and their love for France, though none of them gave up her United States citizenship. Because of their status as U.S. nationals they could have left France at any time before America's entry into the war. They chose to remain. Even after the Axis countries declared war on the United States and they risked internment, they stayed in France and helped its people resist the Germans with all the means at their command. Their actions paralleled those of innumerable Frenchwomen who adapted their peacetime pursuits to their country's cause, with the one difference that the country the American women served was not their own.

Notes

1. Between 1927 and 1945 American women marrying Frenchmen could acquire French citizenship only by a formal request before the ceremony. République Française, Commissariat aux Affaires Etrangères, Decree of August 10, 1927, Article 10.

2. Unless otherwise noted, information in this section was obtained directly from Virginia Hall in telephone conversations and letters to the author between 1977 and 1982.

3. Ambassador Eldridge Durbrow, telephone interview, Washington, D.C., October 1984.

4. Ibid. Mrs. Lorna H. Catling, niece of Virginia Hall, and Mrs. Glen M. Clarke, a friend, also provided the author with information.

5. Virginia Hall, *New York Post*, September 4, 1941.

6. M. R. D. Foot, *SOE in France*, p. 211; Benjamin Cowburn, *No Cloak, No Dagger*, p. 93; Philippe de Vomécourt, *Who Lived to See the Day*, p. 212.

7. Memorandums of March 18 and April 3, 1944, Central Intelligence Agency. Hereafter cited as CIA.

8. Foot, *SOE*, p. 372.

9. Virginia Hall, "Activity Report," September 30, 1944, OSS (SO), WE Section, p. 1, CIA.

10. Carte d'Identité no. 302, February 7, 1942, CIA.

11. Hall, "Activity Report," pp. 2–4.

12. Ibid., pp. 1, 3–4, 10.

13. Ibid., pp. 4–5.

14. Ibid.

15. Hall, telegram, May 26, 1944, CIA.

16. Vera Atkins, interview, London, October 1976.

17. Hall, "Activity Report," p. 5.

18. Hall, letters to author, June 8, 1979, and November 17, 1980; memorandum to Maj. Robert H. Alcorn, April 3, 1944, CIA.

19. Hall, "Activity Report," pp. 6, 10–12; memorandum, August 14, 1944, CIA.

20. OSS Aid to the French Resistance in World War II, "Report of Jedburgh Team Jeremy," no. 980, Marquat Memorial Library, Ft. Bragg, NC.

21. Hall, "Activity Report," pp. 6–7; G. M. Hallowes, "Report of Jedburgh Team Jeremy." According to Hallowes, he and Fontcroise obtained permission from the regional military delegate to take the battalions to the northeast. They never reached Belfort, and on September 15 they joined an FFI team 20 miles from Dijon.

22. Hall, "Activity Report," pp. 7–8.

23. Ibid.

24. Charlotte Norris to Barbara Virginia Hall (Mrs. E. L.), letters of June 2, August 23, and September 23, 1944, CIA.

25. OSS cable, Gamble to Director, June 13, 1945, CIA.

26. RG 407, Records of the Adjutant General's Office, AG 095, Hall, Virginia, 5 February 1945, "Recommendation for Award of Distinguished Service Cross to Miss Virginia Hall."

27. In 1950 Virginia Hall married Paul Goillot, who had also taken part in the resistance. They lived in Maryland, where she died in July 1982.

28. Devereaux was then known by her stepfather's name, Reynolds.

29. Devereaux Rochester, interview, East Quogue, NY, March 1977.

30. Ibid.

31. Devereaux Rochester, *Full Moon to France*, pp. 9–10.

32. Rochester, interview.

33. Ibid.

34. Ibid.

35. Rochester, *Full Moon*, pp. 64–69.

36. Rochester, interview.

37. George Millar, *Horned Pigeon*, p. 322; Millar, *Road to Resistance*, pp. 268–69.

38. Rochester, interview.

39. See ch. 7.

40. Rochester, interview.

41. Ibid.

42. Ibid.

43. Richard Heslop, *Xavier*, pp. 74, 77, 81–82.

44. Rochester, interview.

45. Ibid.

46. Ibid.

47. Heslop, *Xavier*, pp. 165–67.

48. For the story of Millar's imprisonment and escape, see his *Horned Pigeon*.

49. Rochester, interview.

50. Ibid.

51. Heslop, *Xavier*, pp. 223–25. Devereaux did not know why she was recalled.

52. Rochester, interview.

53. Unless otherwise noted, the information in this section is from an interview with Virginia d'Albert Lake at Pleurtuit, France, October 1976, and from her letters to the author.

54. Philippe d'Albert Lake, interview, Pleurtuit, France, October 1976.

55. RG 332, ETO, 7707 ECIC, MIS-X, French helpers, Philippe d'Albert Lake. "Report from Philippe d'Albert Lake," p. 1, dossier.

56. Virginia d'Albert Lake, "Autobiography," p. 8.

57. *Dayton Herald*, August 8, 1946, p. 36.

58. Lt. Jonathan Pearson, questionnaire, Air Forces Escape and Evasion Society (AFEES). Pearson saw Virginia and Philippe d'Albert Lake again in October 1980, when they were honored guests of the AFEES in Orlando, FL.

59. Julius D. Miller, questionnaire.

60. Vera Aisenberg, formerly Madame Sakounienko, interview, Gulfport, FL, December 1978.

61. Vera Sakounienko and Violet d'Albert Lake both received a certificate of appreciation signed by General Eisenhower. Philippe d'Albert Lake, "Comète, Paris, phase du 20 mai à 25 juin 1944," dossier.

62. *L'extraordinaire aventure de la forêt de Fréteval*, pp. 4–8.

63. Ibid., pp. 8, 11, 34; Baron Jean de Blommaert, interview, Orlando, FL, October 1980.

64. Virginia d'Albert Lake, "Autobiography," pp. 14–16.

65. Theodore J. Krol, E & E Report no. 1017.

66. "Report from Philippe d'Albert Lake," pp. 3–4.

67. Virginia d'Albert Lake, interview; Mary Lindell, interview. Women war prisoners in Russia also stopped menstruating. R. F. A. Dean, "Women War Captives in Russia," *British Medical Journal*, April 23, 1949.

68. This was true, since her marriage to Philippe did not automatically make her a French national and she had never formally petitioned for French citizenship.

69. Virginia d'Albert Lake, "Autobiography," pp. 78–79, 88, 93, 155.

70. This was the last information Mrs. Roush had before her death in April 1945. The cable sent to Bern was signed by Grew (acting). It was an isolated document found in RG 332, ETO, MIS, MIS-X Section.

71. Virginia d'Albert Lake, interview, and "Autobiography," p. 121. There was a possibility that Virginia, Genevieve, and others would be exchanged for German women prisoners via the Red Cross.

72. Virginia d'Albert Lake, interview.

73. Virginia d'Albert Lake, "Autobiography," pp. 158–61, 165.

74. Ibid., Epilogue, p. 4.

75. Airey Neave, *Saturday at MI 9*, pp. 237, 270–71; Heyward C. Spinks, tape account, August 1979.

76. Drue Tartière, *The House near Paris*, p. 25.

77. Drue Tartière, Paris mailer, 11-13-44, Willicombe, about Tartière, SHAEF field press censor, Tartière dossier.

78. Ibid.

79. Tartière, *House*, pp. 94–97.

80. Ibid., pp. 143–45.

81. T. Sgt. Carroll F. Harrup, E & E Report no. 333.

82. Irving J. Shwayder, letter to author, April 1977.

83. 201-F Tartière, February 5, 1945, dossier. She later married Geoffrey Parsons, correspondent for the *New York Herald Tribune*.

84. Unless otherwise noted, the information about Mrs. Maeght was obtained in an interview in Washington, D.C., February 1980.

85. Fred Boulle, "Interview with Rosemary Maeght," Pau, March 31, 1946, Maeght dossier; RG 332, ETO, MIS, MIS-X Section, Research Branch, histories and Related Records Pertaining to French Organizations and Networks, 1945–46, Patrick Hovelacque, "Statement Concerning His Work in Pau, Including His Connections with Rosemary Wright Maeght," Report of Kümmel Line. Histories of other escape lines have the same citation.

86. M. S. Thomas, E & E Report no. 760.

87. RG 332, ETO, MIS, MIS-X Section, Research Branch, Histories and Related Records Pertaining to French Organizations and Networks, 1945–46, "Réseau Burgundy," p. 29.

88. Shwayder, questionnaire and letter to author, May 19, 1977.

89. "Réseau Burgundy," p. 139.

90. The date of birth of Roberta Laurie was obtained from the General Register Office for Scotland, Edinburgh; letter to author, July 6, 1982.

91. *The Stoughton News* (Mass.), May 6, 1937. Information about Roberta's early life was obtained from her younger brother, William A. Laurie, in letters and a telephone conversation, 1982.

92. WAC Capt. Dorothy Smith, telephone interview, May 22, 1976. She interviewed the countess in 1945.

93. Smith, interview; 2d Lt. Robert E. Kylius, E & E Report no. 45.

94. T. Sgt. Claiborne W. Wilson, questionnaire, and letter to author, May 4, 1977; Smith, interview.

95. Neave, *Saturday*, p. 222.

96. The five Americans were 1st Lt. Louis L. Halton; T. Sgts. Herman L. Marshall and Glen Wells; and S. Sgts. Roy A. Martin and William C. Martin.

97. The countess died in 1975.

EPILOGUE

The large number of women who participated in the resistance and made significant contributions to its activities has never been generally recognized. Those whose achievements are detailed in this book are not the exceptional few, but examples of countless others who joined the struggle to defeat the Nazis. Besides the women whose names are known, there were thousands working in the shadows who will never be identified.

Escape lines, intelligence *réseaux*, clandestine newspapers, and paramilitary groups had different structures and primary functions. Women played important roles in all of them, although they were more prominent in some than in others. They not only served with courage and distinction in so-called traditional activities, but also broke new ground by becoming leaders of resistance units. Many whose exploits are described here demonstrated newfound talents as organizers and managers. The number who became chiefs and subchiefs is remarkable, since most had no previous experience in administration and strong prejudice still existed against women assuming positions of leadership, and married women taking up any career outside the home.

The work of escape lines engaged more women than any other resistance activity. They helped 5,000 Allied aviators, of whom 3,000 were American, to return to their bases in England; and they assisted an unknown number of Free French volunteers and Jewish refugees to escape from France. They did this by organizing and leading escape lines, and by serving as guides and safehouse keepers for those traveling along the routes. Women comprised, on average, 40 percent of the membership lists of the major escape lines discussed in this book.

Many women took the added risk of working with more than one escape line in the course of the war. Some helped two organizations simultaneously, although assisting two lines at the same time violated the security regulations of MI 9 and BCRA, which were designed to keep organizations separate from one another (*cloisonné*). Other women who survived the destruction of one organization by the Gestapo worked for two or three in succession. Some women in Brittany, for example, served first in the Pat O'Leary line, then in Oaktree, and finally in Shelburne. This was permitted, but not encouraged, and they were advised to keep a low profile.

Working in escape lines was especially dangerous. One reason was that the activities of the estimated 100,000 people who were involved were difficult to keep secret. Further, the great need for helpers meant that volunteers were often accepted on faith, and the lines were therefore very vulnerable to infiltration both by French traitors and by English-speaking Germans posing as Allied airmen. Countless men and women in escape organizations were arrested and deported, and many were shot or died in concentration camps.

About 50,000 resisters participated in intelligence *réseaux*, fewer than in escape lines. As a rule, intelligence *réseaux* were smaller than escape lines and more tightly knit. They did not have to run the risk of associating with evaders; they put Allied aviators in touch with an escape line as quickly as possible, in order to protect the security of the intelligence operations.

About 18 percent of the members of the intelligence *réseaux* discussed in this book were women. Some were chiefs and subchiefs of networks, managers of coding sections, radio operators, or specialized intelligence agents. Official records give credit to several women who passed through enemy lines, gathering tactical intelligence for the Allied armies. A few parachuted into France in 1944, as part of intelligence missions after training in Britain or Algiers.

All knew the risks they were running. The German counterintelligence services did their best to disrupt and destroy intelligence *réseaux* as well as escape lines. They ruthlessly tracked down members of organizations. For example, they carried out a series of assaults on the Cohors-Asturies *réseau*, which Suzanne Tony Robert served as secretary-general. They arrested one-third of its 992 registered agents, of whom 130 died. Some 200 of the agents were women, and they shared in the heavy price the *réseau* paid for its success. Ten were imprisoned in France and 54 were deported to concentration camps, where 16 of them died.[1]

Equally dangerous was the work of publishing clandestine newspapers. Some women filled key positions as editors and writers, while many others learned printing skills and devised innovative methods of secretly distributing thousands of copies of the papers. They were all vulnerable to arrest, particularly the printers and distributors, whose work had to be carried on partly in the open.

Few figures are available about the proportionate number of women who worked primarily with the clandestine press. Newspapers were often part of large resistance movements such as Combat and Franc Tireur, which engaged in many types of resistance, including sabotage and guerrilla operations. For example, 10 percent of the official list of members of Franc Tireur were women, but as the historian of the movement has pointed out:

> Numerous girls and young women were in Franc Tireur, but after the liberation many did not legalize their adherence to the movement. There is hence little official trace of their actions.[2]

These women cannot be identified because at war's end they did not apply for cards showing them to be a *combattant volontaire de la résistance*. Some were discouraged by the registration requirements, but an equally important deterrent was that many had been taught modesty as a feminine virtue, and did not seek recognition and medals.[3]

Women also worked in sabotage and combat units such as Groupes Francs and the maquis, and they too have been difficult to trace. They blazed new trails as couriers, liaison agents, doctors, and nurses. Often they stepped forward to assume the unusual responsibilities of radio operators, sabotage and weapons instructors, organizers, and chiefs. Some were saboteurs and fighters. For the first time the British and French, through SOE and BCRA, trained women as special agents to work with these paramilitary groups. Many others picked up the needed skills in the field. The women in these groups faced cruel reprisals when captured by the Nazis. For example, 11 SOE agents dispatched to France were imprisoned, harshly treated, often chained, and executed. Another died in Bergen-Belsen.[4] Many in all branches of the resistance were arrested and deported, and the posthumous honors accorded to some are eloquent testimony to their loyalty and courage.

The divisions between the various fields of the resistance were not rigid, and during the course of the war women and men were sometimes active in more than one. A woman might be a safehouse keeper for an escape line and permit weapons for the maquis to be stored in her barn. When not busy with airmen, another woman might keep track of German troop trains. Mme Suzanne Tony Robert, the secretary-general of the intelligence *réseau* Cohors-Asturies, set up an escape route for fugitives to Spain and kept in touch with the Armée Secrète de Libération Nord. Marie Thérèse Le Calvez of the Shelburne beach party was not only a guide but also a courier of messages for other groups, including the maquis. Micheline Blum-Picard served Libération Sud as a courier before she became a nurse for an FTP battalion near Montluçon. Many resisters were people of all trades (*gens à tout faire*) and did whatever was needed.

Books have been written about a few heroines of the resistance, and the deeds of some of them are included in this book; but many received no recognition. All too often the women safehouse keepers who welcomed evaders into their houses, knowing that the strangers might prove to be tools of the Gestapo, or who moved about on intelligence or sabotage missions, where they might be ambushed by the Germans, resumed ordinary life without any reward but the knowledge that France was once more free.

For most of them, however, life was never quite the same. The humiliation of France's defeat colored their attitudes in many ways. Bitterness lingered toward neighbors who had profited from the black market. In many happy instances, however, the brief but intense comradeship forged with American, British, or Canadian airmen they had helped to escape was renewed through correspondence and visits after the war. The American Air Forces Escape and Evasion Society, as well as the Royal Air Forces Escaping Society and the Canadian Branch, still sponsor visits of helpers to their respective countries; and many of their members returned to France in 1984 to celebrate the 40th anniversary of D Day.

On a larger scale, the achievements of women in the resistance could hardly fail to affect their status. They had proved themselves competent at countless jobs ordinarily assigned to men, and many had shown exceptional ability as leaders and organizers. They had certainly earned the right to be full-fledged citizens of the republic. The test of their acceptance in that role would be their receiving the long-withheld right to vote, a right that in most countries is fundamental to citizenship.

Some Frenchwomen had expected to receive the vote after World War I, as women in 12 other countries had done. They had replaced their husbands in factories and offices, and had assumed the sole responsibilities for families. However, although the Chamber of Deputies voted 344 to 97 to extend the vote to women shortly after the German surrender, the Senate failed to take action for more than three years and finally voted the measure down. Several more times the Chamber passed similar legislation, only to have it ignored by the Senate. In 1936, after all but one deputy voted to enfranchise women, Louise Weiss, who became the editor of a clandestine newspaper during the German occupation, organized a mass demonstration of women to force the Senate to debate the issue. It failed to move the Senate, however, because the Left feared that the conservative clergy would control the vote of the churchgoing women, and the Right was afraid that enfranchised women might be freethinkers and support the Left.[5]

The long struggle for the franchise ended in April 1944, while the resistance was in full swing. General de Gaulle, as president of the French Committee of National Liberation in Algiers, endorsed the vote for women. In March the Consultative Assembly, acting with the support of the Communists and Socialists as well as of Gaullists, voted 51 to 16 for the principle of extending the vote to women.[6] De Gaulle then issued the Ordinance of April 21, 1944, which finally enfranchised the women of France.

Until elections could take place after the liberation, the de Gaulle government recommended that women and men of the resistance be appointed to municipal councils in the liberated parts of France. By the end of September 1944, more than 100 women were members of municipal councils in the Paris area; several of them, such as Marie Claire Scamaroni, were named adjunct mayors.[7] Women voted for the first time in the municipal elections of April 1945, and a few months later in the national elections for the members of the Constituent Assembly. Their right to vote was included in the constitution of the Fourth Republic of 1946.[8]

Did women receive the vote because of their courage and contributions to the resistance? The evidence indicates that their participation was a major factor. In World War I women had assumed economic and social responsibilities, but during World War II they had done even more. They had defied the Germans occupying their towns and cities, and many had paid the terrible price of imprisonment, torture, and death. As Madame Scamaroni, a supporter of General de Gaulle, pointed out, the women had been tested, and they had proven their strength in the resistance. At the same time their political consciousness had been raised.[9] Marie Madeleine Fourcade, Paule Letty-Mouroux, Nicole de Hautecloque, and many others mentioned in this book felt strongly that they should have a voice in the future of the country they had served so courageously.

Men also agreed. René Cerf, a former editor of *Combat* and a member of the Consultative Assembly in Algiers, believed that women had given witness to their patriotism by assuming their duties "in the night of the occupation equal to men." Without their participation in the resistance, he added, the Assembly would not have voted "equality of rights."[10] Fernand Grenier, another member of the Consultative Assembly and a Communist leader, said, "It was the participation of so many French women in the sacred struggle against the invader which was decisive" in the Assembly action.[11]

With the right to vote, French women at last took their place alongside the women of other industrialized countries.[12] Not only did French women vote but many were elected to public offices, including municipal and departmental posts and seats in the National Assembly and the Senate. More women served in French cabinets. Due largely to their record in the resistance and their enfranchisement, they started to gain political power in France. It was a new beginning.

Notes

1. Marie Granet, *Cohors-Asturies*, pp. 98–99; Granet, letter to author, July 12, 1974.

2. Dominique Veillon, *Le Franc Tireur*, p. 256.

3. For information about the number of women registered in the department of Ille et Vilaine, see Jacqueline Sainclivier, "Sociologie de la résistance," *Revue d'histoire de la deuxième guerre mondiale*, January 1980.

4. M. R. D. Foot, *SOE in France*, pp. 465–69.

5. Marie Thérèse Renard, *La participation des femmes à la vie civique*, pp. 19–23.

6. Nine members and the presiding officer abstained.

7. Renard, *Participation*, pp. 23–24.

8. Ibid.

9. Marie Claire Scamaroni, interview, Paris, June 1974. Her brother, Fred Scamaroni, had died in the struggle to liberate Corsica.

10. René Cerf [Ferrière], *Chemin clandestin*, p. 189. French women received after World War II what British and American women received after World War I without having had to become heroines and martyrs.

11. *Les femmes dans la résistance*, p. 261–62.

12. Switzerland was the only Western country to deny women the right to vote in national elections after World War II. The right was granted in 1971.

ABBREVIATIONS

AFHQ	Allied Forces Headquarters
AS	Armée Secrète
ATS	Auxiliary Territorial Service
BCRA	Bureau Central de Renseignements et d'Action
BBC	British Broadcasting Corporation
BOA	Bureau d'Opérations Aériennes
BRAL	Bureau de Recherches et d'Action à Londres
CAF	Corps Auxiliaire Féminin
CAVF	Corps Auxiliaire Volontaire Féminin
CDL	Comité Departemental de Libération
CFLN	Comité Français de la Libération Nationale
CHG	Comité d'Histoire de la Deuxième Guerre Mondiale
CND	Confrérie de Notre Dame
CNR	Conseil National de la Résistance
COSOR	Comité des Oeuvres Sociales de la Résistance
DF	SOE escape section
DGER	Direction Générale d'Etudes et Recherches
DGSS	Direction Générale des Services Spéciaux
DMR	Délégué Militaire Régional
E & E	Escape and Evasion
ETO	European Theater of Operations
F	SOE independent French section
FANY	First Aid Nursing Yeomanry
FFI	Forces Françaises de l'Intérieur
FFL	Forces Françaises Libres
FN	Front National
FTP	Francs Tireurs et Partisans
GESTAPO	Geheime Staatspolizei
GFP	Geheime Feldpolizei
GF	Groupes Francs
MGB	motor gunboat
MI 6	Military Intelligence 6
MI 9	Military Intelligence 9
MLN	Mouvement de Libération Nationale

MTB	motor torpedo boat
MUR	Movements Unis de Résistance
NAP	Noyautage des Administrations Publiques
OCM	Organisation Civile et Militaire
ORA	Organisation de Résistance de l'Armée
OSS	Office of Strategic Services
OVRA	Organizzazione di Vigilanza e Repressione dell'Antifascismo
PC (F)	Parti Communiste (Français)
PTT	Postes, Télégraphes, Téléphones
RF	SOE Gaullist section
SAP	Service d'Atterrisages et Parachutages
SAS	Special Air Service
SD	Sicherheitsdienst
SFHQ	Special Force Headquarters
SHAEF	Supreme Headquarters, Allied Expeditionary Force
SIS	Secret Intelligence Service
SNCF	Société Nationale des Chemins de Fer Français
SO	Special Operations
SOE	Special Operations Executive
SPOC	Special Projects Operations Center
SR	Service de Renseignements
SS	Schutzstaffel
STO	Service du Travail Obligatoire
UFF	Union des Femmes Françaises
WAC	Women's Army Corps
WAAF	Women's Auxiliary Air Force

GUIDE TO FREQUENTLY
CITED SOURCES

The sources are cited in full here, and abbreviated and reduced to a minimum in notes.

Record Group 332, Records of U.S. Theaters of War, World War II, European Theater of Operations, Military Intelligence Service, MIS-X Section, Research Branch, Histories and Related Records Pertaining to French Organizations and Networks, 1945–46, Washington National Records Center (WRNC), Suitland, MD.

Record Group 332, Records of U.S. Theaters of War, World War II, European Theater of Operations, 7707 European Command Intelligence Center (ECIC), MIS-X, French helpers, WRNC. These dossiers, which sometimes contain citations for the Medal of Freedom, are arranged alphabetically by name and are often referred to in the notes simply as dossiers.

Record Group 332, European Theater of Operations, Adjutant General Section, correspondence regarding Medal of Freedom awards, 1945–46. This records series, arranged alphabetically, includes the entire European Theater of Operations.

The Medal of Freedom was authorized by Executive Order 9586, July 6, 1945. Congress established the medal in four degrees: gold, silver, bronze, and basic. It was to be awarded to U.S. civilians serving outside the continental United States and to foreign civilians for meritorious acts or services on or after December 7, 1941, that aided the United States in the prosecution of the war or furthered the interests of any nation allied or associated with the U.S. The names of the French recipients of the Medal of Freedom are in RG 332, ETO, MIS, MIS-X Detachment, French Office, "France Master List, Medal of Freedom Cases," grades I through IV, June 8, 1948. The names of Belgian recipients are in RG 420, "Belgian Master List, Medal of Freedom Cases," grades I through IV, A48-184.

With some exceptions, Escape and Evasion reports are referred to in the notes only by report numbers. Full citations follow, but the most commonly used were the Annotated (Typed) Narrative Sections.

Record Group 332, European Theater of Operations, Military Intelligence Service, MIS-X Section, Narrative Sections (Appendix Cs) of E & E Reports of American Airmen, 1942–45. These are the "raw" reports.

Record Group 332, European Theater of Operations, Military Intelligence Service, MIS-X Section, Annotated (Typed) Narrative Sections (Appendix Cs) of E & E Reports of American Airmen.

Record Group 332, European Theater of Operations, Military Intelligence Service, MIS-X Section, IS9 (WEA), E & E Reports, 1943–45.

Témoignages were statements that resisters made in interviews conducted under the auspices of the Comité d'Histoire de la Deuxième Guerre Mondiale in Paris. They are usually cited as *témoignages*, but sometimes CHG is added, the abbreviation for the Comité d'Histoire. They are now in the Archives Nationales.

In February 1943 the Free French created the Medal of the Resistance with two grades: the basic medal and the medal with rosette. Because of wartime conditions, the use of pseudonyms, and the death of many resisters on the field of honor, verification of their achievements was impossible, and therefore they did not receive the medal. The names and often the birthplaces and birth dates of those who received the award are listed in the Association Nationale des Médaillés de la Résistance Française, *Annuaire des médaillés de la résistance française*. Since the citation for the medal is always the same, it is not given in the notes.

BIBLIOGRAPHY

The bibliography is limited to works cited in the text plus those that provide background information about the various aspects of the resistance.

Unpublished Documents

Archives of the Comité d'Histoire de la Deuxième Guerre Mondiale, Paris.
These documents were transferred to the Archives Nationales after the Comité went out of existence in 1980.
Témoignages or statements of former resisters.
Biographical files of "héros de la résistance."

Bibliothèque Marguerite Durand
"Femmes dans la résistance" file, 940.4 RES.

Bibliothèque Nationale
Collection of clandestine newspapers.

National Archives, Washington National Records Center, Suitland, MD
RG 331, Allied Forces Headquarters (AFHQ) Records.
RG 332, Records of U.S. Theaters of War, World War II, European Theater of Operations, Military Intelligence Service, MIS-X Section. For details about the records series used in RG 332 see Guide to Frequently Cited Sources.

National Archives, Washington, D.C.
RG 18, Army Air Forces.
RG 165, American, British and Canadian files.
RG 218, Joint Chiefs of Staff/Combined Chiefs of Staff.
RG 226, Records of OSS.
RG 242, Collection of captured records (mostly German).
RG 407, Records of the Adjutant General's Office.

Central Intelligence Agency
Declassified documents about three deceased OSS women and their missions in France, nine OSS cross-Pyrenees chains, one from North Africa, and one Jedburgh team mission.

Department of the Army, Chief of Military History and Center of Military History, Washington, D.C.

French Resistance Unit, Historical Section, European Theater of Operations, U.S. Army, "Participation of the French Force of the Interior in the Liberation of France."
Staff Support Branch, "Women in Combat and as Military Leaders: A Survey," March 1, 1978.

Ellen Clarke Bertrand Library, Bucknell University, Lewisburg, PA
Musée de l'Homme Collection.

George C. Marshall Library, Lexington, VA
Francis Pickens Miller Collection.

Albert F. Simpson Historical Research Center, USAF, Maxwell Air Force Base, AL
"Heavy Bombers Dispatched and Missing 1944-45."
Escape and Evasion reports of about 2,000 British soldiers are there.

Air Forces Escape and Evasion Society
132 questionnaires of members who escaped or evaded from France.

Albert Lake, Virginia d'. "Autobiography." 1945.

Auvert, Dr. Bertranne. "Mémoires 1940-45." February 1979.

Bourdonnaye, Countess Elisabeth de la. "Souvenirs de Madame Elisabeth de la Panouse de la Bourdonnaye." 1946.

Bradley, John J. "Diary." 1945.

French Press and Information Service. "French Women in the War." 2 vols. New York: 1944.

Mainguy, Joseph. "Le réseau d'évasion Shelburn, plage Bonaparte." Plouha, September 1966.

Patton, Ralph K. "Notes on My Evasion." 1965.

Woodhouse, Kenneth. "Escape Account." 1973.

Interviews

France

Philippe d'Albert Lake
Virginia d'Albert Lake
Leslie Atkinson
Jean Badaire
Madeleine Barot*
Anne Marie Bauer

Jacqueline Bernard
Georges and Suzanne Bidault
Henrietta Bidouze
Madeleine Braun
Georges Broussine
Genevieve Camus

---

*Taped interview with my research assistant, Constance Greenbaum.

Marguerite Claeys
Henri and Pearl Cornioley
Josette Dumeix*
Yvette Farnoux
Marie Madeleine Fourcade
Henri and Chilina Frenay
Georgette Gérard
Marie Granet
Nicole de Hautecloque
Simone Lahay
Andrée Le Tac
Paule Letty-Mouroux
Mary Lindell
Irene de Lipkowski
André Manuel
Madeleine Marzin*

Cletta Mayer
Jacqueline Pardon
Gabrielle Buffet Picabia*
Genevieve de Poulpiquet
Gilbert Renault*
Suzanne Tony Robert
Jacqueline de Romilly
Madeleine Sarda de Caumont
Marie Claire Scamaroni
Maurice Southgate
Elisabeth Terrenoire
Marie Claude Vaillant-Couturier
Denise Vernay
Hélène Viannay
John White

United States

Hélène Deschamps Adams
Vera Sakounienko Aisenburg
Leo Arlin
Marguerite Petitjean Bassett
Jean de Blommaert
Martin Blumenson
Ann Willets Boyd
Anne Brusselmans
Marie Tréhiou Cosse
Paulette Declercq
Lucien Dumais
Elbridge Durbrow**
Mary Eddy Furman
Robert Grimes**
Anita Lemonnier Hartman
Dorothy Smith Hentic**
Henry B. Hyde**
Jacqueline Bordelet Kelley**

Paul Kenney
François Kerambrun
Annie Kriegel
Raymond Labrosse
Jacques Le Grelle**
Rosemary Wright Maeght
James S. Munday
Gabriel Nahas
Jacqueline Nearne
Jean François Nothomb
Josephine and Marcel Pasco
Ralph K. Patton
Jonathan Pearson
Devereaux Rochester
Richard M. Smith
Heyward C. Spinks
William H. Spinning
John Weidner

Belgium

Andrée Dumon Antoine
Elvire de Greef
Bernadette Greindl
Marie Eugénie Jadoul

Simone Lamquin
Yvonne Lapeyre
Marcelle Lietard Deleu
Micheline Dumon Ugeux

---

*Taped interview with my research assistant, Constance Greenbaum.
**Telephone interview.

England

Vera Atkins	Donald Darling
Mireille Best	M. R. D. Foot
Maurice Buckmaster	James M. Langley
Yvonne Cormeau	Peggy Van Lier Langley

Correspondents Who Sent the Author Extensive Information

Mireille Albrecht	Pauline Jones
Lucie Aubrac	Victor Le Calvez
Bertranne Auvert	Yvonne Le Four
Madeleine Baudoin	Anny Lévy [Latour]
Christiane Beaujolin	Joseph Persico
Kenneth Cohen	Michel Pichard
Madeleine Devlin	Alfred Satterthwaite
Donald E. Emerson	John Slonaker
Arthur L. Funk	Lise de Baissac Villameur
Génia Deschamps Gemahling	George Whittinghill
Louis Genevois	Kenneth Woodhouse
Micheline Glover	

Published Documents

Assemblée Consultative Provisoire. *Débats, Alger puis Paris, 4 novembre 1943-1 août/ 20 octobre 1945*. Algiers and Paris: Imprimerie officiel.

Granet, Marie, ed. *Le journal "Défense de la France."* Paris: Presses Universitaires de France, 1961.

Journal officiel de la République française, September 1, 1939–January 3, 1941, September 1944–May 14, 1945. Paris: Direction des Journaux officiels.

Journal officiel de l'état français, January 4, 1941–August 1944. Vichy: Imprimerie des Journaux officiels.

Noguères, Louis. *Le véritable procès du maréchal Pétain*. Paris: Fayard, 1955.

Pétain, Henri Philippe. *Actes et écrits*. Edited by Jacques Isorni. Paris: Flammarion, 1974.

Red Cross, International Committee. *Documents Relating to the Work of the Red Cross for the Benefit of Civilian Detainees in German Concentration Camps Between 1939 and 1945*. Geneva: International Committee of the Red Cross, 1975.

Books

Amicale de Ravensbrück. *Les françaises à Ravensbrück.* Paris: Denoël/Gonthier, 1971.

Aron, Robert, and Georgette Elgey. *The Vichy Regime, 1940–44.* Translated by Humphrey Hare. New York: Macmillan, 1958.

Astier de la Vigerie, Emmanuel d'. *Seven Times Seven Days.* Translated by Humphrey Hare. London: MacGibbon & Kee, 1958.

Association Nationale des Médaillés de la Résistance Française. *Annuaire des médaillés de la résistance française.* Paris: Brodard et Taupin, n.d.

Aubrac, Lucie. *La résistance, naissance et organisation.* Paris: Lang, 1945.

Bair, Deirdre. *Samuel Beckett.* New York: Harcourt, Brace, Jovanovich, 1978.

Baudoin, Madeleine. *Histoire des Groupes francs (MUR) des Bouches-du-Rhône de septembre 1943 à la libération.* Paris: Presses Universitaires de France, 1962.

Bellanger, Claude. *La presse clandestine, 1940–1944.* Paris: Colin, 1961.

Bellanger, Claude, et al. *Histoire générale de la presse française.* Vol. 4. Paris: Presses Universitaires de France, 1975.

Bernadac, Christian. *Kommandos de femmes, Ravensbrück.* Vol. 3 of *Les mannequins nus.* Paris: France Empire, 1973.

Bertrand, Gustave. *L'Enigma, ou la plus grande énigma de la guerre 1939–1945.* Paris: Plon, 1973.

Bertrand, Simone. *Mille visages, un seul combat: Les femmes dans la résistance.* Paris: Français Réunis, 1965.

Bidault, Suzanne. *Souvenirs de guerre et d'occupation.* Paris: La Table Ronde, 1973.

Bleicher, Hugo. *Colonel Henri's Story.* Edited by E. Borchers, edited and translated by Ian Golvin. London: Kimber, 1954.

Blumenson, Martin. *The Vildé Affair.* Boston: Houghton Mifflin, 1977.

Bohec, Jeanne. *La plastiqueuse à bicyclette.* Paris: Mercure de France, 1975.

Braddon, Russell. *Nancy Wake.* London: Cassell, 1956.

Brome, Vincent. *The Way Back.* London: Cassell, 1957.

Brown, Anthony Cave. *The Last Hero, Wild Bill Donovan.* New York: Times Books, 1982.

Brusselmans, Anne. *Rendez-vous 127, the Diary of Madame Brusselmans.* London: Ernest Benn, 1954.

Buckmaster, Maurice J. *Specially Employed.* London: Batchworth, 1952.

_____. *They Fought Alone.* London: Odhams, 1958.

Calmette, Arthur. *L'O.C.M., Organisation civile et militaire; Histoire d'un mouvement de résistance de 1940 à 1946.* Paris: Presses Universitaires de France, 1961.

Calvocoressi, Peter, and Guy Wint. *Total War.* London: Allen Lane, 1972.

Camfield, William A. *Francis Picabia.* Princeton: Princeton University Press, 1979.

Carré, Mathilde Lily. *I Was the Cat.* Translated by Mervyn Savill. London: Four Square, 1960.

Cerf, René. [Ferrière]. *Chemin clandestin.* Paris: Julliard, 1958.

———. *L'Assemblée consultative.* Paris: Français Réunis, 1974.

Chatel, Nicole, ed. *Des femmes dans la résistance.* Paris: Julliard, 1972.

Churchill, Peter. *Duel of Wits.* London: Hodder, 1957.

Cline, Ray S. *Secrets, Spies, and Scholars.* Washington, D.C.: Acropolis, 1976.

Cole, Hugh Marshall. *The Lorraine Campaign.* Washington, D.C.: History Division, Department of the Army, 1950.

Corday, Pauline. *J'ai vécu dans Paris occupé.* Montreal: L'Arbe, 1943.

Cowburn, Benjamin. *No Cloak, No Dagger.* London: Jarrolds, 1960.

Craven, Wesley Frank, and James Lea Cate, eds. *The Army Air Forces in World War II.* 7 vols. Chicago: University of Chicago Press, 1948–58.

Czerniawski, Roman Garby. *The Big Network.* London: Ronald, 1961.

Darling, Donald. *Secret Sunday.* London: Kimber, 1975.

———. *Sunday at Large.* London: Kimber, 1977.

Debré, Robert. *L'honneur de vivre.* Paris: Stock, 1974.

De Gaulle, Charles. *The Complete War Memoirs.* Translated by J. Griffin and R. Howard. 3 vols. in 1. New York: Simon & Schuster, 1964.

Delbo, Charlotte. *Le convoi du 24 janvier.* Paris: Minuit, 1965.

Delperrie de Bayac, Jacques. *Histoire de la milice.* Paris: Fayard, 1969.

Deschamps, Hélène [Hélène de Champlain]. *The Secret War of Hélène de Champlain.* London: W. H. Allen, 1980.

Dewavrin, André [Colonel Passy]. *2e bureau, Londres.* Vol. 1 of *Souvenirs.* Monte Carlo: Solar, 1947.

———. *10 Duke Street, Londres.* Vol. 2 of *Souvenirs.* Monte Carlo: Solar, 1947.

———. *Missions secrètes.* Vol. 3 of *Souvenirs.* Paris: Plon, 1951.

Diamant, David. *Les juifs dans la résistance française.* Paris: Le Pavillon, 1971.

Doenitz, Karl. *Memoirs.* Translated by R. H. Stevens. New York: World Publishing Co., 1959.

Dogan, Mattei, and Jacques Narbonne. *Les françaises face à la politique*. Paris: Colin, 1955.

Dumais, Lucien. *The Man Who Went Back*. London: Leo Cooper, 1975.

Duquesne, Jacques. *Les catholiques français sous l'occupation*. Paris: Grasset, 1966.

Les églises protestantes pendant la guerre et l'occupation. Paris: Messageries Evangeliques, 1946.

Eisenhower, Dwight D. *Crusade in Europe*. Garden City, N.Y.: Doubleday, 1948.

Evrard, Jacques. *La déportation des travailleurs français dans le Troisième Reich*. Paris: Fayard, 1972.

Les femmes dans la résistance. *Actes du colloque tenu à l'initiative de l'Union des Femmes Françaises, Paris, 22 et 23 novembre 1975*. Paris: Rocher, 1977.

Foot, M. R. D. *SOE in France*. London: Her Majesty's Stationery Office, 1966.

———. *Resistance*. London: Eyre Methuen, 1976.

———. *Six Faces of Courage*. London: Eyre Methuen, 1978.

Foot, M. R. D., and J. M. Langley. *MI 9*. London: Bodley Head, 1979.

Fourcade, Marie Madeleine. *Noah's Ark*. New York: Dutton & Co., 1974. Abridged; translated by Kenneth Morgan from the French *L'arche de Noé*. 2 vols. Paris: Fayard, 1968.

Freeman, Roger A. *The Mighty Eighth*. Garden City, N.Y.: Doubleday, 1970.

Frenay, Henri. *The Night Will End*. Translated by Dan Hofstadter. New York: McGraw-Hill, 1976.

———. Volontaires de la nuit. Paris: Laffont, 1975.

Fuller, Jean Overton. *Noor-un-nisa Inayat Khan*. London: Barrie & Jenkins, 1971.

Funk, Arthur L. *Charles de Gaulle*. Norman: University of Oklahoma Press, 1959.

———. *The Politics of Torch*. Lawrence: University of Kansas Press, 1974.

Gates, Eleanor M. *End of the Affair*. Berkeley: University of California Press, 1981.

Gourfinkel, Nina. *L'autre patrie*. Paris: Seuil, 1953.

Granet, Marie. *Défense de la France*. Paris: Presses Universitaires de France, 1960.

———. *Ceux de la résistance, 1940–44*. Paris: Minuit, 1964.

———. *Cohors-Asturies*. Bordeaux: Cahiers de la Résistance, 1974.

Granet, Marie, and Henri Michel. *Combat*. Paris: Presses Universitaires de France, 1957.

Guéguen-Dreyfus, Georgette. *Résistance Indre et Vallée du Cher*. 2 vols. Paris: Sociales, 1970–72.

Guéry, Mgr. *L'église catholique en France sous l'occupation*. Paris: Flammarion, 1947.

Hallie, Philip P. *Lest Innocent Blood Be Shed*. New York: Harper & Row, 1979.

Hampshire, A. Cecil. *On Hazardous Service*. London: Kimber, 1974.

Hany-Lefèbvre, Noèmi. *Six mois à Fresnes*. Paris: Flammarion, 1946.

Hastings, Max. *Das Reich*. London: Michael Joseph, 1981.

Hayes, Carleton J. H. *Wartime Missions in Spain*. New York: Macmillan, 1945.

Hepburn, Sybil. *Wingless Victory*. London: Allan Wingate-Baker, 1969.

Heslop, Richard. *Xavier*. London: Rupert Hart Davis, 1970.

Hinsley, Francis H. *British Intelligence in the Second World War*. 2 vols. London: Her Majesty's Stationery Office, 1979–81.

Hostache, René. *Le conseil national de la résistance*. Paris: Presses Universitaires de France, 1958.

Huguen, Roger. *Par les nuits les plus longues*. 3rd ed. St. Brieuc, Brittany: Les Presses Bretonnes, 1976.

Hytier, Adrienne Doris. *Two Years of French Foreign Policy*. Geneva: Droz, 1958.

Jones, Reginald Victor. *The Wizard War*. New York: Coward, McCann & Geoghegan, 1978.

Kedward, Harry Roderick. *Resistance in Vichy France*. Oxford: Oxford University Press, 1978.

Keegan, John. *Six Armies in Normandy*. New York: Viking, 1982.

Langer, William L. *Our Vichy Gamble*. New York: Norton, 1947.

Langley, James M. *Fight Another Day*. London: Collins, 1974.

Lemkin, Raphaël. *Axis Rule in Occupied Europe*. Washington, D.C.: Carnegie Endowment for International Peace, 1944.

Lévy, Anny [Latour]. *La résistance juive en France*. Paris: Stock, 1970.

Lévy, Claude, and Paul Tillard. *La grande rafle du Vel' d'Hiv*. Paris: Laffont, 1967.

MacDonald, Elizabeth. *Undercover Girl*. New York: Macmillan, 1947.

Magdeleine, Paul de la. *Les femmes françaises au service de la patrie*. Paris: Couderc Nérac, 1957.

Marks, Elaine, and Isabelle de Courtivron, eds. *New French Feminisms*. Amherst: University of Massachusetts Press, 1980.

Marrus, Michael R., and Robert O. Paxton. *Vichy France and the Jews*. New York: Basic Books, 1981.

Marshall, Bruce. *The White Rabbit*. Boston: Houghton Mifflin, 1953.

Masson, Madeleine. *Christine: A Search for Christine Granville*. London: Hamish Hamilton, 1975.

Mayer, Daniel. *Les socialistes dans la résistance*. Paris: Presses Universitaires de France, 1968.

A la mémoire des sèvriennes, mortes pour la France, 1939–1945. Paris: Guillemot et de Lamothe, 1946.

Merle d'Aubigné, Jeanne, and Violette Mouchon. *God's Underground*. Translated by William and Patricia Nottingham. St. Louis: Bethany Press, 1970.

Michel, Andrée, and Genevieve Texier. *La condition de la française d'aujourd'hui*. Geneva: Gonthier, 1964.

Michel, Henri. *Les courants de pensée de la résistance*. Paris: Presses Universitaires de France, 1962.

_____. *Bibliographie critique de la résistance*. Paris: Institut Pédagogique National, 1964.

_____. *Histoire de la résistance en France*. 6th ed. Paris: Presses Universitaires de France, 1972.

_____. *The Shadow War*. Translated by Richard Barry. London: Deutsch, 1972.

_____. *The Second World War*. Translated by Douglas Parmée. New York: Praeger, 1975.

Millar, George. *Horned Pigeon*. Garden City, N.Y.: Doubleday, 1946.

_____. *Road to Resistance*. London: Bodley Head, 1979.

Milward, Alan S. *The New Order and the French Economy*. Oxford: Clarendon, 1970.

Minney, Rubeign James. *Carve Her Name with Pride*. London: Collins, 1956.

Mockers, Michel. *Maquis SS4*. Issoudun: Labourer, 1945.

Monestier, Marianne. *Elles étaient cent et mille*. Paris: Fayard, 1972.

Neave, Airey. *Little Cyclone*. London: Hodder & Stoughton, 1954.

_____. *Saturday at MI 9*. London: Hodder & Stoughton, 1969.

Nicholas, Elizabeth. *Death Be not Proud*. London: Cresset, 1958.

Noguères, Henri. *Histoire de la résistance en France*. 5 vols. Paris: Laffont, 1967–81.

Nouveau, Louis H. *Des capitaines par milliers*. Paris: Calmann-Lévy, 1958.

Novick, Peter. *The Resistance Versus Vichy*. New York: Columbia University Press, 1968.

Paillole, Paul. *Services spéciaux 1935–1945*. Paris: Laffont, 1975.

Paxton, Robert O. *Vichy France*. New York: Norton, 1975.

Persico, Joseph E. *Piercing the Reich*. New York: Viking, 1979.

Phillips, Cecil Ernest Lucas. *Cockleshell Heroes*. London: Heinemann, 1956.

Piquet-Wicks, Eric. *Four in the Shadows*. London: Jarrolds, 1957.

Renard, Marie Thérèse. *La participation des femmes à la vie civique*. Paris: Ouvrières, 1965.

Renault, Gilbert [Rémy; Roulier]. *Mémoires d'un agent secret de la France libre*. 3 vols. Paris: France Empire, 1959–1961.

_____. *Réseau Comète*. 3 vols. Paris: Perrin, 1966–1971.

Rochester, Devereaux. *Full Moon to France*. New York: Harper & Row, 1977.

Roux-Fouillet, Renée, and Paul Roux-Fouillet. *Catalogue des périodiques clandestine diffusés en France de 1939 à 1945*. Paris: Bibliothèque Nationale, 1954.

Roux, Catherine. *Le triangle rouge*. Paris: France Empire, 1968.

St. Clair, Simone. *Ravensbrück, l'enfer des femmes*. Rev. ed. Paris: Fayard, 1964.

St. Clair, Simone, and Marianne Monestier, eds. *Cinquante-huit actions héroiques de la résistance*. Paris: Grund, 1971.

Schramm, Hanna, and Barbara Vormeier. *Vivre à Gurs*. Translated from the German by Irene Petit. Paris: F. Maspero, 1979.

Shiber, Etta. *Paris Underground*. New York: Scribner's, 1943.

Smith, Bradley F. *The Shadow Warriors*. New York: Basic Books, 1983.

Smith, Richard Harris. *OSS: The Secret History of America's First Central Intelligence Agency*. Berkeley: University of California Press, 1972.

Sowerwine, Charles. *Sisters or Citizens? Women and Socialism in France Since 1876*. New York: Cambridge University Press, 1982.

Stafford, David. *Britain and European Resistance 1940–1945*. London: Macmillan, 1980.

Sweet-Escott, Bickham. *Baker Street Irregular*. London: Eyre Methuen, 1965.

Sweets, John F. *The Politics of Resistance in France, 1940–1944*. De Kalb: Northern Illinois University Press, 1976.

Tartière, Drue. *The House near Paris*. New York: Simon & Schuster, 1946.

Terrenoire, Elisabeth. *Combattantes sans uniforme*. Paris: Bloud et Gay, 1946.

Téry, Simone. *Du soleil plein le cour*. Paris: Union des Femmes Françaises, 1946.

Teyssier-Jore, Raymonde. *Le "corps féminin."* Paris: France Empire, 1975.

Thomas, Edith. *The Women Incendiaries*. Translated by James and Starr Atkinson, New York: Braziller, 1966.

Thomas, Georges-Michel, and Alain Le Grand. *Le Finistere dans la guerre, 1939-1945*. Brest and Paris: Editions de la Cité, 1979-81.

Tickell, Jerrard. *Odette*. London: Chapman & Hall, 1949.

Tillion, Germaine. *Ravensbrück*. Translated by Gerald Satterwhite. Garden City, N.Y.: Anchor Press/Doubleday, 1975.

Tillon, Charles. *Les F.T.P.* Paris: Julliard, 1962.

Tollet, André. *La classe ouvrière dans la résistance*. Paris: Sociales, 1969.

Le Trividic, Dominique Martin. *Une femme du réseau Shelburn*. Les Sables d'Alonne: Cercle d'Or, 1979.

Troy, Thomas. *Donovan and the CIA*. Washington, D.C.: Central Intelligence Agency, 1981.

United States War Department, Strategic Services Unit, History Project. *War Report of the OSS*. 2 vols. New York: Walker Co., 1976.

Vagliano-Elroy, Sonia. *Les demoiselles de Gaulle 1943-1945*. Paris: Plon, 1982.

Veillon, Dominique. *Le Franc Tireur*. Paris: Flammarion, 1977.

Vie et mort des français 1939-1945. Paris: Hachette, 1971.

Vigneras, Marcel. *Rearming the French*. Washington, D.C.: Office of the Chief of Military History, Department of the Army, 1957.

Les Voix de la Liberté. *Ici Londres 1940-1944*. 4 vols. Paris: La Documentation Française, 1975.

Vomécourt, Philippe de. *Who Lived to See the Day*. London: Hutchinson, 1961.

Walters, Anne Marie. *Moondrop to Gascony*. London: Macmillan, 1946.

Ward, Dame Irene. *FANY Invicta*. London: Hutchinson, 1955.

Wilkinson, James D. *The Intellectual Resistance in Europe*. Cambridge, MA: Harvard University Press, 1981.

Winterbotham, F. W. *The Ultra Secret*. New York: Dell, 1975.

Wittek, Suzanne [Jouan, Cecile]. *Comète, histoire d'une ligne d'évasion*. Brussels: M. Thomas, 1948.

Wormser, Olga, and Henri Michel. *Tragédie de la déportation 1940-1945*. 4th ed. Paris: Hachette, 1955.

Wynne, Barry. *No Drums . . . No Trumpets*. London: Arthur Barker, 1961.

Young, Gordon. *The Cat with Two Faces*. London: Putnam, 1957.

Articles and Pamphlets

Albrecht, Berthie. Héroines d'hier et d'aujourd'hui. Paris: Union des Femmes Françaises, n.d.

Association Nationale des Anciennes Déportées et Internées de la Résistance. *Voix et visages,* January-February 1974.

Cahiers d'histoire de l'Institut Maurice Thorez, no. 10, November–December 1974.

Confédération Nationale de Combattants Volontaires de la Résistance. "Echo de la Résistance," no. 100. Paris: 1964.

Casanova, Danielle. Héroines d'hier et d'aujourd'hui. Paris: Union des Femmes Françaises, n.d.

Dean, R. F. A. "Women War Captives in Russia." *British Medical Journal,* April 23, 1949.

L'extraordinaire aventure de la forêt de Fréteval mai-août 1944. Vendôme: S. Lembeye, 1967.

Granet, Marie. "Dessin général." *Revue d'histoire de la deuxième guerre mondiale,* November 1950.

_____. "Défense de la France." *Revue d'histoire de la deuxième guerre mondiale,* April 1958.

Grégoire, Ménie. "Interview du ministre Simone Veil." *Marie Claire,* September 1974.

Grell, William F. "A Marine with OSS." *The Marine Corps Gazette,* December 1945.

Huguen, Roger. "Les débuts et le fonctionnement d'un réseau d'évasion: Le réseau Shelburne." *Revue d'histoire de la deuxième guerre mondiale,* January 1972.

Josse, R. "Le 11 novembre 1940." *Revue d'histoire de la deuxième guerre mondiale,* July 1962.

Michel, Henri. "Le Comité d'histoire de la deuxième guerre mondiale." *Revue d'histoire de la deuxième guerre mondiale,* October 1981.

Northcutt, Wayne, and Jeffra Flaitz. "Women and Politics in Contemporary France: The Electoral Shift to the Left in the 1981 Presidential and Legislative Elections." *Contemporary French Civilization,* Winter 1983.

Revue historique de l'armée. "Le Réseau F2." December 1952.

Sainclivier, Jacqueline. "Sociologie de la résistance: Quelques aspects méthodologiques et leur application en Ille et Vilaine." *Revue d'histoire de la deuxième guerre mondiale,* January 1980.

Tillion, Germaine. "Première résistance en zone occupée." *Revue d'histoire de la deuxième guerre mondiale,* April 1958.

Union des Femmes Françaises. *Livre d'or dédié aux femmes héroiques mortes pour que vive la France.* 5 parts. Paris: Foyer Danielle Casanova, n.d.

U.S. Eighth Air Force, 94th Bomb Group Memorial Association. *Nostalgic Notes,* December 1976.

Dr. A. Vourc'h. "Une femme debout dans la tempête: Tante Yvonne." *Cahiers de l'Iroise,* 1958.

Wright, Gordon. "Reflections on the French Resistance 1940–44." *Political Science Quarterly,* September 1962.

INDEX

INDEX

About the Author

ABOUT THE AUTHOR

MARGARET L. ROSSITER received her undergraduate degree from Douglass College of Rutgers University and her Ph.D. from Bryn Mawr College. Since 1965 she has been a professor of Modern European History (now emeritus) at Eastern Michigan University, where she also served as the first coordinator of the Women's Studies Program.

She has traveled extensively, including eight trips to Europe for study and research. She is the author of *The Chaco Dispute and the League of Nations* and of numerous articles and papers on women in history.